THE
BAEDEKER
BLITZ

Hitler's Attack on Britain's Historic Cities

Niall Rothnie

IAN ALLAN
Publishing

Contents

Front cover:
Seen from St George's Terrace, scaffolding has been erected on the remains of the tower of the church of St George the Martyr in Canterbury. In the background the southwest pinnacle of the crossing tower of the Cathedral has been similarly protected, whilst overhead a barrage balloon offers protection of a different sort.
Paul Crampton: The Fisk-Moore Collection

Front cover inset:
The headline from the Exeter Express & Echo records a royal tribute to the city.
Courtesy Express & Echo

Back cover top:
With two of Norwich's superb medieval churches as a backdrop, pedestrians pass the destroyed premises of the wine merchants Barwell & Sons on St Stephen's Street.
Swain Collection

Back cover centre:
Although the damage to York station was severe and temporarily affected the shipment of military supplies to Hull (for onward shipment to Russia), the track was quickly cleared and services restored.
Reproduced from The York Blitz 1942 *courtesy of the co-authors Leo Kessler and Eric Taylor and of the Publishers Sessions of York, England*

Back cover bottom:
With damage resulting from high explosive bombs in the Royal Victoria Park in the foreground, the Royal Crescent in Bath has suffered severe damage.

First published 1992

ISBN 0 7110 2038 3

Published by Ian Allan Ltd, Shepperton, Surrey; and printed by Ian Allan Printing Ltd at their works at Coombelands in Runnymede, England.

Introduction

It is relatively easy to produce a book on some aspect of the blitz on Britain during World War 2, and recent years have seen a number of such publications. With some honourable exceptions, however, the bulk of these are based on a limited, and accessible, number of sources — specifically the newspapers of the time and much later reminiscences by people who were in the cities when they were raided. These help to perpetuate a hazy romanticism about the 'blitz mentality' in which everyone worked together and there was no panic or confusion.

The Baedeker Blitz is based as far as possible on the original documentation of the time and shows that the truth was somewhat different. It is concerned with the Baedeker air-raids of the first part of 1942, a period that has been largely overlooked by the official historians, with their concentration on the raids on the big industrial cities. The Baedeker raids have received only passing mentions in the past, as the historian takes breath between describing the drawn out blitz of 1940-41 on London and elsewhere, and then prepares to move on to the V-weapon raids of 1944.

When they are mentioned, the references are often incorrect. Only five cathedral cities were attacked in this sequence of raids — Exeter, Bath, Norwich, York and Canterbury — and certainly not Coventry as is sometimes claimed. Nor did the appellation 'Baedeker' come from the mouth of Adolf Hitler. As will be shown, it was a much lower-ranking Nazi who linked these attacks with the German *Baedeker* guidebooks to beautiful cities, home and abroad. Yet the Baedeker raids are of great intrinsic importance. As we shall see, they came at a crucial stage in the development of the British area bomber offensive against Germany.

They were also the first test of the Civil Defence forces that had been reorganised as a result of lessons learnt during earlier raids.

The Baedeker raids are also a convenient and self-contained series of attacks which can be studied to show more general results: how people reacted to air-raids, the efficiency of local authorities and Civil Defence organisations, and even how such experiences are remembered long after they occurred. In order to facilitate this process, this book is divided into a number of sections. The first and last sections look at the growth of the bomber offensive, the reasons for the Baedeker raids and their significance. The main body of the book is devoted to the raids on the five Baedeker cities. To avoid needless repetition of similar event, each chapter is devoted to a particular aspect of the effects of air raids. Thus Exeter is considered in relation to the workings of Civil Defence; Bath considers the reactions of the ordinary civilian; Norwich highlights the reaction of people to frequent but intermittent raiding; York concentrates on the effects of high explosive bombs; Canterbury raises the question of how much each city learnt from the experience of others. In all cases the main events in each city's raids are also described. The result is a composite that shows that bravery and efficiency did exist, but that some were certainly more brave and efficient than others.

This book could not have been written without the help and assistance of many individuals and institutions. The Archivists at Bath Guildhall, Canterbury Record Office, Devon Record Office, Norfolk Record Office and York City Archives Department gave invaluable assistance. So too did the staff at the Reference Libraries in each of the cities. The archives of Mass Observation at Brighton, the Public Record Office and the Imperial War Museum provided much that was of use. I also received assistance from the following: Caversham Park, Reading; the University of Exeter Publicity Office; the cathedral staff at Exeter, Norwich and Canterbury; the Bar Convent Museum, York; the National Railway Museum, York; Nuffield College; Stothert & Pitt, Bath; Marks & Spencer, London; Norwich Arts Centre; Rowntrees Mackintosh, York and Norwich.

I must also thank the following newspapers for publishing my appeals for information: *Adscene, Bath and Wilts Evening Chronicle, Brecon and Radnor Express*, Eastern Counties Newspapers Ltd, *Express and Echo, Kentish Gazette, MidWales Journal, Yorkshire Evening Press*.

My main thanks must go to all those who took the trouble to write to me with their reminiscences. There are too many of them to list here, but all are noted under the relevant chapter headings. Some people gave me specific advice: Michael J. F. Bowyer, David Irving, Eric Taylor; Dr S. Greenwood gave me access to the work of Jeremy Mac-Dermott on the Canterbury blitz. Alistair Vass provided valuable assistance in translating original German documents.

My thanks for help with photographs and other illustrations go to the archivists of Marks and Spencer Plc; F. W. Woolworth; Rowntree Mackintosh Ltd, York and Norwich; the National Railway Museum, York; the libraries at Exeter, Bath and York; the *Kentish Gazette,* Wessex Newspapers; Peter Thomas; and in particular, Judy Swain, Paul Crampton and Andrew Dalton.

Finally there are some personal thanks. Judy and Viv Pimenta gave much needed support. Fiona Wylie did the herculean task of converting my writing into a readable typescript. My son, Andrew, frequently helped me to look at my notes in a new and interesting way. Most of all, I should like to thank my wife, Norma, for moral support and much else besides.

Niall Rothnie
Bath, 1991

Right:
A prewar photograph of the Norwich branch of F. W. Woolworth & Co Ltd. *F. W. Woolworth*

Below:
The potential damage caused by a single high explosive bomb is graphically illustrated in the scale of this bomb crater.

THE
BACKGROUND

Bomber Offensives

It might be queried why one should look at the Baedeker raids. If you put together the two German and five British cities that made up this series of attacks, then a maximum of 1,450 people were killed in total, spread over some 17 raids. Coventry lost nearly 600 in one night; London some 29,890, although over a much longer period. In Germany, Hamburg, Berlin, Dresden and others had losses measured in many tens of thousands. But you can get a false impression by merely looking at those raids that inflicted the most casualties. Although Bomber Command was to consistently avoid facing the consequences, it was almost inevitable that if it were to make a success of a raid, and thus destroy much of a target city, then there were bound to be heavy casualties. It was not until July 1943 that Bomber Command achieved massive success with the devastation and heavy casualties inflicted on areas of Hamburg, but it had been attempting to achieve just such a result from much earlier on; if they had not destroyed a sizeable area of a German city beforehand, it was not for want of trying. Thus if one is to try to understand the reason why Hamburg and Dresden were raided with such dreadful results you must go back a number of years to the early part of the war. The decision to attack cities, at first along with precision targets, was being contemplated at least as early as mid-1940. That few outside of the senior echelons of Bomber Command realised this at the time speaks volumes for the inability of most aircrews to find even large cities at night, let alone isolated oil dumps. It was not until March 1942 that Bomber Command finally achieved its first concentrated and successful attack on a German city. It was a great success, but there were some contributory factors: the target city was

easily found, lacked defences, and was relatively inflammable. Its name was Lübeck and its destruction was to provoke the Baedeker blitz.

World War 1 saw the introduction of a number of new weapons that, for various reasons, had little time to show their real potential. The tank was one such device, the aircraft another. In particular the bomber aircraft was to develop into what was seen as a massive threat in any future conflict. The relatively few raids by German Zeppelin and Gotha bombers and the casualties they inflicted were used as a basis to calculate the number of people killed per bomb. When these figures were multiplied by the number of bombs carried by more modern bombers that enemy countries possessed by the mid-1930s, one arrived at cumulative casualty figures of truly horrifying proportions. It is no exaggeration to say that in some quarters the bomber aircraft excited the same fear in the interwar years that nuclear weapons do today.

Accordingly, in the years after World War 1 there were numerous attempts to reduce the likelihood of such devastation from the air. They came to nothing, yet on 1 September 1939, the day Hitler invaded Poland, President Roosevelt of the United States issued an appeal to the countries of Europe, asking them to promise they would never bomb civilian populations or unfortified cities. The French and British swiftly agreed the following day. So did Germany.

Both Britain and Germany restricted themselves to only the most obvious of military targets where there was no threat to the civilian population. In the 'Phoney War' this meant each other's navies. As the war grew more intense, both sides threw accusations at each other. Britain said it was wrong of the Luftwaffe to bomb Warsaw and Rotter-

Above right:
The area south of St Paul's Cathedral in London showing the considerable damage resulting from the fire-bombing during the London blitz in 1940-41.

Right:
Industrial centres were the most obvious targets. Amongst those most severely attacked was Coventry on 14/15 November 1940 by a force of 552 bombers. The severe damage suffered by the city is exemplified by this engineering works.

dam; Germany replied that both were defended cities and therefore valid targets. Hitler accused Britain of killing German civilians in the town of Freiburg-im-Breisgau (even though it was soon discovered that the bombs had been dropped by errant German crews). Up to the summer of 1940, such incidents were few. This was partly because — contrary to prewar fears — bombers did not cause wholesale slaughter, but also for the simple reason that neither side saw any real value in killing large numbers of civilians.

With the fall of France, the Luftwaffe began to bomb Britain directly. There were still limitations. London was off limits, by direct order of Hitler. The Luftwaffe bombed military targets such as airfields — and in daylight — when greater accuracy could be achieved. When heavy losses forced them to night attacks, two Luftwaffe crews became lost and on the night of 24 August 1940 they dropped their bombs on London. Churchill launched a retaliatory raid on Berlin. Hitler ordered major attacks on London but, to the despair of his advisors, they were still limited to military targets alone.

The fact remains that even though the Luftwaffe aimed at military targets, the width of definition of what constituted such a target — docks, public utilities, railway stations — and the succession of nightly raids meant that civilian casualties soon began to mount. By December 1940 some 13,596 Londoners had already been killed and the attacks continued even though Hitler had abandoned his plans for the invasion of Britain in September.

The British government emphasised the more scandalous 'near misses', notably the destruction of the cathedral at Coventry (the city, as a centre of manufacturing industry, was in itself a legitimate target). However, Bomber Command was soon to adopt the same approach: bombing military targets within German cities. Unfortunately, it soon became obvious that flying long distances in complete darkness meant that most aircrews would be lucky to find the target city, let alone precise military points within it. Accepting this fact, on the night of 16 December 1940, Bomber Command launched its first deliberate area attack, against the city of Mannheim. The whole of the city was to be treated as an industrial centre with no specific targets. Over the following months further theories were put forward to bolster the morality of area bombing. The aiming point for bomber crews would be the centre of cities so that bombs that missed factories did not waste themselves on open ground. (This assumed, often incorrectly, that the industrial zone was always in the city centre.) Stray bombs would hit targets that were, strictly, non-military; but civilian morale was a legitimate target. Civilians would become despondent if their workplaces were destroyed, their public utilities cut off, roads blocked, homes damaged. The fact that civilians would also be killed was rather glossed over.

In fact, the Germans did not immediately realise that this was a change of tactics. Bomber Command had still so few aircraft and such poor navigational accuracy that, as the Butt Report of 18 August 1941 reported, two-thirds of aircraft could not even find their way to within five miles of the target. Up to the end of 1941, Bomber Command was simply not effective enough to cause accurate or widespread destruction.

After a winter lull, Bomber Command began the spring of 1942 with much greater optimism. Many of its shortcomings were gradually being rectified. More, and heavier, bomber aircraft were introduced into service; night-time navigational devices were developed along with more effective bombs. Most importantly, it gained a new head, Sir Arthur Harris, who was a publicist of the first order. By March 1942 the British public badly needed some good news. The entry of Japan into the war had seen huge losses of men and material in the Far East. In North Africa Tobruk had fallen and on Britain's own doorstep the German battleships *Scharnhorst* and *Gneisenau* had escaped back to Germany, sailing up the English Channel with apparent impunity. These developments threatened the very existence of an independent Bomber Command; critics noted its limited success in the war so far and urged that its aircraft be dispersed to the ever increasing number of battlefields worldwide.

Harris decided to silence his detractors by a display of what his Command could achieve. A strong believer in area bombing, he looked through the list of target cities in the latest directive and chose carefully: better to hit a smaller city than a larger one for then the damage would be, proportionately, all the greater. His first raid was actually a precision one. On the night of 3/4 March

1942, Bomber Command attacked the Renault factory at Billancourt near Paris. It was a great success and the biggest raid by the RAF on a single target so far, but unfortunately not all the bombs hit the target. Casualties were heavy in the surrounding industrial suburbs with at least 340 French civilians being killed.

Hitler was annoyed, although this was no doubt more at Britain's new ability to mount successful night operations rather than any real regret at the deaths of French civilians. He ordered a heavy reprisal raid on London as soon as weather conditions improved. They remained poor for a number of days, however, and in the interval his anger evaporated. The order was cancelled. Hitler explained to Jeschonnek, the Luftwaffe Chief of Staff, his reasons for this change of plan: he had no desire to provoke air raids on German cities when the British were still conspicuous by their absence over German skies; and he was also enough of a realist to admit that Germany, at full stretch attacking Russia, did not have enough aircraft in Western Europe to produce an adequate destructive response.

Harris next attacked the major cities of Essen and Cologne but with very little success. Now, at last, he returned to his first idea which was to bomb a small target city. In the directive, under the heading of alternative industrial targets, was the North German port of Lübeck. Of course, it was not preferable to bomb a city purely because it was small but Lübeck must be a genuine industrial target if it was on the approved list in the first place. Its full entry read: 'Lübeck (Baltic port) (Industrial and armament centre)'. The port was used for supplying the military needs of the German armies in Northern Russia and for the importation of iron ore and other goods from neutral Sweden. There was the Drägerwerke factory which produced oxygen apparatus for submarine crews and the works of the Deutsche Waffen and Muniton branch factory. None of these were close to the city centre. Indeed, taking into account the whole city with its modern suburbs and scattered housing and factory units, 'in general, it is not as vulnerable to blitz tactics as the average town of this size'.

However, there was one part of the city that was a fire-raiser's dream. Lübeck, in the Middle Ages, had been the chief town of the great North German trading confederation known as the Hanse and although it had failed to maintain its supremacy in later centuries, there were many reminders of its days of greatness. One part of the port area still retained large numbers of 17th and 18th century warehouses with their multiple stories and steep gables. The best of the old architecture remained in the very centre of the city, the Altstadt or Old Town. This had very definite limits: the medieval site of the original town was situated on an island at the confluence of the Trave and Wakenitz rivers. As it was surrounded by water, and space was at a premium, the area had at a very early stage in its development become crowded with buildings, forcing new developments to be squashed together and to expand up into the air. The only open spaces were in the eastern part around a series of large, public buildings, — usually medieval — such as the cathedral and the market hall. The very centre of the city therefore consisted of an old, closely packed residential district with a number of 'medieval buildings of historic significance': and it was this area that was to be the chief aiming point in the forthcoming raid.

On the night of 28/29 March some 234 aircraft of Bomber Command were sent to attack the city of Lübeck. It was a tremendous success and 191 aircraft claimed to have attacked the target, leaving the city ablaze by the time that the raid had ended. A daylight reconnaissance flight brought back the good news: some 200 acres of the centre of Lübeck appeared to have been completely burnt out with patchy but substantial damage to the surrounding suburbs. The docks had received some damage, the Drägerwerke factory was destroyed. It had been a most successful raid. The first real example of area devastation. Harris was pleased. Although, as he admitted, it was not a major target he had shown what could be achieved using the tactics of 'concentrated incendiarism': German cities could be devastated by Bomber Command. Churchill was pleased too; his next letter to President Roosevelt referred to the raid and he was still talking about it when he met the Russian leader, Stalin, in August of the same year.

The inhabitants of Lübeck, of course, did not see it the same way. It was not until noon on 29 March that the fire services had the situation under control and over a number of days much destruction had ensued. By that time

the old town had been gutted. The cathedral had been destroyed, as had the church of St Mary's and the Market Hall. Many of the most impressive old burgher houses had gone up in flames along with hundreds of others, smaller but equally vulnerable. The death toll stood at 312, low by the standards of some raids over Britain which had used more aircraft and a greater proportion of high explosives, but a breakdown of these statistics revealed some worrying trends: 50% of the dead were found in air raid shelters, places that often appeared to be untouched by high explosives, with bodies that seemed to be only asleep, but many of which had died from extreme heat and asphyxiation.

Once again, Hitler was furious but this time his temper was not to be assuaged. He had not in the end reacted to the raid on the Renault works near Paris, but Lübeck was different. The British Air Staff had argued that it was not a major military target, but that it deserved inclusion in a target list because it was at least a minor one. The Germans did not agree with even this assessment: the city had minimal anti-aircraft protection and only the previous month its sole searchlight unit had been removed and sent to the Eastern front. However, it was not just the matter of Hitler being upset at the wanton destruction of what the Germans merely perceived to be a rather beautiful city in the manner of, say, Stratford-on-Avon or Cambridge and with about as much value to the war effort. It was also recognised that this raid was a major development in the British bomber offensive against Germany. For the first time the RAF had been able to mount a raid that had really hurt a German city and there was obviously more to come.

Such a successful attack could not go unpunished. Hitler was not one to take an affront without responding and he now ordered not one but a whole series

of raids. But he was also a realist and knew that the Luftwaffe forces available in the west at present could not match British numbers and their powers of destruction. Limited German resources had to be used to the best effect: why not play the British at their own game and attack cities there that were the equivalent of Lübeck? Match terror raid with terror raid. At the very least it would show that the Germans could retaliate; at the best it would deter the British from further raids in a similar vein. Hitler told Goebbels: 'There is no other way of bringing the English to their senses. They belong to a class of human beings with whom you can talk only after you have first knocked out their teeth.' Of course, raids on British cities that had no military value had other advantages. They would have little or no defences, so German losses would be minimised and the propaganda value of attacking new and unexpected targets would be all the greater. Accordingly, on 14 April 1942, Hitler issued the following order to the Luftwaffe forces in the West:

'The Führer has ordered that air warfare against England is to be given a more aggressive stamp. Accordingly when targets are being selected, preference is to be given to those where attacks are likely to have the greatest possible effect on civilian life. Besides raids on ports and industry, terror attacks of a retaliatory nature are to be carried out against towns other than London. Minelaying is to be scaled down in favour of these attacks.'

It was the order for what become known as the Baedeker raids. It was also the first time that anyone on either side of the air war had admitted that the sole purpose of a series of attacks was to cause 'terror'. Full and unrestrained attacks on the civilian population of defenceless cities had finally arrived.

Left:
An RAF reconnaissance photograph of the historic port city of Lübeck.

Below left:
The damage to the *Altstadt* **in Lübeck as the result of the RAF's raid on Palm Sunday, 28/29 March 1942, by 234 aircraft.**

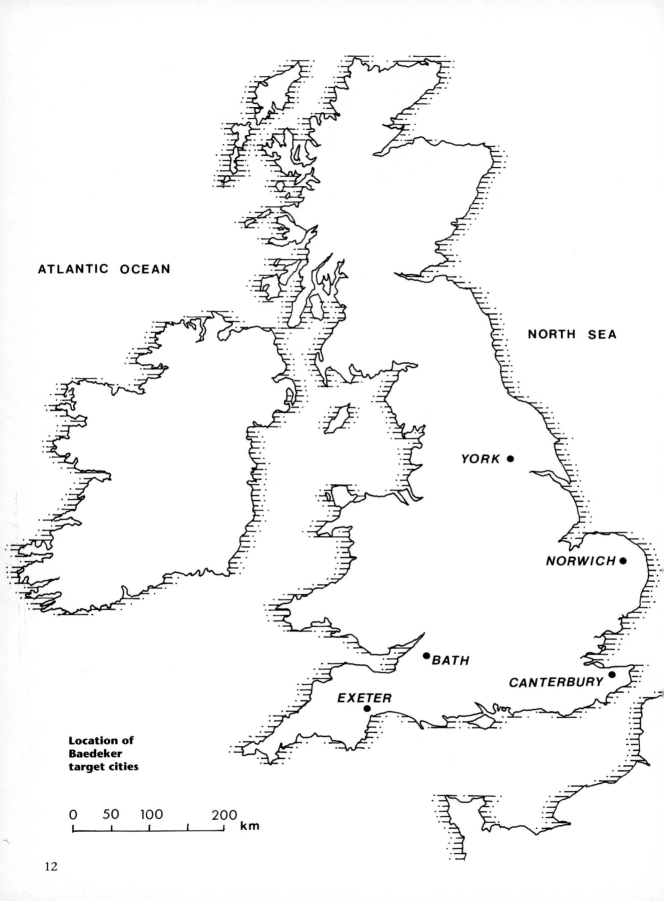

ATLANTIC OCEAN

NORTH SEA

YORK ●

NORWICH ●

● BATH

CANTERBURY ●

EXETER ●

**Location of
Baedeker
target cities**

0   50   100   200
|——|——|————|————| km

Attack and Defence

Hitler's snap decision to launch serious air-raids against Britain again cannot have been met with much enthusiasm by the Luftwaffe. The plain fact was that since May 1941, when the bulk of the German bomber force had been hurled into the campaign against Russia, the rump of Luftflotte III had been left to continue the illusion that they were maintaining an effective threat towards Britain. At the height of the blitz, towards the end of 1940, the Luftwaffe had possessed upwards of 600 aircraft capable of attacking in the west; since the onslaught on Russia had begun, they were lucky to have 60, one-tenth of this capacity and these were limited to minelaying and other such activities.

The Baedeker offensive therefore necessitated not inconsiderable transfers of Luftwaffe squadrons from as far away as Sicily. The British, having broken many of the German codes, including those produced by the 'Enigma' machines, intercepted some of these references and realised that a major movement was afoot.

The surviving records of the Luftwaffe and especially of Luftflotte III are often fragmentary — and in particular for the period January-July 1942 — and so it is difficult to be accurate on exactly which units were transferred. It is certain that at least one experienced 'pathfinder' unit was brought back to France. This was probably the most famous of them all, KG100, although some reports suggest that the task of finding and illuminating the target for the main force had now been handed over to Reconnaissance Gruppe 123. What does appear certain is that this augmented force was being put together to launch a renewed attack on Britain's industrial cities such as Birmingham when the raid on Lübeck forced an abrupt change of policy. As the units continued to gather, Hitler gave the instructions that they should concentrate on historic cities with a series of terror raids against the civilian populations. By the end of April 1942 it was calculated that the German bomber strength in the west had increased by more than 50% since January. The Luftwaffe in France, the Low Countries and Norway was assessed as having just over 200 serviceable aircraft.

Unfortunately British Intelligence drew every conclusion other than the correct one. There was a slight worry that the Germans might attempt some form of retaliation for the bombing of Lübeck with their newly acquired additional aircraft, but the Joint Intelligence Committee decided that for the foreseeable future German tactics would probably not differ from those of the latter half of 1941. Throughout the Baedeker raids, decoded radio intercepts failed to provide advance warning of any of the targets that were about to be hit.

There was a second source of information. Partly from decoded intercepts, and from other sources, the British had discovered in early 1940 the existence of a number of radio signalling devices that enabled German aircraft to find their way to a target at night.

The first to be discovered was the *Knickebein* receiver, based on the prewar *Lorenz* system which enabled civilian aircraft to make safe and accurate landing at night. The *Lorenz* system consisted of two directional-beam aerials which would be set up alongside each other to produce two wide beams of radio signals, broadcasting a series of Morse dots and dashes. The two beams would have a narrow overlap along the centre of the airfield runway and when the pilot was on the correct line of approach he would hear one continual tone on his earphones; if he strayed too far to one side or other, the tone would degenerate into either the dots or the dashes thus warning him that he was beginning to veer off course. *Knickebein* worked on the same principle if on a very much larger scale. It consisted of two main rotational beams that were positioned some hundreds of miles apart. The first one gave the direction; the pilot when he took off would find the beam through listening for the continual tone in his headphones and follow the beam as it led him towards the target. When he was close to it, he would pick up a second, intersecting, beam which would tell him he was within range. The *Knickebein* equipment could be provided for each German aircraft and was to prove very successful for a few months until the British found ways to jam it.

Once the beam had been identified in June 1940, a special unit, No 80 Wing, was set up to concentrate on technical countermeasures. Once they had identified the beams they set out to jam them. At this stage of the war the beams were relatively easy to find as the Germans had the habit of leaving them on for most of the day. The first jammers were a crude attempt to drown the dots and dashes heard on the enemy pilots' earphones by sheer noise.

Proper jammers called 'Aspirins' were then introduced to work on the same frequency as the *Knickebein* beams. They produced their own series of dashes. The German pilot would be flying along the correct route listening to a continuous tone on his earphones when the 'Aspirins' would cause him to hear a whole series of dashes instead. Assuming he was drifting off his route the pilot would change course in an attempt to find the continual tone again and in doing so would get lost even further.

It was not long before the Luftwaffe realised that *Knickebein* was being interfered with but they had already created other beam devices.

X-Gerät was one such device and involved a number of beams. The German aircraft would once again take off and fly along a single directional beam but, as the aircraft came near the target, it would pick up two cross beams, at a predetermined 15km apart, the second beam being 5km from the target. The time measured between crossing the two beams would enable the aircraft to work out its ground speed. In the aircraft, a clock would then be set in operation to activate the release of the bombs 5km beyond the second beam

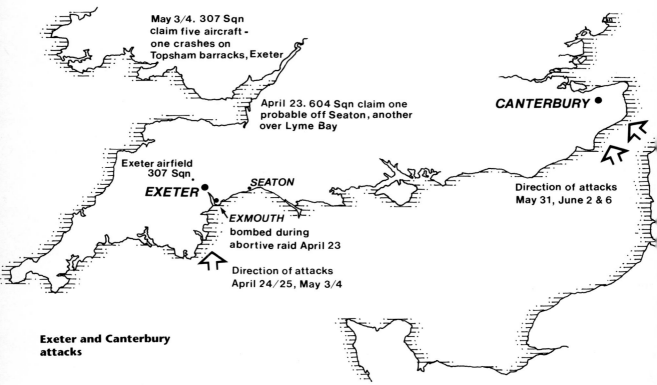

May 3/4. 307 Sqn claim five aircraft - one crashes on Topsham barracks, Exeter

April 23. 604 Sqn claim one probable off Seaton, another over Lyme Bay

CANTERBURY

Exeter airfield 307 Sqn.

EXETER

SEATON

Direction of attacks May 31, June 2 & 6

EXMOUTH bombed during abortive raid April 23

Direction of attacks April 24/25, May 3/4

Exeter and Canterbury attacks

and, hopefully, directly on the target. This was a very accurate blind bombing technique and the 'Enigma' intercepts soon revealed that it was complex enough to be restricted to one particular unit of the Luftwaffe. KG100 was equipped with *X-Gerät* devices and given the instruction to start fires on the target which the rest of the bomber forces could then bomb visually.

Although *X-Gerät* was much more accurate than *Knickebein*, the British countermeasures were also improving. In the early days of finding the beams it was the practice to send up a suitably equipped British aircraft to fly around the night skies until it flew across and picked them up. By the autumn of 1940 it was found that VHF ground stations could also pick up the beams. Even more important, the 'Enigma' intercepts frequently gave beam settings, bearings and references to numbered targets. Six *X-Gerät* transmitters were identified and two of them were known by position. Decodes of radio traffic to and from KG100's base at Vannes in Brittany often revealed target instructions for the night to the various stations in France. As early as 5 October 1940, one of the main scientists involved was able to say that it would be possible in the immediate future to work out all the elements of the system. The British were even able to predict the targets that the Germans were aiming for thanks to the enemy's continued habit of operating the beams long before it was absolutely necessary. On the afternoon of 14 November 1940, for example, the beams were detected over the city of Coventry and the city was raided heavily that night.

No 80 Wing now introduced a new set of 'Bromide' transmitters but, although they operated on what appeared to be the correct frequency, the Germans' accuracy continued to be impressive and the jammers appeared not to be working. It was only when a Heinkel 111 came down just off the shore of Bridport that the British found out why the jamming was proving so ineffective. By luck it was found that it had an audio filter set to peak at 2,000 cycles. The British had assumed the modulation frequency would be 1,150-1,500 cycles as had occurred with *Knickebein*. The wrong setting was, as one put it, 'the difference between a whistle and shriek', but it meant that the Germans could filter the beam signals out of the jamming without much trouble. There was some criticism on the British side that only a tone-deaf person could have missed this and that Coventry might have been saved as a result, but the jammers were swiftly altered to radiate on the correct tone and *X-Gerät* soon proved to be as ineffective as *Knickebein* once it was blocked. From mid-January 1941 the Germans realised once again that they needed to change beams or modify existing ones. The third beam, *Y-Gerät*, was identified by 80 Wing in November 1940 but it was easily blocked and was to play no part in the Baedeker raids.

The Germans learnt from their mistakes. From June 1941 they stopped transmitting radio orders for the beams which were also only activated just before a raid took place. They also took to changing the radio frequencies even during attacks until by August 1941 beacon call signs and frequencies were being altered by up to 15 times a day. Finally, they tried to alter the beams and a new variant of *X-Gerät* was introduced. Despite all the secrecy, the British soon knew of its existence. Radio intercepts, although now far less frequent than before, noted that the German Air Signals Experimental Regiment was developing a new variant of *X-Gerät* codenamed *Taub*. In October 1941 a German prisoner-of-war referred to the idea of a 'dog whistle' frequency. The Germans had partly given the game away by exhibiting their delight in word games. *Taub* is German for 'deaf' and it did not take the British long to work out that the new *X-Gerät* involved ultrasonic sound frequency, inaudible to the human ear. In *Taub* the old modulation frequency would be transmitted so the British could hear it and jam it, but superimposed on it would be an ultrasonic frequency that could not be heard and which the Germans could follow after filtering out the ordinary jamming. Instructions were therefore given to add ultrasonic modulation to No 80 Wing's jammers but not to switch them on until this modulation had been picked up from the German beams. It was quite rightly feared that if the British used this jamming before the beams even appeared then the Germans might begin to realise how effective British Intelligence was; if they realised 'Enigma' could be broken and then changed their entire system British Intelligence would be right back at square one.

Accordingly, when the Baedeker raids did begin, the jammers waited for the ultrasonic modulation to start. It did not or, at least, it did not appear to do so. Yet KG100 appeared to be back in action, presumably carrying *X-Gerät* receivers, and their accuracy was of such a generally high standard that it was assumed they must be using some device that was not being affected by the *X-Gerät* jammers. No 80 Wing, the unit responsible for combating the German beam devices, continued to insist that it was not picking up ultrasonic modulation (and this was in fact correct), but it was not that this modulation was not being used. After some weeks of Baedeker raids a closer look was taken at the listening receivers and it was found that they had been adapted incorrectly. Ultrasonic reception involved a far wider waveband width than normal in the existing high frequency circuits of the receiver. As these had not been modified properly, the ultrasonic modulation was cut out in the early stages of the receiver, so as a result the operators could not detect that which they were not even receiving. Once this mistake was realised the receivers were adapted and proved much more successful than previously at lessening the effects of the beams. By this time it was late May and there had been a series of devastating attacks on Exeter, York, Norwich and Bath.

It would be unfair to stress this point unduly. Most of the Baedeker cities were chosen because they were easy to find, beam or no beam; none was more than 50 miles from the coast, and most raids took place on bright moonlit nights. The target cities were also undefended and it can be no coincidence that once guns and balloons were moved to the more beautiful cities in England, the accuracy of German bombing dropped appreciably.

The Germans had learnt other new lessons as well. Their tactics were a mixture of tried and tested blitz ideas, plus some of the new policies being adopted by Bomber Command over Germany. They tried to emulate, as they put it, the tactics used by the RAF at Lübeck and Rostock with the idea of a first force — possibly KG100 — using the new *Taub* variant of *X-Gerät* to locate the target and then illuminate it with flares and incendiaries for the main force following behind in a tight pack. They planned that each attack should take place in a concentrated period of half an hour or so. There were good up-to-date aircraft available, the latest marks of the Junkers Ju88 and Dornier Do217. They now carried more incendi-ary bombs and twice as many high explosive bombs than the earlier marks in terms of weight, once again emulating the tactics used by Bomber Command in Lübeck. The aircraft were also encouraged to engage in shallow dive-bombing to create greater accuracy over targets where there were known to be no barrage balloons. Many were also to indulge in random machine-gunning of the streets and buildings below. Such tactics were rarely admitted to — the Germans were frequently to complain that the British were doing the same over Germany — but they rarely killed anyone and were largely to deter Civil Defence teams from tackling fires. It was hoped, therefore, that a concentrated raid involving accurate dive bombing, a large proportion of incendiaries and the occasional high explosive bombs and burst of machine-gun fire would combine to overwhelm the defences and set large areas of the target cities ablaze.

Radio intercepts and the jamming of beams failed to provide the British with advance knowledge of the German intentions although it might be argued that even if more information had been available to the defending forces it would in a practical sense have made very little difference. There had been complaints in 1940 that even when the intercepts were so good that the British knew the target, numbers and types of German bombers involved, and even their height and route, very few of them were actually intercepted. This was not because of lack of effort but the simple reason that in the early years of the war the aerial night defences of Britain were quite inadequate. The need to bomb at night had been an unexpected move, necessitated by the heavy losses inflicted by fighter aircraft in daytime raids. As we have seen, flying in the dark over a blacked-out countryside and with only the stars to navigate by meant that many bombers could count themselves lucky to find a target as large as a medium-sized city. It was obviously near impossible, therefore, for nightfighters to be able to find single bombers in the darkness even if they had prior knowledge of which cities were being bombed. The only hope was based on the fact that in the earlier stages of the war, before the major navigational aids were introduced, the bombers preferred to fly at the time of a full moon when visibility was better. The first nightfighters merely cruised around the target city in the vain hope that they might see one of the enemy, silhouetted against a cloud. The fighters themselves were often unsuitable aircraft such as the Boulton Paul Defiant and early marks of the Hawker Hurricane which by now were becoming outdated in the more deadly arena of daytime dogfighting. They were then painted black and known as 'Catseye' fighters but however many carrots the pilots ate, the simple truth was that it was almost impossible to achieve a 'kill' by visual contact alone. In late 1940 it was calculated that during 12,000 enemy sorties, only eight enemy aircraft had been brought down by nightfighters — a figure hardly calculated to strike terror into the hearts of German aircrews. This use of 'catseye' tactics continued even after the first, early airborne radar sets were introduced, and catseye aircraft were still being used during the Baedeker raids. By that time their operational tactics had been improved. The 'Layers' system involved putting up between 12-20 catseye aircraft over a target, each fighter being given a particular altitude at which it should patrol with a vertical separation of 500-1,000ft between them. All other aircraft were barred from the area and so, in theory,

if any fighter saw another aircraft then it could assume it was one of the enemy. This system was renamed 'Fighter Nights' in early 1941 but however well organised, visual sighting tables do not appear to have achieved much success.

The real need was for some type of radar system, one that could see in the dark and guide a nightfighter close enough so that it could then guarantee a visual contact. Such a system was contemplated before the start of the war but until 1942 the radar types that were invented, although each was an improvement on the former, were just not accurate enough to be of any real use at night when a few hundred yards could make all the difference between a contact and a total miss. A radar that could be carried in an aircraft was developed in 1939 but although by 1940 the Mk IV Airborne Interception (AI) radar had been developed, it was still of limited practical use. Under 5,000ft, the signal became confused as it was reflected from the ground below and results could only be obtained if the enemy aircraft flew in a long straight line at a sufficiently high altitude. The nightfighters would receive a preliminary warning from the long

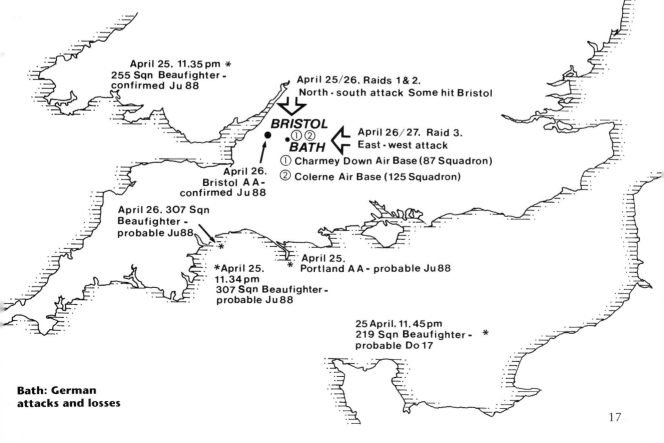

April 25. 11.35 pm *
255 Sqn Beaufighter -
confirmed Ju 88

April 25/26. Raids 1 & 2.
North - south attack Some hit Bristol

BRISTOL
① ②
BATH

April 26/27. Raid 3.
East - west attack
① Charmey Down Air Base (87 Squadron)
② Colerne Air Base (125 Squadron)

April 26.
Bristol A A -
confirmed Ju 88

April 26. 307 Sqn
Beaufighter -
probable Ju 88

*April 25.
11.34 pm
307 Sqn Beaufighter -
probable Ju 88

April 25.
* Portland A A - probable Ju 88

25 April. 11.45 pm
219 Sqn Beaufighter - *
probable Do 17

**Bath: German
attacks and losses**

range Chain Home radar. An individual aircraft would be then directed into the general vicinity of an enemy aircraft by the medium range and medium precision Ground Controlled Interception (GCI) radar. The fighter should then be close enough to pick up the enemy on its own short range high precision AI radar which, in turn, should bring it close enough for a visual sighting. In practice the system was far from perfect, at least at the time of the heaviest nights of the blitz in late 1940 and early 1941. Chain Home radar could give only a very general indication of the enemy's approach; there were too few GCI sites and radio contact between them and the nightfighters was unreliable; AI Mk IV radar was not very accurate; and the available nightfighters were inadequate for the task.

All these problems were to be gradually overcome but not in time to have a significant impact on the Baedeker raiders. In 1941 there was a great increase in the number of GCI sites. VHF radio was introduced which greatly enhanced communications between ground and air. The last two necessities – an accurate AI radar and a suitable nightfighter – were also created but in too small numbers to have any real influence in the early months of 1942. The Beaufighter could stay up longer and could keep up with the faster German bombers but it took time for squadrons to re-equip and many nightfighter squadrons were still flying Hurricanes and Defiants. Some were still using the catseye tactics, aircraft without inbuilt radar. The greatest breakthrough came with the introduction of AI Mk VII, centimetric radar. As its name suggests, this was a radar that worked on a much shorter wavelength (10cm rather than the previous 1.5m) which created a more accurate and narrower beam. This produced a much firmer contact on the radar screen and was less likely to be confused by ground echoes when tracking low flying aircraft. After the Baedeker raids, Beaufighters equipped with AI Mk VII were to begin achieving much better results at night. The new radar scored its first success on 5 April 1942 but the squadrons equipped with the device were too few and at the wrong bases to achieve anything significant in the Baedeker raids. New equipment tended quite naturally to go to the squadrons based near obvious targets, the oft-raided industrial cities. The fighter airfields near Bath, Colerne and Charmy

Down, had a much lower priority and at the time of the Baedeker raids were still equipped with Catseye Hurricanes and Defiants, and Turbinlite Havocs. The Baedeker cities also possessed none of the ground defences afforded to more obvious targets. At the start of 1942 major towns were being surrounded by a complicated series of searchlights and gun batteries to assist and complement the nightfighters. Some searchlights were to illuminate the enemy, others to bathe the whole area in light. Guns could only operate in certain areas or at certain heights. This system, codenamed 'Smack', was to play little or no part in the Baedeker raids as the Germans generally avoided the larger cities that this system was set up to protect.

The pioneering nature of nightfighting was best illustrated by one other tactic introduced just prior to the Baedeker raids – a flying searchlight. A number of twin-engined Douglas Havoc fighter-bombers were converted during 1941 to carry AI Mk IV radar and fitted with a powerful 'Turbinlite' searchlight in the nose. Known as Turbinlite Havocs, these aircraft operated singly in conjunction with a pair of Hurricane nightfighters. All three aircraft would take off together, the Hurricanes formatting on the Havoc with the assistance of lights in its wing trailing edges. Enemy aircraft were tracked by the Havoc crew using GCI and AI radar. Once in range, the quarry was then illuminated with the powerful searchlight and the accompanying Hurricanes would close in for the kill. There were high hopes for this rather cumbersome arrangement, but it was far too unwieldy to be a success and there were no confirmed kills.

This is not to suggest that the Germans had it all their own way. The units that the Luftwaffe had scraped together were rarely of the highest quality, many being novice crews or those recuperating after injury. The first Baedeker raid on the night of 23/24 April was a complete failure: not even the pathfinder unit KG100 found the target city of Exeter. The anti-aircraft guns at Plymouth claimed to have shot down two enemy bombers as did the experienced nightfighter pilots of No 307 Squadron, based at Exeter and flying the new radar-equipped Bristol Beaufighters. Unfortunately all four bombers came down into the sea and could not be confirmed. The following night, 24/25 April, the Luftwaffe went for Exeter again with 44 bombers and with rather more success. Some 92 nightfighter sorties claimed nothing. The anti-aircraft guns at Portland said they shot one bomber down into the sea.

The British High Command was mystified at these seemingly aimless attacks with limited German resources. However, the next night, 25/26 April, saw the Luftwaffe pull out all the stops. Some 80-90 aircraft attacked Bath at around 11.00pm. Half of them, on returning to France, refuelled and launched a second attack on the city at about 4.00am. Again, inexperience showed. At least 20 towns and villages in the West Country received bombs from errant German crews. A sizeable minority flew too far down the Avon valley and attacked east Bristol by mistake. One Ju88 crew of KG3, its beam receiver out of action, flew on and was over mid-Wales before being shot down by a radar-equipped Beaufighter of No 255 Squadron. Two more bombers, a Do17 and Do217 of KG2 and KG40 respectively, were claimed by other similarly equipped squadrons. The local units based near Bath were less successful. No 125 Squadron at Colerne was in process of converting from the Defiant to the Beaufighter, but the latter was very new to them and the German tactics of dive-bombing proved too much for the airborne radar that preferred its quarry to fly straight and level. No claims were made. No 87 Squadron at Charmy Down did even worse. One of its 'catseye' Hurricanes developed a fault and the pilot had to bail out. The only local success was to the anti-aircraft guns at nearby Bristol which managed to shoot down one intruder. The Germans decided to maintain the pressure and on the night of 26/27 April they went for Bath again with some 83 bombers. The raid was another success. Nightfighters claimed a mere two probables; the Luftwaffe lost one Do17 of KG2 and a Ju88 of a reconnaissance unit.

At last the authorities realised that the Germans had launched a new offensive and with different objectives. The decision was taken on the afternoon of 26 April to move some guns from the industrial cities, particularly those of the north and northwestern areas, to a variety of possible targets. A list was swiftly drawn up of historic cities that could be attacked and other nearby towns of less historic interest that might still be bombed while air-

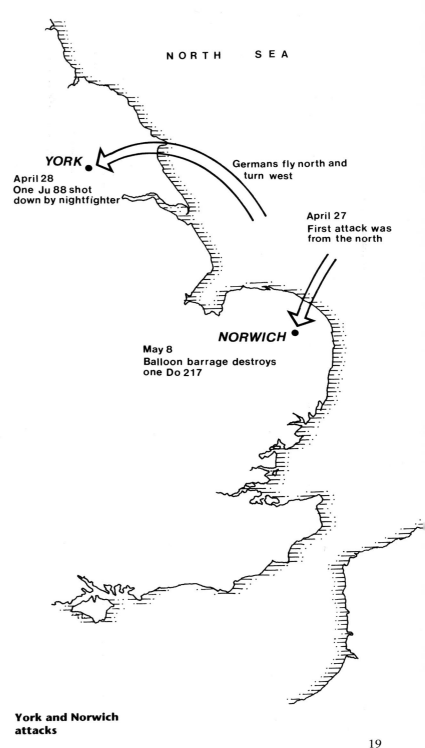

York and Norwich attacks

craft were in the neighbourhood. This first list of towns to be provided with AA defences included the following: Penzance, Truro, Hayle, Exeter, Bath, Basingstoke, Salisbury, Aldershot, Andover, Winchester, Taunton, Guildford, Maidstone, Tunbridge Wells, Ashford and Canterbury. It should be noted that all of these towns were in the south of England. This was quite natural as on the first four nights of renewed heavy bombing the Germans had struck twice at both Exeter and Bath, two southern cities. On the night of 27 April six of the newly positioned guns awaited a third night attack on Bath, but the Germans changed tack and went for Norwich instead.

The German aircrews themselves had not realised that this tactic of bombing historic cities was to be a continued idea until the afternoon of 26 April when Hitler made a public speech stressing that this new onslaught was to be long term. Yet after only four nights of continual effort the Luftwaffe was already beginning to feel the strain. There were no more attempts at two raids on the one night as had occurred at Bath. The Germans still managed to put together a force of 73 aircraft to attack Norwich although perhaps half of these were now provided from the Reserve Training Units. The raid achieved limited success but at least one German aircraft was lost. It also provoked a further rethink by the British defences and by the following evening Norwich had become a Gun Defended area with a battery of eight 3.7in guns. AA Command also decided to send guns to other targets away from the south including Ipswich, Cambridge, Colchester, Chelmsford, Lincoln, Peterborough and York. Many hopes rested with these redeployments. Unfortunately it was difficult to move guns around as quickly as was desired. The decision on the morning of 28 April to deploy some guns to historic cities in the north and east came too late for the next German target. By moving various units to more advantageous airfields, the Luftwaffe was able to send 74 aircraft to the northern city of York on the night of 28/29 April. Damage was again limited because of the relatively few aircraft involved. A catseye Hurricane did shoot one bomber down over the city of York. The 'Turbinlite' system was also in action for the first time, but without success. The minute that the Havoc turned on its searchlight, the German bomber took evasive action before the accompanying Hurricane could open fire.

The following night of 29/30 April the Luftwaffe returned to Norwich. A force of 70 bombers was despatched to the city which was now equipped with a number of mobile AA guns. They seemed to make no difference; indeed, this attack was both heavier and more concentrated than the first raid on Norwich and the centre of the city was badly damaged. This had been the seventh night in succession of continual raiding, however, and it seems that the crews needed a short rest as well as take time to relocate some Luftwaffe units for another change of target.

After a brief lull, on 3/4 May the Germans returned with a vengeance and their most successful raid by far on the city of Exeter. RAF nightfighter crews claimed five bombers destroyed, of which one actually crashed on to Topsham barracks at Exeter. Overall, and despite the obvious skill and commitment of those involved, the Baedeker raids could not be seen as a great defence for the British defences. With the primitive technology available to the British, German losses were low. In the entire Baedeker blitz 23 April – 6 June, some 900 Luftwaffe sorties were flown against Britain; and of these, a mere 33 aircraft failed to return, a loss rate of 3.66% and one that seemed well within acceptable limits.

Civil Defence

It was not only the proponents of the bomber offensive who expected heavy casualties in a second world war; so did the possible recipients of such an attack. The British government certainly took the threat very seriously indeed. In June 1937 the Air Raid Precautions (ARP) subcommittee of the Committee of Imperial Defence reported its findings. It announced that on the basis of World War 1 figures, it could be assumed that one ton of bombs would cause 50 casualties (17 dead, 33 injured). An all out attack by the Luftwaffe using gas, incendiary and high explosive bombs would, it was calculated, bring about some 200,000 casualties in a week, of whom 60,000 would be killed outright. Some form of Civil Defence was therefore essential, if only to minimise the casualties. Yet there were immediate problems when the idea was first raised in the mid-1930s: who should organise Civil Defence and, more important still, who should pay for it? Local councils were suspicious that their traditional freedoms were to be usurped.

The 1937 ARP Act made it law that all local authorities must undertake to set up Civil Defence organisations and went further in specifying some 17 matters which should be included in such schemes from giving advice to the public to setting up rescue parties. However it was up to the local authority to decide what level of Civil Defence was required; in other words, the county or county borough was responsible for assessing how many wardens, for example, that the area needed in relation to key industries or other targets within the area, and enemy attack. This meant some 230 or so separate schemes. All schemes were then sent forward to the Home Secretary for approval. It could be argued that this was a questionable arrangement: in order to preserve the sanctity of local independence, central government was being asked to rubber stamp a local authority's possible blinkered assessment of its own importance. Some cities were later to attempt to deflect criticism of how they failed to cope with air-raids by criticising the government for having approved their Civil Defence schemes in the first place: Exeter was one such. There was also later complaint that civic pride kept cities isolated from each other. Instead of pooling knowledge beforehand, each city made similar mistakes as each was attacked in turn.

Most areas followed the same basic framework of Civil Defence, and one that took care to create as few new organisations as possible. Civil Defence structures were set up and run by Emergency Committees, usually made up of a number of councillors. The Controller, in charge during an actual raid, was often the local Chief Constable and someone with former military experience.

The ARP Controller did not have control over one single structure of Civil Defence, for in the grouping together of the various parts of Civil Defence the idea of grafting new bits onto existing systems created a system of potential confusion. For a start, he had no real control over the Fire Brigade. This remained separate from the main body of Civil Defence to such an extent that when a Warden observed an explosion or fire — an incident as it was known — he had to make two separate telephone calls, the first to inform the Control Centre and the second to tell the Fire Station Headquarters. The Fire chiefs then made their own decision as to how many appliances should be ordered out. The Fire Service itself did make some preparations for the outbreak of war, in particular by recruiting large numbers of new personnel to create the Auxiliary Fire Service (AFS), but it was not incorporated into the Civil Defence system proper. The Police Force also occupied an ambivalent position. It, too, maintained a separate headquarters during a raid.

In London a warden was responsible for taking charge at an incident; everywhere else this was the job of the policeman.

The ARP Controller was still directly responsible for a variety of forces. He was dependent on the wardens for information about incidents. Once the details were received as to the location of an incident and its estimated importance, the message would be passed around the Centre for the attention of the various personnel: Rescue Parties, First Aid Parties, Ambulance Services. Most were volunteers, with a backbone of professionals, for if the proud boast of Civil Defence in general was that it was a local matter, the ethos of Civil Defence in particular was that it was a voluntary organisation.

There was certainly no shortage of volunteers for Civil Defence at first. Apart from those mentioned above, who went out during the raids there were all those in the second line of Civil Defence who helped after the attack had ended, the people who manned the Rest Centres which took in the temporary homeless, the staff who tried to find them new billets, all the voluntary groups that provided food and other assistance to the bombed-out, such as the Queen's Messengers, the WVS and the YMCA. The enthusiasm was certainly there at the start of the war; but there were no raids.

When the blitz finally did arrive in the autumn of 1940, many of the fears and expectations were not fulfilled. The death toll was far lower than expected, and the feared collapse in civilian morale did not occur, either. This belief had never been based on sets of statistics, accurate or otherwise. It had just been assumed that the civilian population would crack under the strain of continual bombing and a rapidly rising death toll. But morale did not crack, at least not in the prewar sense of millions of crazed civilians fleeing the ruins of their cities and seeking refuge in the countryside.

Some observers noted that if morale was to crack then the Germans would have to use different tactics. Civilians became accustomed to air raids; so the trick was to make sure that there was

no pattern to the attacks so that the population could not build up a protective routine. Some experts suggested that a more effective approach would be to raid a city on a number of occasions but with widely varying gaps between each raid. In such a way no pattern would emerge. This was to be the method used by the Germans during at least some of the Baedeker raids.

Other differences from expectations were less palatable. Bombs killed fewer people but caused far more structural damage than had been predicted. For every one person killed, 35 were made homeless. Civil Defence adapted; fewer First Aid parties, but an increase in Rescue Squads. The second line of the service had most problems with far more homeless people than had been predicted, those not injured but still requiring assistance. Many authorities were also criticised for failing to publicise after-raid facilities, to a population often dazed and confused by the bombing.

Herbert Morrison succeeded to the joint office of Home Secretary and Minister of Home Security in October 1940. He was to preside over many of the changes in Civil Defence that had been found necessary in the light of actual air raid experiences; notably the provision of alternate Control Centres and more despatch riders. He also gave his name to the new type of indoor air-raid shelter. Morrison was most noted, however, for his work with the fire services. There was no suggestion that the bravery of the firemen was in question but the raids had exposed a number of weaknesses and in the lull in the bombing after May 1941, a number of new procedures were introduced. To avoid the problem of broken mains, static water tanks were set up, linked by above ground lengths of piping. This was a major undertaking and by the start of 1942 many towns had not completed their system.

To avoid the farcical situation where reinforcing Fire Brigades from out of town found their equipment incompatible with other cities' hydrants, greater uniformity was introduced. Some 1,450 separate Fire Brigades were consolidated into 38 Fire Forces to make up the National Fire Service. By the time this was fully implemented in the summer of 1941, the main blitz had ended.

It was a pity this innovation had taken so long to be introduced; and the same might be said of the institution of the Fire Guards. Morrison not only

Left:
Civil Defence: the Civil Defence squad, Combe Down, Bath.

Below left:
After the raid the slow process of clearing up commenced. In this sadly typical scene, civilians and civil defence workers remove the casualties from a bombed out house, 'somewhere in England'.
IWM/D24337

Bottom left:
Civil Defence: a pre-blitz photograph of members of the Exeter National Fire Service.

cherished the principle of local auton-
omy; like many, he was also a firm
believer in the idea that Civil Defence
should be primarily a voluntary activity. This was fine as long as there were
sufficient volunteers available to do all
the required tasks. But it was a simple
fact that there was really very little
incentive to become a fire-watcher. The
demands of war meant that most workers were already putting in extra hours
at their place of work. Few would wish
to leave the comparative safety of their
homes to spend a long night patrolling
their bosses' properties for no pay and
with the constant worry that if a raid
did start there was always the nagging
fear as to how the family at home were
coping, and whether indeed they were
still alive.

Watchers themselves often felt that
their work largely consisted of long
periods of isolated boredom as they
paced around the darkened and
deserted offices and factories. If a person was to volunteer for Civil Defence
work there was at least a sense of purpose and more contact with fellow
human beings if they opted to go into
the warden service, for example.

It was also a simple fact, unfortunately, that incendiary bombs were little danger if dealt with promptly but
deadly if left to spread their flames. On
29 December 1940 the Luftwaffe scored
a major success. The largely empty
offices in the heart of London were gutted by widespread fires, some of which
spread for a full half-a-square mile
across the very centre of the city. St
Paul's Cathedral survived, in a sea of
flames; but it had a large and caring
band of fire watchers.

As a result of this needless destruction, Morrison announced the principle
of compulsory fire watching. But a
whole series of orders over the next 12
months were sufficiently vague that, as
the official historian pointed out, it was
soon a cliché that anyone bar a congenital idiot could find a way to avoid Fire
Guard duty and a congenital idiot was
exempt from duty anyway.

It seems that by August 1941 the well
of volunteers — those who had gone

into the Auxiliary Fire Service, First Aid
Squads, Home Guard — had finally
dried up. Perhaps as many as 75% of
potential Fire Watchers tried to avoid
compulsory duties. The job was unpop-
ular and by the August date when it
was finally spelt out that such duties
were compulsory, it no longer seemed
that they actually were necessary. The
Luftwaffe had moved en masse to the
Eastern Front a number of months previously. It was no wonder then that
local authorities were both ready to
complain at the lack of suitable fire
watchers and yet at the same time did
not pursue the cases of exemption with
what seemed like any real zeal. City
after city reported difficulties in making
up quotas of fire guards and the lack of
enthusiasm for any form of real training. This report comes from the Eastern
regional Commissioner at the time of
the Baedeker raids:

'The results of compulsory enrolment
are not only disappointing in quantity
but also in quality. Conscription is only
of value in so far as it can be combined
with discipline. The men brought in by
compulsory enrolment consist largely
of those who have previously shirked
all forms of voluntary war work and the
local authorities possess no means of
keeping them under continuous and
disciplined control. Business firms are
most reluctant to have such men
brought into their premises at night,
and the local authorities are also
unwilling to put them in premises
where there are opportunities for damage or theft. Night inspections by
Regional Officers have made it clear
that the conscripts are much less reli-
able than those who are either working
at the premises or have volunteered for
this duty.'

Some Fire Guard leaders felt such
despair that they even put forward the
hope that there might be further air
raids. These at least might raise morale
by giving the unwilling conscripts an
idea that they did have a purpose.
Unfortunately, they were to get their
wish.

THE
RAIDS

Exeter:

Civil Defence

The beautiful city of Lübeck had been attacked and so Hitler decreed that similarly attractive cities in England should be bombed in retaliation. The comparison went further. Lübeck had been famed for its *Altstadt* with its large numbers of late medieval buildings; the Germans also seem to have targetted cities in England that owed their popularity to having important buildings from the same period. In the early 16th Century, three of the six largest towns in England (excluding London, which Hitler had also placed an embargo upon in his new directive) were Exeter, Norwich and York; and these were to be three of the first four targets. Only Bath, which had been comprehensively redeveloped by the Georgians, had effectively covered up much of its early origins and was famed for architecture of a later date, that of the 18th Century. The other three cities still revealed much of their medieval past: each possessed cathedral and castle, areas of closely packed and vulnerable buildings, all enclosed by the remains of their original defensive walls.

Appearances can be deceptive. At first glance, Exeter retained much of its medieval past. The cathedral was not as large as some and it did not dominate the city as others did, but many people remarked on its beauty and that of the Cathedral Close. Only a few pieces of Rougement Castle remained, but the great mound that it had stood on added dignity to those parts that did exist. The medieval walls of the city were remarkably complete but they suffered from the same problem as the Cathedral. Later building had so encroached upon the walls that there were large expanses that could not be observed with ease.

The buildings in the central area were tightly compact, as in Lübeck, but here the comparisons ended. Only the ground plan remained medieval in Exeter; many of its buildings were of a far more recent date. Aside from the area of the Cathedral Close, medieval and early modern buildings were scattered about the city rather than grouped together in one picturesque spot. Nor were there that many of them. In the words of one postwar planner: 'the sober truth is that, outside the Cathedral Close, there were hardly more than half of a dozen buildings that remained from the period before 1600'.

It is perhaps a good example of selective historical recall to discover that the Cathedral Close apart, much of Exeter's best architecture that had survived into the 20th Century was not medieval, but of the Georgian period. It was generally agreed that by far the best example of a development from this time was the oval-shaped Bedford Circus. This stood just east of the High Street and only a short distance from the Cathedral itself. The Circus led on to other 18th Century streets of equally good style: Southernhay West, Barnfield Crescent, Dix's Field. Further out still were the far less impressive Victorian districts, areas such as Newtown, packed with small terraced houses with as many as 62 to the acre.

Also on the outskirts were the limited areas of industry, one between the city walls and the river, at Haven Banks. Here stood the nearest things that Exeter had to military targets: the power station and Willey's engineering works. The latter had a peacetime workforce of some 1,400 out of a total population of some 76,000. The next biggest industrial employer was Wippel's, although its products — church furnishings — obviously had little immediate role to play once war was declared. No other single firm in peacetime Exeter employed more than 150

workers. By no stretch of the imagination, therefore, could Exeter be considered a major industrial target.

The war naturally brought some changes as more people went into engineering, vehicle and aircraft production. Some departments of the Admiralty moved down to the city but, as in Bath, it was largely those departments that were not too important and did not have to be kept in London. None of these developments appreciably increased the chances of Exeter being designated a military target because of any vital war industries. It had none. Its only possible claim to attention was as a major centre of road and railway links.

It is most important to bear in mind the layout of the city. The general theme of prewar Civil Defence was the idea that you should organise a service that was commensurate with the perceived threat to the city. If your city had plenty of essential war industries, then it would probably be raided and so the local authorities ought to lay out Civil Defence services that could deal with a major attack. Exeter did not possess such important targets and so it had no need to provide as comprehensive a service; it did not expect a major raid. Unfortunately, there was another way of estimating Civil Defence needs. Instead of considering the likelihood of attack, you might consider the vulnerability of the city; in other words, forget for the moment the reasons why you might come under fire. If we assume that Exeter could be raided, were there then any particular features of the city that could lead to problems? In Exeter, the answer was most definitely in the affirmative: its central shopping area was so congested that it was a major fire risk. A concentrated incendiary attack on any one part of it could very easily spread flames across the whole lot, so tightly packed were the cafés and banks and shops. In that case, it could be argued that Exeter required a greater degree of Civil Defence than might first appear to be the case. In 1973, official government records released to the public included wartime reports that were somewhat critical of Exeter's Civil Defence preparation. The ARP Controller of the time, C. J. Newman, was more recently asked to give his opinion on these newly released documents. He said:

'None of us expected that in a city like Exeter we would be an air-raid target like we turned out to be. We could have understood that cities like Bristol and Plymouth would be hit, but Exeter was not counted as a war target.

'The government of the day evidently held that view as well, for it never sent us any protection like the barrage balloons with which the war production cities were served. If there were any shortages in Exeter the higher authorities were to blame. We erected everything they let us have.'

The final sentence might be queried: local authorities usually assessed their own potential as a target and central government rarely questioned their judgement. The initial work was a local responsibility, therefore. But the rest of Mr Newman's response is quite true. In a sense, neither central nor local government were to blame for the devastation that was to wipe out so much of the centre of Exeter. The city was not a major target and so it did not need a high level of Civil Defence. No-one considered the possibility that it might be attacked for the very reason that it was a particularly beautiful city with no real industry or defence. Then, because of its congested heart, it would burn quite spectacularly.

By the time that Exeter was raided, it possessed some 90 full-time firemen along with 17 part-timers. It also had 17,000 registered Fire Guards. These sound impressively high figures, but in order to provide general cover for every night of the month, only some 1,100 Fire Guards would be on duty each night. These were divided into teams of five, and so 220 teams had the job of looking after an estimated 1,735 premises; a tall order, indeed. The sad thing was, that this number of Fire Guards was deemed more than enough under normal conditions and according to central government guidelines. Although the system shared many of the problems found in groups across the country, the Fire Guards of Exeter seemed less of a problem than most. There had been a large number of volunteers, more than in many cities. Most had been taught the theory of dealing with an incendiary; many had tackled practice bombs. It was admitted that few had gone on to Part III training with fire bomb parties, learning to work as teams in their business premises and streets, but this was being planned.

An inspection by the Regional Headquarters had intimated that there was

Above:
In more peaceful days prior to the outbreak of war, Exeter Cathedral is seen from the southwest. It was the area to the south of the Chancel which was to suffer severe bomb damage; fortunately, the main structure of the Cathedral was to survive remarkably intact although much of the medieval stained glass was lost.

Left:
Two of the leading Civil Defence figures in Exeter: on the left is Newman, head of the local Civil Defence, whilst on the right is the local head of the National Fire Service, Willey.

nothing inherently wrong with the Exeter Fire Guard system and that it was developing well. One suggestion was made: for the first time it was accepted that the centre of Exeter was a particular high fire risk and therefore 'it might be considered that the minimum standard of cover which had been taken as the general standard here was not sufficiently high and that steps should be taken, where possible, to improve it by increasing the number of fire watchers, particularly in business groups. . .' The Exeter Fire Guard leaders agreed and did attempt to increase numbers, but at the same time they recognised a fundamental problem: there were just not enough people available.

With increased air activity over Britain in the summer of 1940, Exeter began to receive the odd bomb. For the most part the war seemed to pass it by, quite literally in some cases: many believed that Exeter was on the Luftwaffe's route as they headed towards the industrial cities far to the north. If Exeter did suffer occasional damage then this was usually seen as being accidental: the bomb, no doubt, had been intended for somewhere else. This still seemed the case on 23 April 1942,

when the warning sirens began to sound over the city at 10.44pm. As far as the Germans were concerned, this was the first of their revenge raids but, although the moon was full, there was a haze across much of the West of England and perhaps for this reason the attack went very wrong. It was not until the next morning when the British intercepted a message from a German reconnaissance aircraft flying over the city, that the British authorities realised that Exeter had been the intended target. Instead of one concentrated raid, the Germans had dropped their bombs over a wide area of Somerset, Devon and Cornwall. Only one aircraft had dropped bombs on Exeter itself. Flying at about 9,000ft, a sole bomber let fall four high explosive bombs at about 11.30pm. Even these landed nowhere near the centre of the city but fell across the river in the district of St Thomas. They missed both the main road bridge and the nearby station of St Thomas. All landed on the roads. One fell near the junction of Okehampton Road and Manor Road. The explosion threw debris up into the air which crashed back down again, on top of a woman Fire Watcher. She was dead when the rescue squads dug her

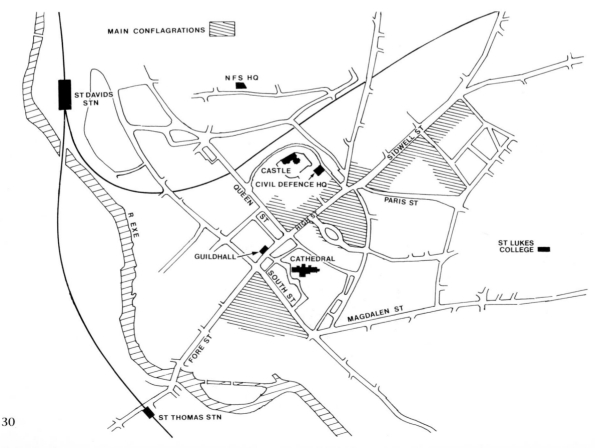

out. Another five people were killed in two separate incidents along Okehampton Road, one man's body being found at the top of a partially wrecked house.

The attack did seem rather more impressive at the time. There were many flares illuminating the sky at one point but if they were intended as markers, no main force ever arrived. They were not particularly accurate either as they all fell to the west of the city and beyond. As a result scores of incendiaries fell across St Thomas, and also the more outlying areas of Ide and Alphington. The Fire Brigade was sent out to deal with these fires but as there were no high explosives dropped in these areas, there were also no serious casualties to be dealt with. The other deaths in the area that night were further out again. The mental institute at Exminster took a hit from a high explosive bomb and a rescue squad was sent from Exeter to assist in clearing up. When they arrived, it was obvious that parts of the hospital had been damaged quite badly. The staff had taken a roll call but some patients were still missing. A careful search of the twisted wreckage in one ward eventually located the body of a man who had been buried beneath a heap of bedsteads and other debris. Local troops arrived and helped to remove the body. The rescue squad then turned their attention to another part of the building where the staff believed another man was still unaccounted for. It was a repeat of the first case. A careful sifting through the accumulated wreckage eventually revealed another body, again trapped underneath a whole heap of debris on the bottom floor. The rescue squad had to use crowbars to get him out. These appeared to be the only two deaths at the institute, the injured having been dealt with before the rescue squad arrived.

Within the Exeter district, therefore, a handful of bombs had killed a total of only eight people. This was good for the area, but hardly satisfactory as far as the Luftwaffe was concerned and when the reconnaissance aircraft reported back the next day that little damage had been done to the city, a second raid was immediately ordered for that same evening.

So on the night of 24 April the sirens sounded at 10 minutes after midnight to signal another attack. This time visibility was much improved and far more of the German aircraft were able to find the target. This time a number dived to low altitude before releasing their bombs. It is perhaps all the more surprising that the main destruction was to the outskirts of Exeter as some 60 high explosive and perhaps 2,000 incendiary bombs fell within the city limits. Once again, St Thomas on the eastern edge suffered some damage.

The main brunt this time, however, was felt by the eastern and northern parts of the city just beyond the main High Street. Two of the main eastern roads suffered badly, Paris Street and Sidwell Street. High explosives killed a number of people in Paris Street. A series of high explosive bombs in this part of the city added to the death toll. At least 14 dead in Paris Street; twos and threes killed in nearby Sidwell Street, Prospect Place to the north and Kings Road. Fire added further complications. There were some 54 fires recorded that night but none were major. Sidwell Street received incendiaries as well as high explosives. Powderham Crescent to the north of the city probably suffered the worst of the fire, but the flames did not spread to adjoining streets. The Fire Guards were later commended for their prompt and efficient action in all parts of the city that were affected by incendiaries. Many areas escaped almost completely and this included the centre of the city: that is, apart from one particular bomb which landed very close to the Cathedral. Later reports claimed that it must have been a deliberate attack on the Cathedral. This is quite possible, especially in the light of what was to happen to the building in the heaviest of the raids on the night of 3 May. But if there was deliberate intent, this does appear a little odd, because the Germans seemed to take great care in the other Baedeker raids to avoid hitting cathedrals and thus handing over to the British a great propaganda victory as had happened over Coventry.

On this night, the 24th, the Cathedral itself avoided major damage but a lone bomb landed some 70yds away across the Close on the Abbot's Lodge. It could have been a major incident. The Lodge had been the medieval town house of the Abbots of Buckfast although it had been much reconstructed in the 16th Century. It was now the residence of the headmaster of the Cathedral School which stood close by the house. The school was not large, having only 25 pupils, but luckily it was on its Easter holiday and so all the boys were away. The headmaster himself, Richard Langhorne, was also absent along with his son. Unfortunately his daughter Elizabeth was still in residence in the Abbot's Lodge. When the bomb fell and completely demolished the building she was killed instantly along with three of the domestic staff who also lived there. Four people were killed, but it could have been a lot worse.

As the all-clear sounded at 1.55am, this was a feeling shared by many. At first sight this might appear odd. Exeter had suffered some 73 dead, as many as York was to lose in what the latter considered a major raid a few days later. To some extent the limited nature of this Exeter raid is only seen as such with the benefit of hindsight. It was rapidly overtaken by the far worse destruction of the night of 3 May which made the previous week's raid seem small in comparison. It should also be noted, that by its very nature the 24/25 April raid did not appear to be that heavy. There was neither widespread damage across the entire city, nor concentrated damage in the very heart. With the exception of the Abbot's Lodge, the main destruction was to the less visible periphery of the city, notably Paris Street, the bulk of which had already been earmarked for demolition for the purposes of road widening and urban renewal. Casualties had been high in a few areas, but most had escaped very lightly and there was no great destruction of major buildings in the centre of the city, historic or otherwise, to suggest that a major raid had occurred. The Civil Defence services received praise for the way that they had coped with the situation. While the raid had not been heavy enough to really stretch them, the Fire Guards and Fire Brigade could be congratulated for having dealt with the incidents that did occur in a swift and efficient manner.

If damage was obviously limited, it was less easy to estimate the effects of this raid on civilian morale. Bombs had now fallen within the city limits on two nights in succession and there seemed every possibility that there might be further raids. This appeared to be the case the following night when in the early hours of 26 April the air-raid sirens sounded yet again. It seemed that Exeter was in for another serious raid and in fact the all clear was not sounded until two hours later. But Bath was the main target that night and there was only one aircraft that dropped its bomb load over Exeter. A single high explosive bomb came down on the closely packed terraced houses of Portland Street. It killed four people. A scattering of incendiary bombs started several small fires but these were extinguished without difficulty.

These were the last bombs to fall on Exeter for a number of days but obviously no-one knew this at the time; a third successive night of casualties, however light, proved to be the last straw for some. It was natural that the heaviest raid, of 24 April, had the most effect. The following day the Emergency Committee met and decided that in the light of already obvious movements of the city's inhabitants, they would not interfere with those who wanted to trek out into the countryside, but at the same time they would not give them actual encouragement. The 25th and 26th of April were a Saturday and Sunday and so it was not until the following day that many municipal offices re-opened for normal business. The department that dealt with requests for Morrison shelters found that Monday 27 April was anything but normal. Prior to that date, there had been a steady rate of some 300 applications for an indoor shelter per week. Now the demand increased dramatically as people suddenly realised the necessity for having a proper shelter. On Tuesday 28 April there were 1,400 applications for Morrison shelters. The staff were not always sympathetic. One member of the department wrote of 'belated applicants for shelters, who swarmed round the shelter office following the raids, after having neglected to apply during the quiet months previous to then'. Nor did the demand subside after a few bombless nights, for it remained high throughout the following week. Trekking also showed no signs of going into decline. On 28 April the Emergency Committee was sufficiently worried to begin making arrangements to limit the trekkers' numbers. Loudspeaker vans drove around the city broadcasting appeals for people to stay put.

Events were to prove the pessimists right. The Germans appeared to agree with the local assessment that the city had not yet been dealt a body blow and on the evening of 3 May the Luftwaffe revisited Exeter. This was by far the worst of the raids; no wonder the attack of 24 April subsequently became known as the 'Minor Blitz'. With pardonable exaggeration, the mayor of Exeter was later to call it the worst dis-

Location of buildings in central Exeter

aster to have befallen the city since its devastation by the Vikings back in 1003.

It was a very clear night and the Germans had no difficulty in finding the city. The attack began at 1.36am and went on for an hour and-a-half. In the first 10 minutes the bombers dropped masses of incendiaries. Some fell, once again, on the long suffering eastern districts, Newtown in particular, but this time the aircraft made no mistake and hundreds of incendiaries cascaded down upon the centre of the city as well. This was then followed by a fair number of high explosive bombs and then the main part of the raid when the two types of bomb were dropped together. It was later calculated that at least 160 high explosive bombs and 7-8,000 incendiaries had been dropped on the earlier nights.

The greatest fears of those who recognised the particular vulnerability of the centre of Exeter were about to be realised. 'The worst fire risk in the region' was showered with incendiaries. The German aircraft often came in very low, despite the newly installed anti-aircraft guns, and dropped their incendiary loads so close to the ground that they landed in great concentrated masses. St Luke's College stood away from the centre but its experience was reflected elsewhere. In the morning after the raid, the remains of over 200 incendiary bombs were found in and around the college, a massive concentration that was bound to overwhelm the fire watchers. In the city centre the situation was worse still as fire in one building swiftly spread to others. The compactness of the city centre had already been noted. There were few squares or open spaces, save for the Cathedral Close, to lessen the chance of a fire spreading. The streets themselves were no barrier to flame: even the High Street was only 40-50ft wide and many of the side streets were little more than alleyways. Many of the buildings were constructed of wood with only a thin outer facing of stone to suggest a more expensive building material and the large numbers of shops in the centre also contained significant amounts of combustible materials. Finally, a light wind also proved strong enough to spread the fires across the area.

The Fire Guards in the centre of the city were in a quite unenviable position. The Germans knew exactly what to do to cause them maximum discomfort and to hamper their efforts as far as possible. High explosives could kill. If they were dropped by far the safest thing to do was to take cover and thus be forced to abandon the job of fire fighting. In fact the centre of Exeter did not suffer a great deal of blast damage on the night of 3 May. Some 14 high explosive bombs fell there and they had limited physical effect. The very fact that buildings were so tightly packed together in the centre meant that a handful of shops absorbed the blast and acted as cover for others. In the more open residential areas, damage was much more widespread. High explosives did of course pose one additional problem; the odd bomb could quite effectively blast open a store's windows, leaving it vulnerable to encroaching flames. But one of the chief uses of the high explosive bomb was as a deterrence to Fire Watchers. Fourteen bombs might not appear many, but as no-one knew when or where they might fall, some Fire Guards might take shelter when the first did fall and remain undercover from then on. Other cases were less obvious. In one incident a mixed Fire Guard team of men and women were dealing quite adequately with incendiary bombs on the roof of a multi-storied building when high explosive bombs were heard to fall, apparently close by. Showing a possibly misplaced example of chivalry, the men ordered the women to take shelter in the basement of the building while they stayed on duty. With half the squad gone it was soon found that the men were too few in numbers to deal with the fires which rapidly got out of hand. Nor had the danger been as great as had been first thought: the high explosives had not landed close by, indeed they had not even broken the building's windows.

The Germans had other tricks as well. Many aircraft encouraged their machine-gunners to open fire across the city. High explosive bombs and machine-gun bullets forced many to keep low.

Within a short time the NFS headquarters had received details of over 500 separate fires. What was worse, some of them were beginning to join up and it was not long before there were three conflagrations in the very heart of the city. The most serious conflagration extended over some 23 acres of the city just to the north of the Cathedral and gutted much of the High Street as well as important roads leading off it to either side. This fire destroyed many of the principal department stores, a number of the best Georgian parts of the city, as well as the Post Office and the Public Library which also happened to hold the Civil Defence Control Centre for Exeter. The Germans systematically strafed and bombed this area so that each group of Fire Guards was reduced to fighting its own little battle to defend its particular building. Incendiaries fell on roofs, high explosives threatened to wipe out entire fire watching parties and blew open windows and doors. Flames threatened to spread from adjoining buildings or, even, from across the street. In the face of this onslaught, the Fire Guards struggled valiantly but in most cases could only delay the inevitable for a little while. Much of the west side of the High Street was burnt out. At the northern end of the street a high explosive bomb struck the Plaza Cinema, practically demolishing the building at a single stroke. A sheet of flame seemed to envelop the building and fanned by a northeasterly wind, fire began to spread into adjoining buildings down the street. At the southern end of this small block of buildings a number of incendiaries landed on the roofs of further properties. It was very difficult to get on to the roofs of any of these buildings and as the fires began to develop, high explosives close by forced the Fire Guards to vacate the premises and take shelter. As a result this fire at one end of the block advanced to meet that spreading down from the Plaza and the whole lot was gutted.

The fires on the west side of the High Street had now reached what might appear to be a natural break, the gap in the street that was the side road off Castle Street. On the opposite corner to the already blazing premises further up the High Street stood the Westminster Bank. But Castle Street was a very narrow thoroughfare and the lead Fire Guard on the bank, a Mr Thomas, began to worry for the building's safety as flames began to reach across the road. A bomb that had fallen on the opposite, east side, of the High Street had already rendered the bank more susceptible to fire as the blast had blown out its windows and doors. At this time the NFS had still not arrived in the High Street and so Thomas tried to contact them, only to be told that the Fire Brigade was unable to give any assistance at present. The inevitable happened. Fanned by a stiff breeze, the

flames jumped across the gap of Castle Street and in through the gaping windows of the Westminster Bank. The Fire Guards soon found the situation was out of hand and had to vacate the premises.

The fires now began to work their way down this next block of buildings on the west side of the High Street. Here the situation was still more confused as fire spread from one direction, interspersed with high explosives, dropping mostly to the rear of the street and a continual carpeting of incendiaries across the whole lot. The two adjoining buildings, Whippell Brothers and the Devon and Somerset Stores, had already lost their windows in the same blast on the opposite side of the street that had opened up the Westminster Bank. Then both stores were hit by a very large number of incendiary bombs. The Fire Guards on the roof of the Devon and Somerset stores were able to deal with all the fire bombs that landed there, and also went out into the streets to the front and back to deal with a further scattering of incendiaries. But there were just too many bombs falling onto the Whippell Brothers' store and despite help from the fire-watchers of the Devon and Somerset Stores, a serious fire began to develop. This obviously threatened the adjoining store and so Mr Mathews, the leader of the Devon and Somerset Fire Guards, sent a desperate message to the Fire Brigade for assistance, even for just the use of one hose pipe as he was sure that this could make all the difference. This request was refused; nor did any unit of the NFS turn up. There was a hydrant outside the front of the store that was not being used; there was a static water tank at the rear of the premises which held hundreds of gallons of water and was also not in operation. But Mathews had no hoses, only stirrup pumps, and without further assistance all this water was of no use to him whatsoever. The Devon and Somerset store went up in flames, along with its neighbours.

Further high explosive bombs landed at the rear of these premises demolishing the Baths and the Musgrave Club. Another series of incendiary bombs set fire to the adjacent buildings including Bruford's, and as the fire proceeded to gut yet another whole block of buildings there was some fear that it would engulf the whole of Castle Street, too. But here the fire watchers were to have a certain amount of success. They could do nothing to prevent the flames from reaching across and into the Castle Hotel which was eventually burnt to the ground. But there were a few large separate buildings with some open ground in this area; and more importantly, the NFS had sent some fire crews to deal with fires in two important buildings: the main telephone exchange and the city library next door, which also housed the Civil Defence Control Centre in the basement. The latter had to be evacuated and the library was gutted. The Fire Brigade had more success with the Telephone Exchange which was saved from destruction, although this was partly attributable to appropriate forethought. The exchange was a modern building with a fire-resisting roof deck. It only received some three incendiary bombs which were easily quenched by Fire Guards. The obvious threat was the possibility that fire could spread from adjoining buildings and, indeed, one side of the exchange faced an alley barely 9ft wide, across which there was an old three-storey building. This building had caught fire during the raid and flames easily crossed into the wooden window of the exchange. This had been foreseen, months ago, and long before the raids a 4½in thick brick wall had been built inside the window. This proved a completely effective barrier to the flames and the interior of the room remained quite unmarked.

The telephone exchange was saved by the Fire Brigade. Fire Guards also played their part in stopping the spread of flames. Two who were actually on duty in the castle went out to chop down the small bridge that linked the city library to the museum at Rougemont House and thus saved the latter building from catching fire. Fire Brigades and Fire Guards thus prevented fire from spreading down the street to the castle itself although that building was relatively safe in that it stood in its own grounds. There was little to stop fire spreading further up and down the west side of High Street, though. At the northern end there was something of a gap in the shape of Northernhay Place. The Plaza Cinema, on the corner of High Street and Northernhay Place, had been one of the first buildings to be hit but the width of the Place was just enough to hinder the spread of fire northwards. The Fire Guards were able to hold the flames long enough for the Fire Brigade to arrive and to stop them from spreading over and beyond at least part of Northernhay Place.

There were fewer obvious breaks at the southern end of this side of the High Street: the side roads were quite narrow and, as we have seen, flames had already crossed the gap that was Castle Street with relative ease. The eastern and opposite side of the High Street was also soon well ablaze. The first incendiaries on this side appeared to fall on to the Arcade, near the top — or north — part of the street. The Fire Guards had great difficulty in getting up to the roof and dealing with the very large numbers of bombs which had fallen there and they were forced

Area destroyed along the High Street

36

to abandon the Arcade and leave it to burn. It seemed that adjacent premises were doomed to destruction as well. The Co-operative shop stood to one side of the Arcade, and on the corner of High Street and Southernhay although the very corner itself was occupied by another and older building. The Co-op was a modern department store building of fire-resisting construction but within a short time it was completely surrounded by fire. The small corner building was ablaze, as was the Arcade to one side and other premises to the rear. The two fronts of the store also faced across to fires on the opposite sides of the road, in High Street and Southernhay East respectively. Yet the Co-op did not burn. This was solely due to the efforts of the Fire Watchers on the premises, led by a Mr Restorick. He led a team of four others that was particularly well prepared.

Restorick had long realised that the greatest danger was of fire coming in through the windows from other buildings that were as close as a mere 10ft away. Accordingly, he had developed the habit of laying out 60ft lengths of hose alongside the windows on all floors and connected to taps fed from the large water tank on the roof. This was even done on nights when there was no air raid alert. He positioned his four men so that each one looked after one storey while he stood on the roof as a watcher. Each man was also equipped with a stirrup pump and bucket, as well as a whistle to attract help from the others, should fire break out on his floor. When the actual attack began, the fire watchers acted on a prearranged plan and immediately began to remove as much combustible material as they could from the vicinity of the windows. Blackout curtains were torn down, boxes of shoes and other items for sale moved into the centre of the rooms. Restorick himself dealt most efficiently with the four incendiaries that landed on the roof of the building and snuffed them out with buckets of sand. The greatest danger, though, was obviously the flames that were belching out from every building that surrounded the Co-op.

The Fire Watchers proceeded to perform an epic task; for the whole length of the raid and for some time afterwards they ran from window to window, hosing each one as flames threatened to burst in. In two or three places fire was able to set alight some wooden fittings but a concentrated defence pre-

vented it from going any further. Walls and ceilings were blackened, fittings scorched and charred but when daylight came the Co-operative Store was still standing. Thomas Pike, one of the Fire Watchers involved, was to recall later that when the Fire Brigade finally found him and his colleagues, the firemen could hardly believe they could be alive, surrounded as they were by so much devastation.

It was, in truth, an isolated success and practically the only building that survived in its block. To the other side of the Arcade stood the main Post Office. This received a large number of incendiaries which started a fire that was soon well beyond the control of the Fire Watchers. They attempted to leave the building but a series of explosions now appeared to rock the street and sent debris flying everywhere. One high explosive bomb landed just a little further down the east side of the street, demolishing Singers' premises (it was this bomb that also shattered the glass of most of the buildings on the west side as well). The resulting fires coupled with even more incendiaries to set further parts of this area alight. Kendalls went up in flames. Fire shot across from the other side of the street to ignite more premises on the east side of the High Street. The Fire Guards at Bobby & Co were driven from the roof of the building by German machine-gunning but when they returned to their duties the flames had taken too strong a hold. Fire then spread to Dellar's Café. It is possible a high explosive bomb hit it at the same time; certainly fire seemed to break out quite suddenly as flames flashed through the kitchen quarters. Lloyds Bank, Cann Bros, each caught on fire in turn until half the High Street was a tunnel of fire, with both sides alight.

The fire burnt back as well as along. On the west side it had petered out in the face of determined fire prevention groups, aided by a low density of buildings in the area in front of the castle. This advantage was to be denied to the fire-fighters on the eastern side where the shops and houses were much more closely packed together. Bedford Street ran into the High Street on this side and flames from the main fire soon spread into Hughes' premises and the Bedford Garage. But the street was only a short one, linking the High Street to Bedford Circus and within a short time this fine area of 18th Century architecture was well ablaze. One high explosive bomb landed on the exit nearest to the High Street, demolishing the Devon and Exeter Savings Bank and killing a number of Fire Guards who were on duty there. Another bomb fell near to the exit at the other end of the Circus, setting alight to a drill hall. The ammunition and explosives that were stored there only added to the incendiaries and machine-gunning to make fire fighting well nigh impossible within the Circus itself. The fires spread further: narrow Chapel Street and Catherine Street went up in flames, the former behind Bedford Circus, the latter behind the High Street. Half of another Georgian masterpiece, Southernhay West, was completely destroyed by incendiaries. It was later claimed that the scale of destruction was partly due to the fact that so many premises were under so many different authorities, that 'it would appear that united effort to deal with the fires here was lacking'.

For the most part, the situation was basically beyond the capacity of the ordinary Fire Guard; the fires could only be dealt with by the heavier equipment of the Fire Brigade. Yet by the time the Fire Services were able to send pumps to the area the situation was already well beyond simple fire-fight-

ing. It was not that the pumps could not deal with the fires in Bedford Circus, they never had the opportunity to try, at least not in the early part of the raid. With fire shooting from one side of the High Street to the other, high explosives at either entrance, it was just not possible to get into Bedford Circus. Reg Vincent had found it impossible to get along the High Street in the early part of the raid. With the fire engines unable to reach the heart of the conflagration, the premises in the centre of the fires just had to burn themselves out and the fire services could simply try to stop them spreading out any further. This was no easy task. If an area was ablaze, it was not the case that every building was on fire at once. Most Fire Watchers had been able to escape once they realised their efforts on their particular building were hopeless. A number of premises, parts of Bedford Circus included, did not catch fire until some hours after the actual raid had finished. On the outskirts of the conflagration, the fire services concentrated their attentions on areas where there were natural fire breaks in the form of wider streets and open areas. The successful stoppage of the fires up Castle Street and across Northernhay Place has

Area destroyed around Sidwell Street

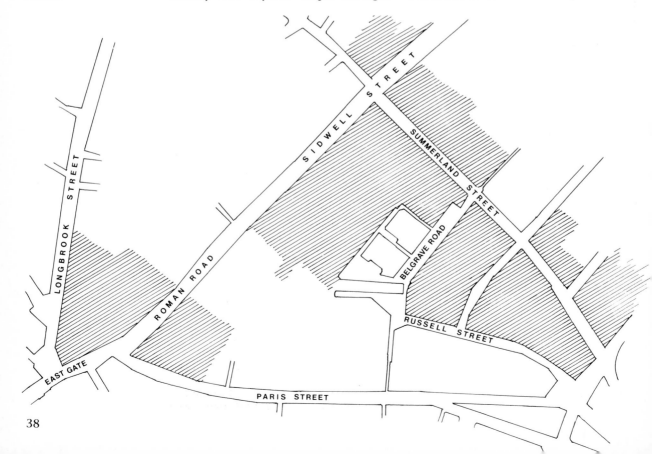

already been noted. On the eastern side of this great inferno the expanse of open land that separated Southernhay East from Southernhay West provided another welcome barrier. But with the wind blowing from the northeast, there was still the danger that the fire would continue to work its way down the High Street and right through the centre of the city and here there were no open areas or wide roads to retard the passage of the flames. In these circumstances, the achievement of the NFS was all the more impressive. Pumps were brought up the High Street to the limits of the fires. Here, outside Colson's Stores, water was played on to the properties just beyond the flames. This tactic worked and at last the fire was stopped in its tracks so that the lower half of the High Street was saved, including both the Police Station and the Elizabethan Guildhall.

Meanwhile, a second conflagration had developed in Fore Street and threatened to burn up the High Street from the opposite end of the city. This never developed to such a degree as the first inferno although it did consume some seven acres of buildings. A large market building went up in flames. Marks & Spencer's store was hit by incendiary bombs which the Fire Guards were dealing with quite successfully when a high explosive bomb hit the store, shattering the building, and causing such a fire that the duty personnel were forced to evacuate. Other properties had less dutiful Fire Guards; it was said that at one store, the Fire Watchers took cover as soon as the air-raid siren was sounded and without protection the building was soon ablaze. The fire made only limited progress up Fore Street, however, the main fires sweeping down one of the side roads, Queen Street. Here there was much damage although the street did produce one hero. The priest of the Roman Catholic Church of the Sacred Heart spent the entire raid on top of his church tower, throwing and kicking away the incendiaries as they landed. In this he was successful; the church did not go up in flames.

So a crucial central section of Exeter was not consumed by fire. Half of the High Street remained intact and, beside it, the Cathedral Close also escaped serious damage by fire. High explosives were another matter. A number of incendiaries fell across the Close in the early part of the raid. Some landed on the Cathedral but the Fire Watchers were able to deal with them promptly and no damage was done. The Deanery caught fire, but the Dean himself was able to extinguish the flames with a stirrup pump. However, a sole German aircraft then circled the Cathedral before dropping a single 250kg bomb. This crashed down on to the south choir aisle before exploding at ground level so that much of the blast went upwards rather than down. Three bays of the aisle were demolished and two of the flying buttresses were completely sheared off; luckily, the choir vault did not collapse. The chapel of St Thomas was also destroyed as was a crypt below and a chamber above it. This upstairs chamber was the muniment room and a large number of rich, ceremonial garments were ruined. Blast also played havoc in the interior of the building. The 15th Century screens that separated the Quire from the aisles were blown into thousands of pieces. The organ was badly damaged, the Quire pulpit ruined. A thousand tons of masonry came crashing into the Cathedral, with another thousand tons outside. Almost all the glass was destroyed. This was not quite as disastrous as it appeared; the best glass and the more venerable pieces of furniture having been taken away for safe-keeping. The explosion also did not cause an outbreak of fire nor, by luck, did it kill any of the Fire Watchers, all of whom had taken cover when high explosives had begun to fall in the vicinity. There was still an impressive hole in the side of the cathedral, however, and some fears for the safety of the roof.

There was one other large area of fire that night although this was less of a conflagration and more a series of separate block fires. The area just to the east of the High Street had received some attention in the earlier raids and now it once again found itself coming under attack. The story of the centre was repeated. A mixture of incendiaries and the occasional high explosive set light to large parts of Sidwell Street and Paris Street with at least 40 smaller shops going up in flames along the former road. Machine-gunning again hampered the work of the Fire Guards although the manager of at least one dairy was able to thank the Civil Defence services for saving his premises the following day. Large patches of Paris Street were not so lucky; nor were parts of Dix's Field, another area of Georgian housing that suffered badly in this raid. Just beyond the Sidwell area, the closely packed Victorian streets of Newtown were hit again. At least two roads went up in flames, the Fire Guards being assumed to have left the city after the raids of the previous week.

The German bombing on the centre of the city was so accurate that the damage to the outer districts was relatively light. A few larger buildings on the outskirts of the city were badly affected by fire. Along the Heavitree Road, the City Hospital suffered serious damage from incendiary bombs and high explosives. Practically opposite, St Luke's Theological College came under intense incendiary attack and showed how even the best Fire Guard system could be overwhelmed. The students were all young men of 18 to 20. They had a trailer pump, six trained stirrup pump teams and six Fire Watchers. Every student had been trained in fire guard duties. There was even a swimming pool to provide static water. 'The Fire Guard organisation was a model of its kind' – yet almost all of the buildings were gutted. The college was attacked by an initial salvo of incendiary bombs that were quickly disposed of. Then followed a set of three high explosive bombs that fell on the ground, although one failed to explode.

Soon after came an intense concentration of incendiary bombs and despite the presence of the Fire Brigade, the number of bombs was so heavy that nothing could be done to save most of the college buildings. It was a salutary lesson. As a ministry report noted: 'This incident . . . appears to show that the enemy can fairly easily overcome the most efficient and courageous Fire Guard organisation that it is possible to provide, even when it is quickly reinforced by the NFS'.

It is worth bearing this pronouncement in mind, for as dawn broke on the morning of 4 May, it was clear to all that Exeter had been damaged most severely by high explosive and especially so by fire. At least 40 acres of the built-up area had been burnt out and most of this in the centre of the city. The main shopping centre from the High Street up to Sidwell Street had gone up in flames taking with it the Public Library, the main Post Office and many of the city's department stores. Paris Street had suffered badly from fire. Bedford Circus, Southernhay, Dix's Field, Georgian buildings housing at least six banks and other professional businesses were no more. Valuable records had also disappeared: the Pro-

Area destroyed around South Street

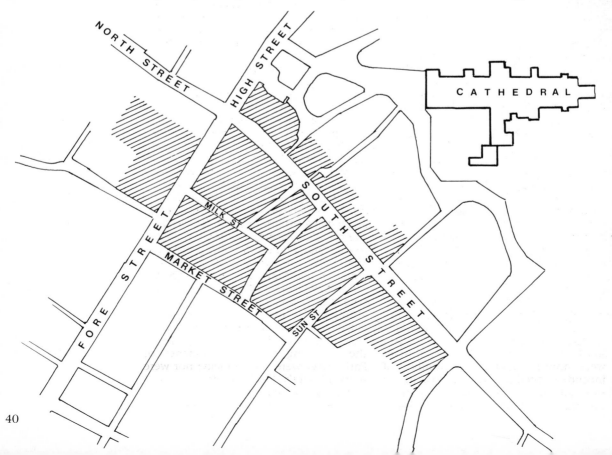

Above left:
Firemen climb their ladder in amongst the debris of the High Street.

Above:
With the twin towers of the Cathedral in the background, this was the site of Bedford Square and the High Street once the bomb damage had been cleared away.

Left:
Although the Cathedral was fortunately spared serious damage, the area south of the Chancel was destroyed.

Below left:
All that remains of an elegant terrace in Southernhay West are the facades of half a dozen houses, whilst behind all the living accommodation has been reduced to rubble.

bate Office stood on one side of Bedford Circus and with its destruction also went that of thousands of old wills.

It was obvious that a major disaster had hit the city and in the early hours of 4 May there were already some people who were asking why it had happened. Some blamed the Fire Guard. There were few complaints concerning the residential parts of the city. Apart from two streets in Newtown, all other incidents in the outer districts were dealt with promptly and efficiently and no fires were allowed to spread. Most Fire Guards had turned out to do their duties.

The business area was another matter entirely. Later investigators found various anomalies and some glaring omissions in the fire-watching schemes there. Some commercial buildings appeared to have no Fire Watchers at all and when they started to burn the Fire Brigade had to break down the doors in order to get in and tackle the flames. Other teams seemed to take shelter a little too quickly and could be observed leaving their posts by Fire Guards on the roof of the adjoining buildings. One party, based on the roof of the Royal Devon and Exeter Hospital, just beyond the centre of the city, went even further: 'When Exeter seemed to be burning all the way round, and at that time the hospital appeared safe, the Fire Watchers apparently thought their first duty was to their own homes and families, for which nobody can blame them, and I was left on my own'.

Most parties had not yet done any stirrup pump training at the actual premises where they worked. In the main, however, it is hard to criticise the Fire Guards. A highly combustible city centre, scattered high explosives and a veritable deluge of incendiaries had given the Guards little chance. They had simply been overwhelmed.

If the fires were too much for the Fire Guards, then the next line of defence was obviously the Fire Brigade and, indeed, the NFS came in for criticism from fire watchers who telephoned for help and received none – or, at least, none until it was too late.

It is easy to be over-critical. The Fire Guard team was concerned to protect its own building and could sense when the fire was about to get out of control. It was easy to request assistance and be annoyed when this was not given, especially when it seemed so often that a single pump could have prevented a

great deal of destruction. But the Fire Brigade had to take a much broader view of the situation and to make decisions on the basis of which incidents needed immediate attention and which would just have to be left to burn, at least for the present.

This report did note one 'bright spot' as it put it: apart from a very few isolated cases the fire services never lacked for water. This seemed a remarkable vindication of the measures that had been put into practice on the basis of experience gained after the blitz of 1940-41; Exeter centre had a whole series of static water tanks and overground steel pipelines that had obviously proved their worth. The mains supply had also continued to function for most of the raid which was equally encouraging as 'the water system of Exeter is of very low power and great antiquity'. Much more modern systems were to fail in other Baedeker cities such as York and Norwich, and not only because of damage by high explosive bombs. Another interpretation could be put on this one encouraging aspect. In Norwich the mains had failed partly because too many pumps were attempting to draw water at the same time so that the water pressure became so low as to be almost useless. This did not happen in Exeter for in the carefully chosen words of one later report: 'The water supply seems to have been sufficient for the number of pumps available'. In other words, there were so few pumps around that even an antiquated mains water supply had no difficulty in coping with the limited demands put on it.

In such circumstances it was essential that reinforcements arrive from other areas as quickly as possible. But matters conspired to further aggravate the already considerable problems. In previous raids reinforcements from the local Exeter Division had been very prompt but by the early morning of 4 May there were large numbers of fires burning on the hills and commons surrounding the city which forced the incoming fire crews to make considerable, and lengthy, detours. Other problems were of an organisational nature. Exeter Division of the NFS came under the control of Fire Force Area No 19 which had its headquarters in Plymouth, some 35 miles from Exeter. Early in the raid, Exeter NFS tried to put out a request for assistance but the telephone communications had been badly damaged by the bombing and it took some time to get the message through. Plymouth was not exactly close to Exeter either. Some Fire Force areas were relatively small in area, encompassing only one large conurbation for example, but there were few large towns in the West Country and the original organisers of the NFS had decided to put both Plymouth and Exeter into one area, plus all the surrounding countryside. The Fire Force Commander now put out orders for other Divisions to send reinforcements: a section leader was sent with five pumps from Barnstaple, others came in from Torquay, Taunton and other nearby towns. But it took time for these to get there and it was not until 4.35am, a good 1 hour 45 minutes after the all-clear sounded, that the first area assistance arrived, a Reinforcing Company from Plymouth itself.

By this time the fires had already just passed their peak although as more and more reinforcements arrived it was not until 6.40am could it be said that the majority of the fires were under control. Not that this was evident to many of the harassed Fire Watchers, still trying to deal with their own incidents. Reinforcing crews were under instructions to drive straight to Exeter Fire Station at Danes Castle, to the north of the city centre, where they would receive specific instructions as to where to go next. While it obviously made sense to report in first so that the headquarters knew what resources they possessed and which incidents were being attended, it did nothing for the morale of Fire Watchers who tried to flag down passing fire engines only to see them drive straight by. At one chemist three Fire Guards had begun to fight a fire at the very start of the raid armed only with a stirrup pump. They continued at their task for over six hours until finally relieved by the arrival of a fire crew at 7.00am. There was also still a lot to do of course: 'under control' largely meant that the fires were no longer spreading, and certainly did not mean that they were out. As the full magnitude of the devastation at Exeter began to emerge, even more pumps were sent in and from increasingly great distances. Johnston, the Chief Fire Officer for the entire South West region came down from Bristol to take personal charge of the operation. He decided that the situation was still so bad that the City of Exeter should be divided into fire zones, each under the complete control of a senior fire officer. Alfred Bowden at

Barnstaple had already sent a section of fire pumps in the early hours of Sunday morning in response to one telephone call. At 1.00pm on Monday afternoon he was ordered to go himself to the city. This time the message had to be brought by despatch rider as by then all telephone communication with Exeter had been lost.

Bowden set off by car at once. He called in on the original Control Centre at Danes Court. It was not an impressive sight. The blast shutters were still in place on the windows and as a result the rooms were still in darkness. There were only two people in the building, women plotters who remained in cover under a table clutching on to a hurricane lamp. There were only five fires recorded, as if the staff had noted the first incidents and then became overwhelmed by the sheer volume of fires being reported in.

Bowden now had to tour his area and find exactly what resources he possessed. Accordingly he parked his car, hoisted the incident flag and went for a walk around his zone. Each time he found a fire crew he asked them where they had come from, when they had come on duty and how long they had been in action. These were important questions. Some local crews had been in action since the early hours of the morning without any rest at all; there were stories that at daybreak when the fires seemed to be under control, some local men had gone home to check on their families. Fires had then flared up again in their absence. Other crews had driven a very long way. South West region stretched all the way from Cornwall to Gloucester and beyond. Some crews were worn out by the time they reached Exeter, often an all-night drive. Reinforcements from one distant area were said to be of 'very limited assistance' having driven a very long way and having arrived 'tired and dissatisfied'. By lunchtime on Monday other crews were just too exhausted to care any more. Having battled with fires for much of the night and the following morning, new ones that broke out could prove the final straw. Some were just left to burn in front of their exhausted eyes.

Trekking took place on a very large scale on the night of 4 May. It must certainly have been higher than one local official estimate that put it at some 5,000 people. After such a destructive raid it might be thought that the Germans had achieved their

Above:
The Exeter branch of Dr Barnardo's was damaged by the effects of a bomb blast.

Above right:
Underneath the debris of a demolished house on Roseland Avenue, Heavitree, was a Morrison shelter.

Right:
Adjacent to the undamaged communal shelter on Monks Road a house received a direct hit. Other surrounding property has suffered from blast damage.

Below right:
No 17 Regents Park received a direct hit, completely demolishing the house.

purpose but for many there was still the fear that they would return. After all, the Cathedral was still standing. Rumours were later spread that some people were so frightened that they called for the Cathedral to be dynamited so that the Luftwaffe would have no reason to come back. It did appear to be a target. If it was a brave move to stay in the city that night, then how much greater a risk was it to actually go on duty as a Fire Watcher, and not just at any property, but at the Cathedral itself? Wilfrid Dymond was a Cathedral Fire Watcher and had been unable to get from his home in St Thomas on the night of 3 May. But on 4 May it was actually his turn to go on duty at the Cathedral. His parents begged him not to go yet he did so if not without a great deal of trepidation. As he walked through the city he could see that fires were still burning; the Germans would have no difficulty in finding Exeter that night. At the Cathedral, he found that the numbers of Fire Guards were sadly depleted. Instead of the 20 that should be on duty, there were only five: three student girls, a short-sighted man and Dymond himself. The Canons had been bombed out of their houses in the close and had gone to seek shelter with friends elsewhere in the city. Some Fire Watchers just did not turn up. Most important of all, the Head Verger was also absent. He was meant to be in charge not only of the Cathedral but also of all the Fire Guards in the immediate area. Instead he had taken his wife and mother well away from the city – all the way to Barrow in Furness, in fact. The Dean did stay and offered to lend his assistance: and in the early evening of 4 May, amid the rubble of the earlier bombing, he gave the reduced fire team his blessing. It did look as if this would be needed for at some point in the evening the sirens went again: but there were no bombs on the city that night nor, as it turned out, for many nights to come.

The danger over, the recriminations began. Certain senior members of the NFS felt that insufficient preparations had been made by the local authorities before the blitz. It had been the responsibility of local authorities to submit schemes for Civil Defence at the start of the war as well as the later comment by the ARP Controller, Newman, to the effect that Exeter set up everything that central government gave them, and approved Exeter's arrangements. But the Fire Service staff knew that the letter of the law might not be sufficient. Two cities might have an equal population of 80,000 but one might have a closely packed central zone full of old and combustible buildings while the other had modern low density shops and houses with plenty of parks and open spaces. Common sense would suggest that the former city needed far greater protection than the latter, even if at first they had the same number of inhabitants. The government's regulations did not even go that far: two cities of equal population could have very different levels of fire defence, depending on the assumed danger of attack. Exeter was not expected to be attacked and so it had a lower level of defence than, say, Plymouth.

We have already met Alfred Bowden as one of the senior Fire Officers called in to help deal with the fires in Exeter on the morning after the raid. But before being sent to Barnstaple, he had spent some time with the Fire Brigade in Exeter where he had made continual protests to the local council for, as he saw it, their lack of support for the Fire Service and their failure to provide adequate numbers of men. There was even the suggestion that when the NFS was set up in mid-1941 the Fire Brigade wanted Bowden to be Divisional head at Exeter but the local council refused this. There are some figures to back up these accusations. In April 1942 Exeter (population 80,000) had 107 NFS men, full and part-time; Bath, with a population of a few thousand less, had 220 firemen; York (population 100,000) had 238. Thus Bath, a Georgian city and less of a fire risk, had a similar sized population but twice as many firemen. Exeter had 26 pumps; York had 40. Even Canterbury, perhaps a third of the size of Exeter, had 28 pumps. In comparison with the other Baedeker cities therefore, most of which were rated as the same low risk targets, Exeter had far fewer resources available for the fighting of fires at the start of their raids.

They had other problems as well. The formation of the National Fire Service meant a great deal of reorganisation and a large number of transfers of senior personnel. Exeter Council had appointed a Mr Coles as Chief Officer of its Fire Brigade, but with the formation of the NFS he was taken from them and appointed Fire Force Commander at Taunton. His second-in-command was lost in more tragic circumstances. Mr Townsend had been seconded for service with the Admiralty

Fire Brigade at Plymouth-Devonport Dockyard where he was killed while on duty during an air-raid. The NFS then sent S. F. Willey to take over as Divisional Fire Officer at Exeter. He was judged a great success, in particular for his close links with the heads of the other Civil Defence services and the way in which he made himself thoroughly familiar with the local arrangements and particular fire risks. Then in early March 1942, after a mere six months in this post, the NFS announced that Willey was to be transferred and Exeter was to receive yet another new Chief Officer. Exeter protested most vigorously, but seemingly to no avail. The NFS Chief wrote back to say that as of 13 April (barely two weeks before the first raids) Exeter would have a new Divisional Officer, H. J. Brown, although in a slight bow to pressure, Willey would be allowed to remain in the city as his second-in-command. For whatever reason, this change does not appear to have been implemented: Willey remained in charge throughout the Exeter raids and for some months afterwards before being transferred to the Isle of Wight.

This time there seemed less cause for concern. Reacting to criticism from those who felt that Plymouth was too distant to control most of Devon and Cornwall, Exeter was removed from its command and made a Fire Force area in its own right, with responsibility for most of Devon. The new Fire Force Commander at Exeter, who arrived in mid-1942, was the city council's original choice for the job, Coles; but it was a choice they were soon to regret. Coles had not been based at Exeter during the blitz but he had been another of the five regional commanders brought in to take control of a zone of the city on the day after the 3 May raid. In early November 1942, he held one of his regular meetings of his Fire Force officers during the course of which he made a number of controversial comments. With regard to the fires at Exeter, he had little respect for the local authorities. They had made inadequate preparations for the attack, and in particular there were problems with the main emergency pipelines. It was no good asking for information from them but they could be ignored in any case. As central government paid for the NFS the local authorities should have no right to question them and if they protested they could just be allowed to 'squeal'. Coles also claimed that the police were generally obstructive and under some 'tin-pot' commanders; and that it was interesting to note that the static water tanks tended to have been located outside councillors' houses.

This was radical stuff even if some points, the final one in particular, do look like pure gossip. Unfortunately for Coles, although this was a private meeting, one of those who attended it was not only a part-time NFS officer but also Surveyor to Budleigh Salterton Urban District Council and he repeated these comments to the local authorities at Exeter. Understandably, they were furious. Newman, as ARP Controller and Town Clerk, wrote a series of letters of complaint to the Regional Commissioner. In vain did the latter try to pour oil on troubled waters. Coles was severely reprimanded and expressed regret at the incidents. A Board of Enquiry was set up which found that some of these comments had been taken out of context in what was a very long meeting. The Regional Commissioner also reassured Newman that the pipelines laid out by Exeter Emergency Committee had not been wrong; in fact Coles had been misquoted and had merely said that if too many take-offs were made (ie, pumps using water along the way) then the overall water supply might prove inadequate. The Commissioner assured Newman that: 'It is the view of the Regional Commissioner that the layout of the pipelines at Exeter, and the general arrangements for supplementary water supply, are as satisfactory as they can be with the resources that have been placed at our disposal'.

It could be argued that all of this was rather missing the point: the water supplies were inadequate because there were insufficient pumps available to use them. In any case, all these arguments were to no avail. Although the affair dragged on into the spring of 1943, Exeter Emergency Committee stuck to its guns and to a demand first put into a letter of December 1942: 'While he (Coles) remains in charge of Exeter there cannot possibly be the wholehearted and friendly co-operation between the NFS and the other branches of the Civil Defence services'.

In the face of this opposition, Coles applied for a transfer with, it must be noted the sympathy of the Regional Commissioner who told Exeter the same. Indeed, when the Commissioner had a face to face meeting with the Emergency Committee he felt that they were too intransigent and were biased against Coles. Newman assured him they were not: 'I have also to state that the Committee have no animus whatsoever against the Fire Force Commander, and that any hostility that exists has been created entirely by himself in his attitude to Local Authorities since becoming an Officer of the National Fire Service . . .'

Coles was transferred but he was not the only person to make a complaint about the Civil Defence preparations at Exeter. Bowden also wrote a report that was so critical that the NFS senior authorities decided they could not use it. It is a pity that all this took place, for much of the Civil Defence system had worked very well indeed, and far better than in some other cities which lost fewer dead.

The post-raid services of the Civil Defence system could hardly be faulted. Although a large number of incendiaries had been dropped during the raid, the sheer weight of the attack had produced a death toll twice that of the 24 April raid: some 164 people had been killed on the night of 3/4 May. Most officials agreed that morale remained surprisingly high. Rumours were many, but few were specific. There were only a handful of cases of looting, a few safes in burnt out buildings being broken into. Trekking involved quite large numbers of people, including some Fire Guards, but was quite orderly and most returned home the next morning. Much of the responsibility for this happy state of affairs was directly attributable to the work of the local authority. The ARP Controller and Town Clerk, Mr Newman, was particularly singled out for praise by a Ministry of Home Security report. He was 'a tower of strength throughout' and 'an outstanding personality'. He was credited with having created a real team spirit amid the Civil Defence staff by insisting on regular weekly meetings of the Heads of Services ever since the outbreak of war. Nor was Newman afraid to make his views known: it was a fact that amongst those who trekked out each night were some of the leading citizens of Exeter who used their own private cars for the purpose. Newman was quite ready to say that no-one without an official permit should be allowed to use a private car in this way. Galvanised by his example, local authority staff kept well on top of the situation. There were a number of letters sent by grateful civilians to show

that at least some of the public realised the help that they were being given. This took many forms. Within two days, the Corporation buses were running again; and the Regional Headquarters made sure that there was no lack of certain types of 'essential' goods: some three million cigarettes and large quantities of tobacco were sent direct by van to Exeter.

Great stress was also laid on the fact that the public were kept fully aware of what was happening in the confused days after the 3 May raid. Here the most important figure appears to have been a Mr J. Whiteside who had been appointed Emergency Information Officer sometime before the raids occurred. He had gone about his work with some gusto. On New Year's Day 1942, he was able to issue a *Handbook of Emergency Information on Civil Defence*, to be issued to a 'large inner group of what might be regarded as natural leaders of the people'. Other critics produced similar guides, but this was a particularly detailed one and was not just restricted to Civil Defence leaders. Whiteside made other preparations as well, and to a most efficient degree. There was not one Information Centre, but four possible alternate sites; blank posters were prepared, placards put together. So effective was Whiteside's work that at the height of the post-raid activity, he had 310 people working for him and more volunteers than he needed, a far cry from the situation in other Baedeker cities, Norwich in particular. Three bulletins were issued every day, with details such as the location of Emergency Feeding Centres, reminders to boil water, and pleas for Fire Watchers not to leave the city. These were posted in every feeding centre, the Post Office, and 200 copies were handed out to Civil Defence workers. Whiteside took it upon himself to attend the Emergency Committee meetings and to ask the various personnel what they wanted him to announce. He even had seven loudspeaker vans to tour the city and give out further advice.

The Information Service appears to have been a great success; it was also quite essential in view of the large number of buildings that had been destroyed which necessitated frequent changes of address. A number of municipal offices had been destroyed, including the Billeting department, Public Assistance Office and the Registrar of Births and Deaths. Exeter's officials had been housed in many separate buildings; this proved an advantage during the raid as there was no one central building to be knocked out. Most of the departments vital to post-raid operations were undamaged. In the same way, although a large part of the shopping centre had been burnt out, supplies were rushed in from other parts of the region so there was never any shortage of food and the remaining shops were well able to cope with the demand. The effect on national war production was negligible, which was hardly surprising as there were few industries there in the first place and these were largely on the outskirts of the city which received little attention from the bombers. Transport was also little affected. The city's railway stations suffered little damage and rail traffic was only interrupted for a few hours.

Apart from the relatively heavy loss of life, the most noticeable effects were the sheer scale of the general destruc-tion and, in particular, the loss of much that was of historical importance. The cathedral could be repaired, but little was left of other medieval and Tudor buildings. St Sidwell's Church, famous as the place of imprisonment of Sir Walter Raleigh's father in 1548; Bamp-field House; the Hall of Vicars Choral; the Norman House; Chevalier House in Fore Street, formerly a City Merchant's dwelling in the reign of James I; the Globe Inn and the Seven Stars; all had been burnt out or had to be demol-ished. Eighteenth Century architecture had suffered in particular: there were great gaps in Bedford Circus, Southern-hay West and Dix's Field. The early 18th Century City Hospital was in ruins. All around stood acres of devasta-tion – all that was left of buildings less notable in an historical sense, but each important to someone. The Germans, at least, had clearly decided that enough was enough; no further major attack was to be launched on Exeter.

Above right:
Although the roof of the adjacent house was damaged, the first floor windows remained intact – unlike the house in the foreground, where members of the Rescue Services sift through the rubble. *Exeter Libraries*

Right:
The 1930s had witnessed the first dramatic growth of car ownership. Here, one owner's pride and joy is devastated amongst the destruction. *Exeter Libraries*

Bath:

Citizens Under Pressure

Some cities suffered regular bombardment, others escaped almost intact and gained an enviable reputation for their supposed invulnerability. When the Germans came to Bath they found a Civil Defence organisation that had yet to be tested and a population unaccustomed to such attacks. Bath did not expect such an onslaught; in the event it was to be the most severely damaged of all the Baedeker cities and both Civil Defence personnel and ordinary inhabitants were to be stretched near breaking point.

It was certainly an ancient and beautiful city. Natural hot spring water rushing from the ground had long provided the basis of Bath's prosperity, at least since the Roman period. In the 18th Century Bath had been the most fashionable spa town in England, a fact reflected by the large amount of Georgian architecture that it still possessed. The works of John Wood, father and son — Queen's Square, The Circus, The Royal Crescent — were internationally famous. In the 19th Century, Bath had ceased to be fashionable but after a few nervous years during the Napoleonic wars it had continued to expand. it was no longer fashionable visitors that came to stay for a short while, but the more elderly and lame who came to retire to the city. The population continued to rise although there were some difficulties with accommodation. The large Georgian houses were built for large and rich families. Now they were often sub-divided and in the poorer areas to the west of the city centre such as Kingsmead, there might be a large number of people living in the one house, a factor that was later to contribute to the high death toll when Bath was bombed.

Bath was not just a Georgian city and the 18th Century architecture stood largely to the north and east of the centre. In the late 19th Century there had been substantial housing developments to the west in the Newbridge, Oldfield Park and Weston areas. In a thin band along the River Avon to the west of the city also stood the little industry that the city possessed, notably the engineering works of Stothert & Pitt. There was also a moderately large gasworks in this area. Bath further possessed two main railway stations, serving two railway companies. Green Park station in the Kingsmead area was owned by the London Midland & Scottish Railway Company and also acted as a terminus for the Somerset & Dorset Joint Railways, but this was not a major line. Bath Spa, near the centre, stood on the Great Western main line from London to Bristol and the South West.

This location on the fast railway link to London was to be of some importance. As international tension heightened in the 1930s the British government had accepted the prevailing wisdom that any future war could start with an all-out aerial bombardment by the enemy designed to lay waste the opponent's capital city. Plans were therefore put in hand to evacuate those who were not needed to man the departments or run the factories that had to be located in London. In November 1938 the Admiralty was considering sending records, supply staff and other non-essential personnel to an accessible city large enough to cope with the influx of office staff. They contemplated a city on a main line station, perhaps 100 miles from London, such as Bath and when the war began in September 1939 the less essential and administrative departments moved down to the city where they took over all the major hotels and plenty of other buildings besides. These were still not enough and they soon began to put up purpose-built small offices, notably on

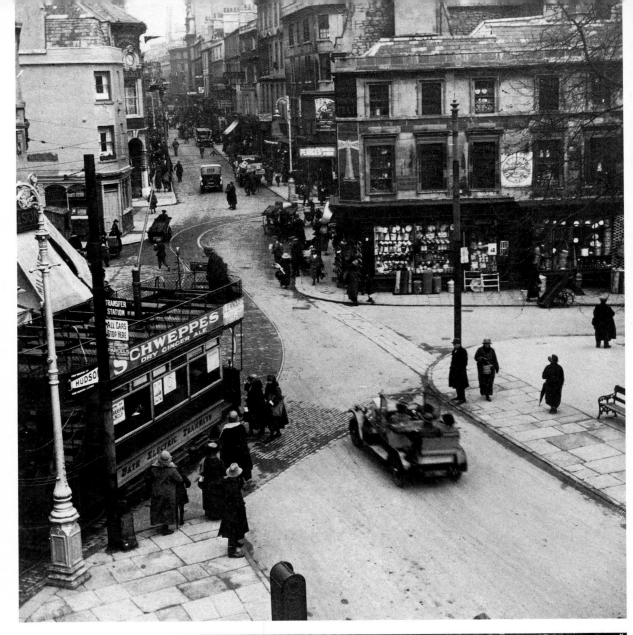

Above:
Kingsmead Square, Bath, photographed before the outbreak of war. Kingsmead Square was the main focus for the Luftwaffe's bombers during the raids on the city. *Bath City Library*

Right:
A prewar view of the Royal Crescent with St Andrew's Church pictured on the extreme right.

the southern outskirts of the city at Foxhill.

Other refugees arrived as well. Train loads of evacuee children from London were arriving at Bath from 2 September 1939 onwards, and although many were distributed throughout the county of Somerset, a sizeable minority remained in Bath. Then there were the less publicised evacuees, the wealthy who could afford to leave London and other possible target cities and could pay for good billets in a safe town like Bath. These were rarely publicised as it was felt that such moves were not generally popular and not to be encouraged; but it is probable that within a few months of the outbreak of the war that with Admiralty, children and unofficial evacuees the population had risen from a prewar total of possibly 67,000 to nearly 80,000. Many of the children were to slowly drift home in the early months of 1940 when the much feared air-raids did not appear to be materialising over London, but the accommodation problem in Bath continued to be intense and the city soon began to gain a reputation that it was to keep throughout the war of being uncaring of others who wished to take advantage of Bath's assumed immunity from attack.

The Civil Defence organisation was based on the same premise, that the war would largely bypass the city. It might be argued — and indeed was — that when the Admiralty moved to Bath because it was not a military target, they did in fact then make it so. Stothert & Pitt turned over to war production. A series of underground Bath stone mineworkings around the city were used to store everything from precious paintings to ammunition and other military stores, although few knew about these at the time. There is no evidence that the Germans knew of these underground stores, but they certainly knew of the Admiralty's presence there: a Luftwaffe aerial photograph of 1941 had the Foxhill hutments clearly annotated, but the Germans took photographs of most cities in England without bombing them all and there were similar hutments scattered throughout the country. It seems unlikely that Bath now saw itself as more in danger with the presence of the Admiralty. All local Civil Defence control centres were required to have an emergency, back-up centre if the main one was put out of action. The secondary control centre in Bath was at the Forester's Arms public house which stood directly opposite the main entrance to the Foxhill hutments. If these were seen as a major target then this location for an emergency centre was foolish to say the least.

At the beginning of the war the Civil Defence Control Centre had been located in the centre of town but it was generally accepted that such a position meant that it might easily be hit in any raid and in 1941 the centre was moved out to Apsley House in Newbridge, a district to the west of the city. The chairman of the Civil Defence Committee that set up the organisation imagined, along with most people, that Bath would never receive a direct attack but only the occasional bomb.

Bristol, just over 10 miles to the north west of Bath, was the obvious source of Civil Defence reinforcements. It was by far the largest city in the area and in the period 1940-41 was to suffer a number of serious attacks that were to test the Civil Defence units there to the full. It was also the headquarters of the South Western Regional Commissioner. At the start of the war, air-raid warning sirens would sound in any area which German aircraft might overfly and so they did on numerous occasions; but only twice did bombs fall on Bath and in each case it was a single aircraft dropping a string of bombs, possibly as it made an escape from a British night-fighter. In January 1941 a number of bombs landed in Twerton High Street to the west of the city. Six people were killed, including three evacuee children aged from 6-12. They had arrived in Bath at the very start of the war and their parents had stayed in Kent, convinced that their children would be safer away from that area. A few months later another stray stick of bombs landed in the city killing another 11 civilians. Eight of the bodies were taken to an emergency mortuary in the crypt of St James' Church and here, unfortunately, they remained. Some days after the raid the verger of the church discovered that three unauthorised people had managed to get into the crypt to 'see the bodies'. Seven of the bodies were then removed but due to some oversight the eighth was not collected and after 10 days the congregation began to complain of an unpleasant odour that was beginning to suffuse the main body of the church. The body was at last removed but the entire incident reflected badly on the morbid interests of some Bathonians and the organisation of at least part of the Civil Defence services.

The stray bombs in Bath did little to dent the confidence of the locals and they studied their guides to Civil Defence with little urgency. There was a great deal of information from both national and local sources on what to do in the event of a raid, largely designed to minimise casualties and to limit the destruction of property. Unfortunately in all this material some was contradictory, some was merely a counsel of excellence and, most important of all, some raised basic questions that were often left unanswered.

When an air-raid siren sounded, everyone should take to a shelter, but which one? The guide to Civil Defence services in Bath was quite specific; unless caught out in the open some distance from home you should use whatever shelter had been prepared in your own house or garden. No one should rush out into the open to a public shelter because there were not enough of them for the entire population of the city. There was only enough public shelter accommodation in Bath for 20% of the population, and no shelter in the city was proof against a direct hit. If too many people packed into a public shelter and it was destroyed then there would be a very heavy loss of life. However, it was widely known that throughout the long blitz on London many people had regularly taken to shelter in the Underground and in ordinary public shelters on the surface and there was a natural feeling amongst some that such public buildings could provide not only better protection but also morale-lifting company. Bath had not been bombed and so almost no-one regularly went to a municipal shelter, until the nights of the raids on the city.

If there is a criticism that can be levelled at many of the guides to Civil Defence, it is that they assumed a passivity amongst the general population that might be difficult to maintain when bombs were actually falling. There were many descriptions of what the active Civil Defence personnel, such as Wardens should do. Everyone else should merely stay put. They should not go out until the all-clear sounded. They should stay in their personal or family shelter.

There was no real advice on what to do if you merely wished to get out of the city to avoid a possible further attack. The phenomenon of 'trekking', or commuting to the country every night for a number of days after a raid had emerged early in the war. The government vaguely felt it smacked of defeatism but knew it was impossible to stop and so they chose to ignore it. In some ways this was the best thing to do, but this did mean that all guides to Civil Defence left the question of self-evacuation as literally that, a question.

The 25 April 1942 was a Saturday night and just before 11.00pm a number of people were still out in Bath when they saw the first chandeliers or clusters of marker flares begin to descend over the city. Even at this late stage some did not understand the significance or assumed that these were a few stray incendiaries that were in fact meant for Bristol. As the first high explosive bombs began to fall, the air-raid warning siren began to sound at 10.59pm. Immediately there were problems and mistakes. Assuming that Bristol was the target, a detachment from the Fire Brigade in Bath was immediately despatched towards Bristol. What happened next was sheer black comedy. As the engines headed out of Bath they found that there was already so much damage in the west of the city that they were unable to go along the Upper Bristol Road and had to negotiate their way via a detour through the nearby Victoria Park. One of the firemen had the doubtful privilege of driving past his own house, already burning fiercely, as the crews continued to obey orders and headed steadfastly out of the city. The Control Centre soon ran into further problems. The bombs that had fallen on the Upper Bristol Road, thus causing the Fire Brigade to make a detour, had also severed a number of the telephone lines in the city. For the rest of the night Apsley House was to be unable to send any telephone messages out and could receive only the occasional incoming call.

Bath lacked any defence and in clear moonlight the bombers were able to descend to a very low level to drop their bombs with some accuracy. If this was the case it might be asked why the first bombs fell well to the west of the city. In fact on the annotated aerial photograph of Bath that the aircrews possessed, it was the gasworks on the Upper Bristol Road that were marked out most prominently and these were in the western sector of Bath. Very early on in the attack two gas mains were ruptured by high explosive bombs, igniting the escaping gas and acting as a marker beacon for further bombs.

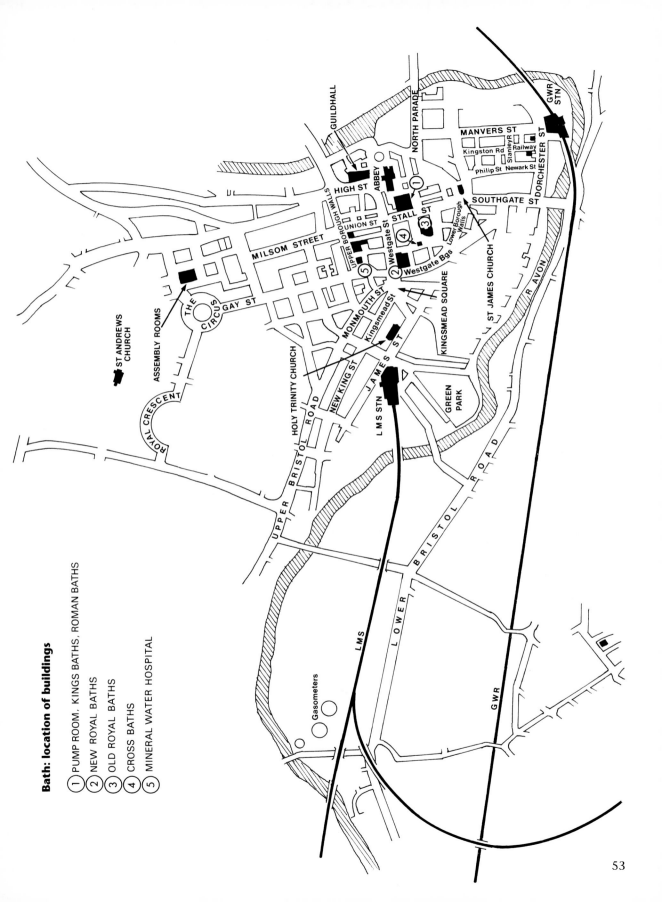

Bath: location of buildings

① PUMP ROOM, KINGS BATHS, ROMAN BATHS
② NEW ROYAL BATHS
③ OLD ROYAL BATHS
④ CROSS BATHS
⑤ MINERAL WATER HOSPITAL

53

As the entire area around the gas-works erupted into flames a further onslaught of high explosives and incendiary bombs showered down to add to the destruction. The low level at which the bombers were able to descend enabled them to drop incendiaries in very concentrated patterns to add even further problems to the Fire Guards below.

Nearby, in Newbridge, other Fire Watchers were also in action. At the start of the raid Frank Selwin was out and about trying to cope with what seemed to be hundreds of incendiaries. Some houses were unoccupied but there was an efficient system by which nominated Fire Guards were given spare sets of keys to enable them to enter the properties if they caught alight. However, even this early in the raid there were some worrying sights. Part of Hungerford Road, near the gas-works, was hit by a series of incendiaries. Frank Selwin went along to help but found that a number of inhabitants were not even trying to stop the flames. While he managed to stop some from leaving the scene, others gave him their keys and disappeared. Two young men just dashed straight past him. Frank felt that the road could have been saved by

prompt action; instead a sizeable proportion of it went up in flames.

Some Fire Guards had not even turned up for duty in the first place. Myrtle Meredith and her mother had a young couple staying with them and the husband should have been on Fire Watching duty on this first night of bombing, but he had not gone on duty as he had a stomach upset. He spent the night under the table with the other inhabitants. Most Civil Defence personnel however did turn out and often at some personal risk to themselves. In Oldfield Park lived a Mr and Mrs Smith and at the start of the raid Mrs Smith's brother called around at their house to leave his wife there with them. He was a special constable and had to go on duty but did not want to leave his wife on her own. Mrs Smith took her in and then saw her brother go off. She was not to see him alive again.

Most non-Civil Defence personnel took shelter as the bombs began to fall and in all the usual places — Morrison shelters, tables and their cupboards inside the house, Anderson or purpose-built shelters in the back garden. The raid had started just fractionally before the sirens had sounded and even if peo-

Loss of life in Shelters

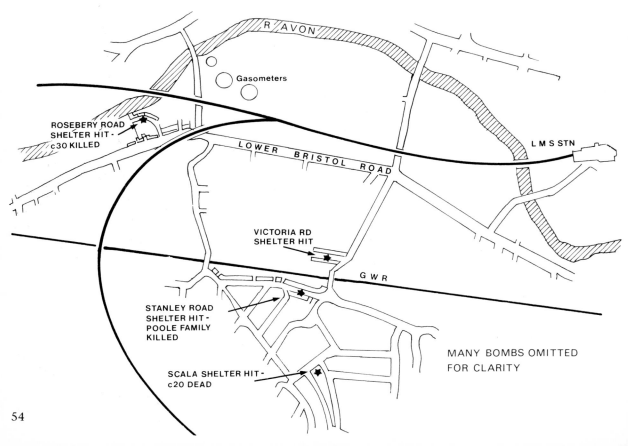

R. AVON

Gasometers

ROSEBERY ROAD SHELTER HIT - c30 KILLED

LOWER BRISTOL ROAD

L M S STN

VICTORIA RD SHELTER HIT

G W R

STANLEY ROAD SHELTER HIT - POOLE FAMILY KILLED

SCALA SHELTER HIT - c20 DEAD

MANY BOMBS OMITTED FOR CLARITY

Left:
The Upper Bristol Road is illuminated by a gas main which ignited early in the first raid. Park Lane is beyond the trees in the centre, to the right. *Wessex Newspapers*

Below left:
New King Street, where the Ford family was killed. *Wessex Newspapers*

Bottom left:
Kingsmead Street viewed from Kingsmead Square, seen after its destruction by high explosive bombs.

55

ple saw some of its first signs such as incendiaries and flares, three years of immunity from bombing meant that not all of them grasped the significance of these strange lights and fires. New King Street was part of Kingsmead just to the west of the city centre. Many of the large Georgian houses there were divided up into series of flats and in one of these lived Anne Marks along with her parents. That night her father was already on Fire Watching duty but this was just part of his regular duties and none of them had expected a raid. When the siren sounded Anne and her mother stayed in bed and continued to do so even when the bombs began to sound a little too close for it be Bristol. Then the elderly lady who lived in the upstairs flat came down to report that she was most worried as she had seen incendiary bombs falling very close by, Anne's mother now decided that it was time to take shelter and as the little group made their way downstairs, a landing window shattered in their faces. None of them was injured but others had been less lucky. The window had been blown in by the last in a series of bombs that wreaked havoc across the Kingsmead area. Working out from the centre, two bombs had landed in Kingsmead Street and a third in New King Street, demolishing the houses next to that which Anne Marks lived in. These, too, were subdivided into flats and because they fell inwards the death toll was high: 19 people, at least, died from this one bomb in New King Street including seven members of the Ford family, mother and six children. The father was away serving in the armed forces and was to return to Bath a few days later, but only to see each member of his family be brought out in turn, dead, from the rubble. In Kingsmead Street at least another dozen people were killed in a similar type of house. Anne Marks and her mother were not injured and took refuge in the bottom flat where the inhabitants took them in. Anne spent the night huddled in a blanket, half under a camp bed, being reassured by visitors there who had had experience of the London blitz. The house shook and the candle flickered but there was no further damage. These Georgian houses were built with very large and fairly strong cellars and in a number of cases these were to stand up well when the floors above were hit by high explosives, but survival often meant being able to get down to the cellar in time and in New

Damage in Central Bath

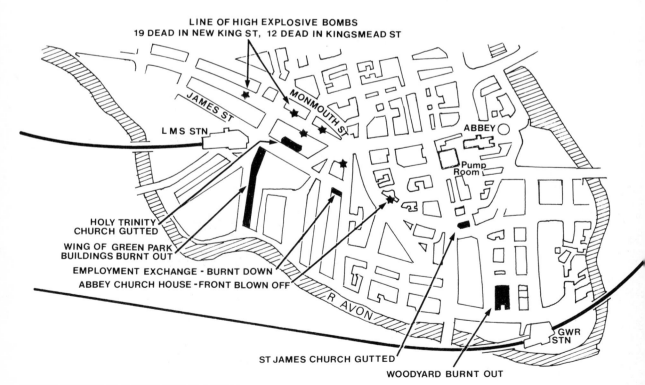

LINE OF HIGH EXPLOSIVE BOMBS
19 DEAD IN NEW KING ST, 12 DEAD IN KINGSMEAD ST

JAMES ST

MONMOUTH ST

L M S STN

ABBEY

Pump Room

HOLY TRINITY CHURCH GUTTED

WING OF GREEN PARK BUILDINGS BURNT OUT

EMPLOYMENT EXCHANGE - BURNT DOWN

ABBEY CHURCH HOUSE - FRONT BLOWN OFF

R AVON

GWR STN

ST JAMES CHURCH GUTTED

WOODYARD BURNT OUT

MANY BOMBS OMITTED FOR CLARITY

King Street not all had been able to do this.

Despite all advice, some people still risked everything to dash out of their houses to seek a public shelter. There are stories that in Kingsmead Street a number of people panicked and ran out in such a way, only to be killed by the blast of high explosive bombs. Two young girls were supposedly sent out by one mother, their bodies, cut by flying glass, being found in the street next morning. One couple noticed at the start of the raid that their street was suddenly full of people rushing around. This would appear a rather foolish thing to do as bombs were falling and there is no doubt that as the siren sounded only just as the raid began, there were few incentives to run along to a public shelter however protective it might appear to be if you had to run the gauntlet of high explosives. Some still did this, and in one area with the full sanction of the Wardens despite all previous official advice.

Faith Dolman lived in the Southdown area of Bath, on the hills to the south of the city, with her mother and grandmother. She was awoken by the sirens and as she and her family came downstairs to take shelter under the dining table there was a knock at the door. It was the local warden, a Mr Harwood, who informed them that they were the last people in the area who had not gone to the nearby public shelter at Twerton Roundhill. The three women made their way along the road escorted by two of the Wardens and quite conscious of the fact that the raid was well underway. The sky would suddenly light up as bombs fell across the city and when Faith Dolman looked up she saw at least one aircraft flying so low that one of the aircrew could be observed in the glass fronted nose of the bomber. She could see the red glowing tracer bullets flying about but the whole party managed to make their way along to the shelter where they spent most of the night close to the main entrance and listening to the bombing. In other parts of the city, other streets were also encouraged, contrary to the Civil Defence guide, to gather in the nearby public shelter. The inmates of the Twerton Roundhill shelter were lucky, it was not hit on either night. Other shelters were to be less fortunate.

Whatever type of shelter you were in, there was a natural desire to know about what was happening outside, especially if you were in a garden shelter and wanted to know whether your house was still standing. The nature of the raid also encouraged some people to investigate for although the all-clear did not sound until 11 minutes past midnight, just over an hour after it began, the German bombers seemed to arrive over the target in ones and twos rather than all at once and so there were lulls in the attack. Indeed, half an hour after the all-clear had sounded there was another warning siren at 46 minutes past midnight which continued until a further all-clear at 1.10am which suggests that some aircraft did arrive very late over the target. A number of people took the opportunity during brief lulls to venture out of their shelters and see what was going on. When what appeared to be the final all-clear sounded at 1.10am, a number of people did venture out to take stock. One such was Alec Clifton-Taylor, the famous architectural writer who was working for the Admiralty in Bath. He was living in Queen Square in the centre of town at the time of the raid and had taken shelter in the cellar while the bombs were falling. He emerged when the all-clear sounded for the first time at just after midnight and inspected the immediate area. There had been no bombs in Queen Square itself but as he walked further he found a large fire at Norfolk Crescent and, as he freely admitted, he could never resist the sight of a fire. Others also owned up to a strange fascination with the flames that they passed, especially as such an event was so unusual in Bath. When the second all-clear sounded at just after 1am, Alec Clifton-Taylor's companion, a Mr Cotter, decided that he had to walk across town to the suburb of Oldfield Park to check on some friends there and the two men agreed to go together. This was accomplished and as they walked back at about 3.00am they came across a family of three adults and two children whose house had been badly damaged. They had nowhere to go and so they were invited back to the house in Queen Square where everyone had a cup of tea and then tried to get some sleep. For many, dozing fitfully in their various types of shelter, the night was one long raid interspersed with the occasional period of quiet. However, a number of people did make use of this one o'clock all-clear to personally check that friends and family were safe and at a time when the telephones were not universal possessions this meant, in some cases, a fair walk across town. Some were cautious. When the all-clear sounded in New King Street, Anne Marks' father had come in for a short while displaying a deep gash on his forehead gained while doing Fire Watching duty. The old lady in the top flat who had first given the warning of the incendiary bombs asked Anne's mother to accompany her to Rivers Street to check on her relatives, but her mother declined.

One gentleman decided to go and check that his pigs were safe. He lived near the gasworks at Rosebery Road and his animals were some distance away. As he crossed the road onto the Lower Bristol Road he passed a dead body, laid out under the nearby railway arch. Rosebery Road had suffered no real damage in the first raid even though it was so close to the gasworks, but some of the inhabitants of this small cul-de-sac had become a little nervous. There were three or four of the oblong brick shelters in the road and during the first raid Fred Short who worked for one of the Rescue Squads had helped put some of the local inhabitants into these for, as they thought, added protection.

When the all-clear sounded most had stayed put. Fred Short took the opportunity to go back home up to Odd Down to check that his family was safe. Other Civil Defence workers did the same. Two men walked home from the centre, one turning into Rosebery Road, the other going on to Twerton. In the east of the city, Mary Middlemas took a rest from working at a first aid post to nip home for a short while, having promised to return later.

It is probable that people felt that the raid had ended, but also few were ready to take chances and in this lull of well over two hours there was plenty of time to consider the questions of what to do next. The coincidence of the sirens with the first bombs had meant that few people had been prepared to risk the run outdoors to the nearest public shelter; but now there was time and, despite the official advice in all the air-raid booklets, a number did decide to leave home and seek the greater protection of a communal shelter. Those already in them largely stayed put. Faith Dolman and her family remained in the Twerton Roundhill shelter, the Rosebery Road inhabitants stayed in theirs. In a larger public shelter opposite the Scala cinema in Oldfield Park most of the 30 or so inmates were still

dressed in their night clothes although there were also a number of special constables who had taken shelter there to deal with a small case of panic, according to some witnesses. Mrs Smith's brother was amongst the constables present. During the lull, one family of six did leave the shelter to return home for a cup of tea but they came back soon after. When they did so they found that some more people had arrived in the meantime and so they were obliged to sit at the opposite end of the shelter to that which they started at. Around the corner and a few streets away stood another smaller brick shelter in Stanley Road. At number 8 lived a Mr and Mrs Poole and on the Saturday evening, as was their custom, they were entertaining their son and daughter-in-law. At the start of the raid they had soon taken cover indoors. During the lull there was something of a disagreement. At first the two men wanted to stay put, but Mrs Poole said she wanted to go to the street shelter and eventually they all agreed. Then the daughter-in-law announced that she wished to return with her husband to their home in Second Avenue, a few streets away, and another discussion ensued.

The general impression after the first raid gained by Alec Clifton-Taylor, as he had walked through town across the large expanses of broken glass, was that there were isolated fires but no large conflagrations; he counted only a handful of fires that might be considered medium and with the arrival of fire-fighting reinforcements from Bristol and elsewhere it was generally felt that the fires were well under control. They were not yet all extinguished and the burning gas mains and the gasworks themselves were something of a problem, but at least the fires were not spreading. Tom Gale was damping down a fire just off the Lower Bristol Road, in Bellots Road, and refilling the static water tank nearby during the lull. The Chief Regional Fire Officer had already assessed the general situation and was pleased with the overall results. It seemed that Bath had taken its first night of bombing and had coped well.

But the first night was not yet over and in the hour or so that was to follow the sound advice that people should not congregate in public shelters was to be proved fatefully correct time and again. The Germans had decided to make a special effort with Bath, an effort they were not to repeat in the rest of the Baedeker raids. When they had returned to their bases in North France and elsewhere at least half of them had been immediately rearmed and refuelled and sent back towards England. This time they had less difficulty in finding Bath as some fires were still burning and at 4.35am the inhabitants of Bath heard the air-raid warning siren sound yet again.

Tom Gale was still refilling a static water tank when the siren went. He then heard a bomb falling nearby and lay down to take cover but the blast made him feel that he was being torn apart. He momentarily blacked out, only to be awoken by a policeman who was slapping his face and calling out that everything was on fire. In fact a factory opposite was in flames but the blast had wrecked Tom Gale's pump and a messenger had to be sent to the Fire Station for more help. The bomb had been intended for the gasworks but it had landed short and exploded in the centre of Rosebery Road. The effects were devastating. Most of the houses were blown apart as was the main street shelter into which Fred Short had escorted the inhabitants earlier. The man who had walked home during the lull was never seen again. The pig owner survived because he had not returned home but his family were all killed. The forms certifying death tended to list home addresses rather than place of death and so it is difficult to say who was in their house and who was in the shelter, but it can be said that in Rosebery Road over 30 people were killed and at least a dozen injured.

The second major raid of the night seemed to begin with a series of high explosive bombs. Leslie Nott was a despatch rider who had taken cover in the Scala public shelter while the bombs were falling. He had just set off again and had gone only a hundred yards or so when a policeman called him to the side of the road and they both lay in the gutter as a bomb demolished one end of the shelter. The blast was so intense in the confined space that it literally ripped some people apart. Amongst the dead was Mrs Smith's brother, the special constable, along with his companions; for one of them it had been both his first and last night on duty. Yet although some 20 people were killed in the shelter, one family had a miraculous escape. The party that had gone home for a cup of tea had come back and occupied the far end of the shelter and survived, if very shaken, to clamber out of the wreckage. It was the end that they had occupied during the first raid that had taken the direct hit.

Nor was this the last shelter to be destroyed. As the sirens had sounded again the Poole family were at the entrance to the street shelter in Stanley Road. The daughter-in-law had just announced that she wanted to go home when a bomb scored a direct hit on the shelter. The father was killed instantly. The mother and a female lodger in their house were pulled from the wreckage of the shelter and taken to the hospital but both were to die there in the following week. The son and daughter-in-law had been in the doorway to the shelter when the bomb fell and the son did in fact survive although the blast rendered him temporarily deaf and he was taken to hospital suffering from severe shock. Of his wife, the daughter-in-law, there was no sign. Two other women were dragged out of the shelter by people eager to help but one was already dead and the other died whilst lying on the ground. The bodies were taken away and one must assume they were identified, but no trace of the daughter-in-law was ever found other than a few pieces of her coat that were strewn among the debris nearby. Three out of the four Poole family members had been killed while seeking cover in a street shelter; the two homes, of parents and son and daughter-in-law, received no serious damage and so if they had stayed at home it is probable that they would all have survived. In a few short minutes three shelters had received direct hits killing at least 50 people. The wisdom of staying at home and not congregating in one place might seem reinforced, but this is obviously a case of being wise after the event. In Victoria Road, a stone's throw from the Scala, a bomb detonated at roof level obliterating possibly 20-30 houses on both sides of the street. However only a dozen or so people died there because most had taken cover in street shelters. Holes were punched in the roofs of two of the shelters but no further damage was caused; in fact they were the only structures left standing in the central part of the road. The safety of a shelter was the illusory safety of numbers rather than protection from bombs, but in the end it depended on the luck of where the high explosives actually fell; and in terms of direct hits on shelters, Bath was just being desperately unlucky.

Once again in this second raid the main attack seemed to be directed towards the west of the city. This is not to say that all other parts remained untouched. Dr Mary Middlemas who had gone home to her house in the Paragon was killed along with her sister and some home helps by another direct hit. Most areas of Bath and the surrounding districts suffered some damage but the major fires that were still burning next morning at the gasworks, Hungerford Road and Crescent Gardens were all in the western sector.

Marjorie Horsell was trying to get across town to the Homestead First Aid Post in Weston where she was the superintendent. After having to abandon a car because of rubble and glass on the road she was then told by a policeman that it was impossible to get along the Upper Bristol Road because the road and the gasworks were a mass of flames. As the German aircraft roared over, she was forced to take cover and it was some time before she was able to reach her post.

Many people tried to carry on with their jobs or duties; indeed, it had been remarked in other cities and raids that one of the best ways to cope with worry and stress was to occupy the mind by doing something. Quite what you should do was another matter. In a sense, Civil Defence workers could cope the best. They had specific jobs to occupy them during a raid and they were trained to react when bombs were falling. It was the ordinary person who had time just to sit and listen to the explosions who had more problems in adjusting. As the everyday, safe surroundings went up in flames before your very eyes, it was easier to try and continue as normal however inappropriate such behaviour might appear.

Brook Road ran down to a junction with the Lower Bristol Road and at the bottom of the street stood a number of the ubiquitous brick street shelters. At the very start of the first raid a gas main had been hit and set alight and another near miss had actually moved one of the shelters a few inches along the road although it had remained intact. At the height of the second raid one of the men inside the shelter had stepped outside to light a cigarette. Immediately one of the others had cried out the standard call of 'Put that light out!'. Yet at that time the gas main was still flaring away, Rosebery Road to the left had

been gutted, Elm Grove Terrace to the right had been devastated by a direct hit and the gasworks were blazing. One match would hardly attract further attention when there was already so much fire and light. Such calls, and other symbols such as the traditional cup of morning tea even if the house was in ruins, were regularly repeated by the newspapers as examples of the indomitable spirit of the British. The reality was often quite different: holding onto normal routine was a way of holding onto one's sanity as the normal world collapsed. Air-raids in Bath were new and were proving very difficult to cope with.

The Control Centre at Apsley House was also having problems in coping with this new experience. At first sight it might seem that the controllers of the Civil Defence system would have the best knowledge of what to do, but in the event many were superfluous during the actual raid. Even the best laid plans could fall apart when damage started to be inflicted, but there was some later criticism that Bath's Civil Defence had not been the best that might have been planned in the first place. There were some complaints that Bath's Civil Defence leaders had not taken the opportunity to study at first hand the experiences of the Bristol system during their raids. There was also some distrust of the overall co-ordinator of Civil Defence in Bath, Major Pickard. He was seen as too military by some and unable to get on with a force that was essentially voluntary and civilian. Others felt he was too old and lacked a firm grip on the Civil Defence organisation. On the night of the raid at his centre in Apsley House it was also suspected that he was not sure quite what was happening or what to do. This may have been a little unfair.

At the start of the raid most of the telephone links had been cut and the whole centre became somewhat redundant. Further dislocations occurred. With the telephones down, it was essential to use the despatch riders and messengers but one of the key organisers did not arrive and the system suffered accordingly. It was only later learnt that he had been killed on his way to his post. Acting on personal initiative, some telephonists set up an alternate Control Centre at the Central Police Station, but not everyone knew that it was in operation and some calls were still received by Apsley House, albeit on a very intermittent basis.

Regional headquarters sent in reinforcements on their own initiative without Bath Control Centre always being informed.

Alec Clifton-Taylor was once again out and about as soon as the raid had ended. He found little to do and assessed correctly that the attack had largely missed the city centre. Like many others he was later to find it difficult to remember what exactly he did on that Sunday, between the two nights of bombing. As it was not a weekday most people did not even have the routine of going to work and many were more worried by the lesser inconvenience caused by the raids. There was no gas to cook with and many areas were without water. Most households had shattered glass and plaster to sweep up. Children found it all quite incomprehensible. Jill Clayton was only eight years old at the time and when an unknown young girl came into their house and was sick all over the carpet, Jill could not understand why her mother did not lose her temper. Her mother was also very upset later when a baby child was brought in from 'no-one knew where' and a doctor pronounced that it was dead.

Clearing up took only a certain amount of time though and as the day wore on a fair minority began to consider leaving the city for the night. Miss Meredith was not the only person to hear a rumour to the effect that the Germans would be returning to finish them off. The official guides to Civil Defence gave no advice on this form of behaviour. The government in ignoring the idea of trekking hoped it would go away, or at least only occur on a manageable level, but no-one knew quite what this meant.

At the very start of the war women and, in particular, children, had been evacuated from high risk areas to those where there was little chance of attack. Bath had itself been host to London evacuees. Most had then returned to London but the principle had been established that non-essential personnel might leave a city that might be attacked. Unfortunately when the heavy raids did hit London it was discovered that one of the greatest potential dangers was empty houses. If no-one was at home then there was also no-one to extinguish an incendiary before it began to burn out of control. It was essential therefore that someone stayed at home. Women and children might evacuate but what if there were

then no men at home, with fathers or husbands serving in the armed forces? Even if there was a man in the house, did he have to stay at home if it was not his night to act as a Fire Guard for the street? National, and local, government tended to answer these questions with a resounding silence and it was left to individual families to make up their minds on whether to stay put or seek shelter elsewhere.

There was no real proof that there would be a second night of bombing and it was hardly the warmest time of year to be sleeping rough. But against this there was a real fear of another attack and perhaps as many as one in eight of the population of Bath – some 10,000 or so – decided to leave the city on this Sunday night. Most went only a short distance to one of the hills around the city. Edwin Stainer and his parents spent the night at Bathampton Rocks sleeping out in the open with only a coat beneath them. Others went to the hill around the popular site of Brown's Folly, possibly without realising that in the man-made caves beneath them were stored many tons of ammunition. At Odd Down and Combe Down people took shelter in old underground Bath stone workings. Mrs Smith and her family went with a neighbour who was a railwayman to the Combe Down railway tunnel. They spent the night in alcoves in the tunnel, terrified of the bombs and worrying that if a train did not hit them, then they might be buried alive by direct hits at either end of the tunnel.

So many people left the city that to Bernard Humphries who lived on the southern outskirts of town, the scene reminded him of the newsreels of Belgian and Polish refugees at the start of the war, great lines of people carrying their possessions with them. Bernard's own family did not trek because they had faith in their own privately built garden shelter but it seemed that all the others in his road had left. One gentleman said he was staying to look after his house. Another old couple felt there was nowhere else for them to go. In Herbert Road, Oldfield Park, Sam Hayward who organised the Fire Guards on his side of the road watched most of his neighbours preparing to leave for the night and was asked by one old lady who could not make the trek whether he was staying. He did remain, partly because it was his duty but also as he was something of a fatalist and felt that if a bomb had his name on it, that was it. A number of people who did decide to stay soon felt as it got dark that they were the last ones left in their particular roads. As 90% of people probably did stay at home this idea of deserted streets was often more apparent than real, but it is probable that in some areas many had followed the lead of a few and there were parts of the city where, if a second attack were to be made, there would be few people around to extinguish the flames.

Meanwhile, the Control Centre had problems of its own that Sunday. When looking at what happened during that day, it is noticeable that by and large the local Civil Defence leadership barely impinged on the consciousness of most people in the city. There were notices and loudspeaker vans but on a limited scale and even if the local authorities were putting out advice and encouragement then very few people seemed to have heard it. In overall terms, a very small percentage of people had been killed or injured and the Civil Defence services were well able to cope with the incidents that had occurred. High explosive bombs had disrupted much of the main water supplies but the static tanks and relay pipes had proved adequate. However, in terms of after-raid care, the Control Centre had enough to do in looking after itself.

Apsley House was abandoned on the Sunday morning and the Civil Defence leadership moved across town to the secondary centre at the Forester's Arms. Not everyone realised this and some messages were still sent to the Central Police Station. The situation at the Forester's Arms was itself somewhat chaotic as the staff moved in and tried to set up a proper communications system to regain a full picture of what was going on. In particular, Major Pickard and his fellow controllers were somewhat unsure as to how much help they had received. Under the mutual assistance scheme, in theory, Bath should have requested help from neighbouring Civil Defence areas. The required squads would then rendezvous with despatch riders at predetermined points on the roads into Bath and be escorted to the various depots in the city to receive further instructions. In the event, some outside squads had missed their rendezvous or had driven straight into Bath. A few had got lost, a handful ended up doing nothing and a number never got around to signing in with the Bath depots.

By Sunday evening there was certainly a much larger number of Civil Defence squads available in the city than on the previous night, but there were fewer Fire Guards patrolling the streets and buildings; and Bath was still without barrage balloons or anti-aircraft guns to hinder any attacker.

The night of 26/27 April was again clear and also very cold and those who were lying out under the stars on the hills around Bath found it difficult to sleep. 11.00pm came and went; if there was to be an attack that night, it was obviously going to be later than the first one. By midnight a few people were beginning to hope that the Germans were not coming back and at least one couple packed up their eiderdowns and decided to go back to the warmth and comfort of their own house. They had not been back 5 minutes when the warning siren began to sound. The couple quickly gathered up their bedding again and ran the entire length of two long roads before diving for cover in a ditch alongside the first open space that they could find. In fact the safety of open spaces and the countryside was far from absolute; over the two days of the bombing a number of stray bombs fell in areas around Bath but no trekkers appear to have been killed. Some were able to observe the city beneath them being attacked. Mark Whiteley, at Browns Folly, could hear the bombs falling and see the resulting flames reflected in the underside of the clouds which were more numerous on this second night. Others could not bear to observe the raid too closely. Eric Davies had seen his house collapse around him on the first night as a result of a high explosive bomb and as most of his family were now in hospital he had gone out to the small village of Southstoke. As the raid began he found that he could not stand being indoors again and spent most of the night in a nearby wood, still able to see and hear the aircraft heading towards the centre of Bath.

In the city itself, even if people said they were not expecting another raid, few failed to take some precautions. Many stayed in their daytime clothes, went to bed late or not at all. Alec Clifton-Taylor did go to bed but was very nervy and found that he could not sleep. He tossed and turned, wondering whether there would be a second attack. At 1.15am the sirens sounded and his question was answered; and answered very abruptly. Whilst he was

still in his room there was a colossal explosion nearby. He went to the window and looked out to see a terrible greenish-yellow light which quickly turned to a dark fierce red. He assumed that this bomb had fallen a few roads away in the Kingsmead area and that this night his area around Queen Square would not get off so lightly. He was not to be proved wrong.

A post-raid report noted that on the first night the Germans had basically flown north-south over the city and on the second night predominantly in an east-west pattern. The two paths crossed over Kingsmead Square, just to the west of the city centre. When the 83 bombers came over the city on the Sunday night it was Kingsmead which took the brunt of the attack. There were fewer aircraft this time but they were to cause far more destruction. On the first night they had dropped a higher proportion of high explosive bombs. These ripped buildings apart or at least blew out roofs and windows, thus exposing the more combustible wooden floors and the furnishings inside. During the first raid houses in Kingsmead Street and New King Street had been torn open. Now came the incendiaries. Holy Trinity Church in nearby James Street was blown up on the first night and gutted by incendiaries on the second. Further high explosives, dropped at irregular intervals, encouraged the Civil Defence workers to take cover and prevented them from tackling the fires. One bomb fell a few yards from Kingsmead Square tearing a great gap in a row of houses. A public shelter nearby was tilted to one side but remained intact as other shell fragments peppered the face of the employment exchange opposite. This was a modern two-storey building and the top floor was already well alight as the two rather elderly Fire Watchers were taking cover from the high explosives. Just along the road a Civil Defence garage took further incendiaries and a number of vehicles were burnt out. Further along still stood the two wings of Green Park buildings close by the Midland Railway Green Park station. Incendiaries began to burn in the roofs of one wing of the buildings. Fire Watchers were pushed back by intense machine-gun fire from other German aircraft and almost the entire wing went up in flames as the fires began to climb across the party walls between each house. Only one survived and that was one in the middle of the terrace. The caretaker in the house was a trained fireman and he went up onto the roof with a stirrup pump and thus saved the building despite the fact that the houses on either side of him were well ablaze. The Fire Brigade arrived too late to save the rest of the terrace.

In truth, the Fire Brigade had too many fires to cope with all at once and where Fire Watchers did operate they were often on their own. Stothert & Pitt factory did have its own brigade but even this did not help on the second night. The engineering firm was based at a number of different sites alongside the River Avon. One unit had taken a direct hit on the first night causing a roof to peel off. At another site a near miss had blown out all the windows of a four-storey office building. There had been no serious damage but with the glass gone the office block was now particularly susceptible to incendiary bomb attack. There was also another problem as, according to a later report: 'on the second night the trained crew had gone home to rest or were looking after their families'. Only a number of untrained personnel were on duty. The Sunday raid began with a sprinkling of incendiary bombs that landed nearby and which set alight a wooden hut. Burning brands were blown across the yard where they brushed against the office curtains which were now blowing freely out of the shattered windows. The office interior began to burn. The inexperienced Fire Watchers brought up their trailer pump only to discover that the suction pump had been damaged by bomb fragments. There was a spare pump but no-one knew where it was. They decided to telephone the Fire Brigade but found the lines were down. One of the Fire Watchers volunteered to drive to the Fire Station instead. However there were only two vehicles available, a van and the general manager's car, and these were locked up in a garage. When they tried the door they found it was stuck; someone had left the hand brake off and the van had rolled forward and wedged the door closed. By the time they had forced the door open both vehicles had been destroyed and a Fire Watcher had finally to run the 2-3 miles to the Fire Station to get assistance. By the time they arrived, the office block was past saving although the Fire Brigade was able to save the fire from spreading to the main factory buildings.

There were far more incendiaries on this the second night and consequentially there were far more fires. In some areas Fire Watchers complained that the Fire Brigade took too long to arrive; in others the Firemen declared that Fire Watchers were conspicuous by their absence. There were faults on both sides. 'It is the general feeling that the Fire Guard largely disintegrated after the first raid' ran one report and that RAF personnel 'only found one man who claimed to have put out any incendiaries, whereas a great many people openly admitted that they had left their houses when the IBs had fallen on them'. At least two factories had no Fire Watchers on duty and the general feeling about fire watching was that it was unsatisfactory: even before the raids it was felt that too many streets and businesses had not been organised to deal with the incendiary bomb threat. Some active Fire Guards had left the city. Other people had caused potential trouble by leaving their homes empty. One rural location suffered a near miss which blew out the blackout curtains in two separate houses. The inhabitants of one had stayed at home and quickly replaced the curtains; the owners of the other house had gone out and left the lights on and so, with their blackout gone, the lit windows quite possibly attracted further bombing. In another case, the owners of a house trekked out to nearby hills but a near miss blew out their smouldering coal fire across the carpet. The house would have probably gone up in flames but for the prompt action of a lodger who had decided to stay in, thus saving his landlord's property. It would be wrong to castigate all Fire Watchers, though some paid for their bravery with their lives. At least one Fire Watcher was killed in Kingsmead by a direct hit on the school where he was on duty. Three others, soldiers of the Gloucester Regiment, were machine-gunned to death by a low-flying aircraft as they stood outside a church, one having his head blown clean away.

The sheer number of fires did put a severe test on the Fire Service even if it was supported once again by the Chief Regional Fire Officer and a large number of pumps from outside the city. But however many fire engines there were, Bath still had the same initial reserves of water. The damage inflicted by high explosive, coupled with the general demand for water, meant that mains water pressure was often low and frequently not to be depended upon.

Static supplies became increasingly important but these had to be topped up and in a few areas relay pipes were damaged and the pumps ran out of water. At Weymouth House School a fire broke out and there were sufficient water supplies but a number of pumps had then to be sent away to Long's factory where there was the danger of a much larger conflagration. The Weymouth House crews tried to co-opt two passing engines but they, like others, refused to stop as they had to report in to the Central Fire Station first. Six pumps did arrive at the school some 30min later but by then it was well ablaze and despite all efforts, flames spread across to the neighbouring church of St James. The firemen then turned their hoses onto the roof of the church but it, too, was soon well alight. The crypt was once again being used as an emergency mortuary and some firemen were sent down for the unpleasant task of rescuing the bodies of the dead — bodies that were soon floating in the water that was cascading down from the main part of the church above. The tower fell in soon after and the church was totally gutted.

The most famous fire incident of the Sunday might well illustrate the bravery and frustration of the fire-fighters. The Assembly Rooms had been built in 1769-71 by John Wood the Younger, who was also the architect of the Royal Crescent. On the Sunday night there were three Fire Watchers on duty. A fourth who should have attended did not turn up and only after the raid was it discovered that he had been killed elsewhere in the first attack. One of the Fire Watchers on duty that night was Harvey Wood who had a vested interest in the building as he was the caretaker and occupied rooms with his family there. At about 2.00am he was on patrol when another of his team rushed to report that the Ballroom was on fire. Harvey went to check only to find that a large portion of the roof at the west end of the room was already well alight and that further incendiaries had penetrated the roof, setting fire to the ceiling of the Ballroom. Other incendiaries had burnt even further and the Ballroom floor was alight, too. Harvey estimated that a good 25-30 incendiaries must have fallen on the roof and with such a blanket coverage the situation was immediately beyond the control of the three Fire Watchers. He tried to telephone the Fire Brigade but without success and so, having told Fire

Watcher Millard to get everyone out of the building, Harvey sprinted the half-a-mile to the Fire Station only to be told when he got there that they had just received a message about the Rooms. He ran back to find several pumps were already in action and so he quickly ran down nearby Broad Street to report the incident to the Central Police Station which was still acting as an unofficial Control Centre. When he returned to the Rooms it was to find that the situation had changed dramatically. One moment it had seemed that the fire had been under control. Then the water had run out as the mains pressure was too low and the nearest static tanks were dry. Another relay from the river was quickly set up but in the interval the fire was able to take too strong a hold and the Rooms were gutted. This was certainly not a case where the Fire Watchers had been absent, but the incident had just been too big for them. Harvey Wood was to write his own report on the incident a few days after the raids. He concluded: 'My family and I have lost our home in the blitz, but I at least lost far more. Words cannot express my sense of loss. I loved the Rooms'.

Close by the Assembly Rooms stood the Regina Hotel and this was to suffer the heaviest loss of life in the Sunday raid. The hotel occupied a large Georgian building and during the raid a single high explosive bomb scored a direct hit on the lefthand side of the building, causing it to collapse. The righthand side remained standing and, as luck would have it, the reinforced cellar which acted as the hotel shelter was located under the undamaged half and all who took cover there were brought out safe and alive. At least 20 people were killed in the demolished section of the hotel and it was assumed later, from the way their bodies were scattered throughout the rubble, that they must have decided to stay in their own separate rooms and had not bothered to seek shelter in the cellar. A second hotel was also half demolished during this raid although there the casualties were far fewer. Another single bomb landed, this time on the south side of Queen Square, wiping out one side of the Francis Hotel. But only five or so people were killed which suggests that most of those in the hotel had taken shelter in the cellars and elsewhere.

The bomb had fallen just a hundred yards or so from the house in which Alec Clifton-Taylor was sheltering and yet when he looked out just after the all-clear sounded at 2.45am, he did not notice the chunks of hotel that were scattered all across the square but merely that there seemed to be fires everywhere. He went out for another

Damage around St Andrews Church and The Circus

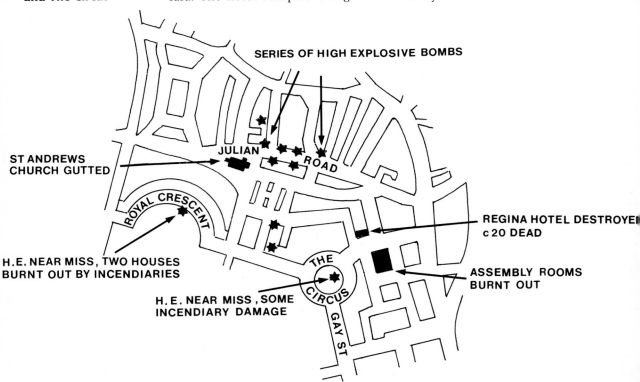

SERIES OF HIGH EXPLOSIVE BOMBS

JULIAN ROAD

ST ANDREWS CHURCH GUTTED

ROYAL CRESCENT

H.E. NEAR MISS, TWO HOUSES BURNT OUT BY INCENDIARIES

THE CIRCUS

GAY ST.

H.E. NEAR MISS, SOME INCENDIARY DAMAGE

REGINA HOTEL DESTROYED c 20 DEAD

ASSEMBLY ROOMS BURNT OUT

Above left:
Firemen replenish water supplies from the Fountain at Laura Place, Great Pulteney Street.

Above:
A Bath chair is salvaged from the Assembly Rooms.

Left:
Incendiary damage to Bath's masterpiece of Palladian architecture, the Royal Crescent.

Below left:
The gaunt and still-smouldering remains of St Andrew's Church in Julian Road.

investigation then and realised that his side of the city had certainly taken more damage on this the second night. He walked up to the Circus where the first thing he noticed was the body of a fireman lying by the side of the pavement. The face had been covered by a coat. Apparently he had been working in the Circus when he and his fellow crew members had heard a bomb falling. They had taken cover behind their pump but this one fireman had looked up just as the bomb had landed and had been hit by a piece of flying shrapnel. The damage might have been far worse. The exploding bomb fell into the lawn in the centre of the Circus rather than on the houses themselves and there were some reports that another two bombs fell with it but did not explode. The only damage to buildings there was that two homes were gutted by fire. The Royal Crescent had a similarly lucky escape. Another bomb ploughed into the lawn in front of the Crescent but again the only damage to buildings was that a couple of houses were burnt out by incendiary bombs. It was not until Alec Clifton-Taylor returned to his home in Queen Square at about 6.00am that he saw the damage to the Francis Hotel and realised how lucky he had been.

Yet, as daylight began to appear and the authorities tried to take stock of the situation, it was apparent that the general damage was still localised rather than widespread and that the 'Grade I' areas of the city had largely escaped damage. The Assembly Rooms were gutted, the south side of Queen Square half destroyed, frontages torn off some of the Crescents and roads up on Lansdown; but the Circus and Royal Crescent were largely intact, the Abbey had lost just a few windows and the Pump Room and the Baths themselves were untouched.

Neither had the Germans much more success with the military targets in the city. The gasworks were admittedly well carpeted with bombs. Some damage was inflicted on Stothert & Pitt and on the aircraft factory on the Lower Bristol Road, but the Admiralty buildings were mostly spared. Interestingly, considering it was highlighted on their aerial photographs, the Germans did not even appear to have concentrated on the Admiralty offices on the southern slopes at Foxhill. Perhaps they were too far from the centre to merit much attention; a near miss would waste itself in open fields rather than in a closely built-up area. Four bombs that had seemingly been aimed at the nearby mansion of Prior Park had caused some blast damage but had caused most destruction to the parkland in front of the house. The main damage in Bath had been to residential districts, especially to the western and southwestern suburbs. It was later calculated that the city had been hit by nearly 400 high explosive bombs and well over 4,000 incendiaries. These had destroyed 329 houses and rendered unfit for habitation at least another 1,000. Add to that the 15,638 that suffered damage and then one can see that few houses escaped completely unscathed, even if it was only a matter of losing their windows. Serious damage was in scattered pockets rather than being general and widespread.

The Civil Defence services took some time to compile statistics because on the Monday after the raids they were still having problems of their own. The transfer of the Control Centre to the Forester's Arms had not been a complete success. Harvey Wood, the Fire Watcher at the Assembly Rooms, had not been the only person to think that the Central Police Station had taken over as Civil Defence control. The telephones had failed once more at the start of the Sunday raid and once again a certain degree of overall control had been lost. Some Civil Defence depots had needed to move after sustaining damage of the first night and so reinforcements were sometimes unsure where they were to meet up with them. The blocking by bomb debris of one main road to the west of the city also did nothing to help ease the situation as far as reinforcements from Bristol were concerned, who could easily find themselves lost. The Rescue Squads in Bath had moved to bases on the outskirts of the city after the Saturday raid. This move had caused some disruption in itself but they were still ready with three duty squads on the Sunday evening. However, they later complained that the Regional Headquarters in Bristol had assured them of immediate reinforcement of another seven squads. These did not materialise at the start of the raid and the three Bath squads found themselves dealing with 15 incidents. Major Pickard later 'regretted' that other Civil Defence regions had not kept him informed as to the movements of their reinforcing squads.

The officials who visited from the Ministry of Home Security were more critical of Bath's own system. One wrote of his visit to the Forester's Arms: 'Conditions there were chaotic . . . my impression — perhaps an unjustified one — was that there was considerable confusion in administration, especially when compared with other blitzed towns which I have visited under similar circumstances'. Even the Bath authorities themselves agreed that some aspects of their Civil Defence arrangements had failed to a serious extent. After the raids, the Chief Warden wrote a report on his part of the service: 'On the first night Fire Guards generally remained on duty and some extinguished fires (preventing larger ones) but in other cases few attempts were made, without any prepared schemes. On the second night many left and what fire prevention there was done was with wardens and local help. It was lucky that the business areas weren't hit by incendiary bombs.' It was hardly an encouraging report which concludes by saying that the only reason the centre of the city was not burnt out was that it was lucky enough to avoid the main bombing.

Another report from the period might give an insight into the problems affecting the city after two nights of heavy bombing. A Ministry official wrote: 'The official bodies have also become quite separated from their normal duties and are not accustomed to the new work. . . Whether it is because of the enormous quantity of work which has arisen, or because of its quite unusual nature, they are obviously working very close to their maximum capacity.' In other words, the concept that Bath might be bombed — and had been bombed — was too new to be easily absorbed. This was seen to be all the more true for the general population of the city. The raids had come as a great shock to a city where many people had felt some kind of immunity from attack and, in the immediate aftermath, the dislocation was all too clear to see:

'When we arrived in the town the general impression we obtained was that it had more or less ceased to function as a town in the normal sense. The mass of the people had become quite detached from their normal routine, and had not yet found any place in the new situation, their only outlet was in wandering around the streets either to the various aid bureaux, or seeking some means of getting out of the town, or just wandering round. . .

'The majority of the people one talks to show signs of having been under severe strain. They seem faintly nervous and agitated, there is a tendency to repetition of the same story. They obviously have not settled themselves down or become adapted to bombing. . .

'The streets are always full of people walking to and fro although the shops are not properly open and there is nothing in particular for them to do.'

In extreme cases, the disruption of an ordinary pattern of life might be so complete as to prevent a person from attempting any kind of adaptation. This was noticeably the case at times where people survived a direct hit on their house and lost all of their possessions. In such cases it was natural for the inhabitants to be in shock and to need to be led and looked after by the Rest Centres and hospitals as and where appropriate. But a handful of people were overlooked in all the confusion after the raids and they were left to cope on their own.

Florence Delve lived in the northern outskirts of the city and during the Saturday raids her house had been destroyed but, along with her husband, child and baby, she had been able to get out without much difficulty. Then had come a second dislocation. The house next door had also been destroyed and Florence's husband helped to dig out the young girl who lived there. She was pulled out seemingly untouched apart from a bruise on her forehead, uttered the one word 'hello' and then fell back dead. Florence felt in a state of shock. She tried to breast-feed her baby, but no milk would come. Her teeth were chattering and she asked her husband for a cigarette although she had never smoked before. An ambulance came to take the young girl away but no one did anything for Florence and her family because they were physically unharmed. They spent the Sunday night taking cover in a stable nearby where at the height of the raid Florence's husband sent a man flying for lighting a match. On the Monday, she just sat in the stable with her two children doing nothing and in a complete daze. Only one neighbour offered any help and that was an hour's rest in her house. Everyone else seemed too busy with their own problems. After three nights in this stable, Florence finally realised that she had to do

something. Her mother lived in South Wales and so she and her husband, carrying the two babies, walked all the way to Bristol to catch the train to Tonypandy. When Florence walked into her mother's home she was still covered in dust and plaster, having not had a wash or eaten properly for the last four days. Her husband had to return to Bath to his place of work at Stothert & Pitt.

This might be an extreme case but it does show how people could become paralysed by the sheer novelty of the post-blitz situation. Anything that smacked of normality was of great importance if one was to try and cope. People cleared up glass and plaster as if the house was just a little more untidy than unusual. Miss Meredith went to work on Monday to her office and found everyone was tidying up there as well. Alec Clifton-Taylor turned up as usual at the Admiralty, the requisitioned Empire Hotel, to find most the windows smashed and his services not required. It was essential that gas and water supplies be provided again and shops re-opened, not just for convenience sake but also to show that normal life could be resumed, and that the city could operate as a going concern again. The outside observers that came to Bath immediately after the raid had noted that many people were in some form of limbo: they were no longer in an unscathed town but they had not yet come to terms with the new reality of serious air-raid damage. Could they adapt, or would there be widespread panic if the raids continued? Experience in other cities had suggested that the first raid, if heavy, would be by far the worst. Successive raids would bring diminishing returns of fear. Indeed, adaptation could be very swift indeed. On the first night the Homestead First Aid Post reported that all the 37 casualties they dealt with had been suffering from shock, as well as other wounds. Some admitted purely for shock were 'really in a bad way', there was a great deal of vomiting and the toilets were in continual use. Yet on the second night of the raids, admittedly fewer cases were dealt with and only two displayed any symptoms of anxiety by bursting out into hysterical weeping. Observers on the Monday noted that people appeared dazed but there were no obvious widespread examples of open depression or hysteria.

What, then, is one to make of the fact that on the Monday night even more people left the city and trekked out into the country? Some 80 people who lived in or near Bath were interviewed or written to by the author in connection with this chapter. All of them were in the city on the first night; 56 were present on the second; only 30 stayed for the third. This is, admittedly, a very small sample but there were certainly fewer people in Bath on the Monday night than on the previous two evenings. To some extent this was because the raids appeared to be becoming a habit. Some people had stayed home on the second night not expecting two raids in a row and had been proved wrong. Others felt that their houses might not be lucky for a third night in a row. Some just wanted a guaranteed good night's sleep. Alec Clifton-Taylor, having been sent home from work, finally fell asleep at 5.00pm on the Monday evening. He had been awake since the first bombs fell on the Saturday night and so had been without sleep, by his reckoning, for the last 57 hours. Many trekkers acted on the belief that anywhere outside the city limits must be safe which indicated a touching trust in the accuracy in the German bomb aimers.

Two other factors also contributed to the mass exodus on the Monday evening. In the afternoon a lone German reconnaissance aircraft had flown over the city provoking a mass rush to the nearest street shelters by those people who were already outdoors. Don Tuddenham was at work with a Civil Defence team when the aircraft came over and one of his companions broke down and cried at the sight of it. Many assumed it was checking up on targets for that night. Secondly, the story went around that the local authorities were encouraging people to leave the city. As we have seen, the government had in 1941 agreed that trekking should be discouraged. It left houses unguarded and seemed to be an admission of defeat, so any idea of active official encouragement might seem far-fetched. The Emergency Committee and other local bodies kept sparse records during the days immediately after the raids and there appears to be no documentary evidence that they would officially sanction evacuation; but it was reported to the War Cabinet on 30 April that Bath's authorities were encouraging evacuation, and other personnel in Bath's Civil Defence later recalled that this was the case. Having said that, there was also a rumour —

Far left:
Mopping up in the Julian Road area. Firemen damp down smouldering debris in bomb damaged houses in either Morford Street or Ballance Street.

Left:
High explosive damage in Somerset Street, close to the city centre.

Below left:
Debris in Circus Mews. The area in the right foreground has been redeveloped twice since the war.

later exposed to be an overstatement — to the effect that everyone, or everyone possible, was being asked to leave the city by 9.00pm on the Monday night. This rumour was later traced back to a very minor truth, that a number of houses had been evacuated because of the danger caused by unexploded bombs.

Whatever the truth in this evacuation story, it is certainly the case that many believed they had official sanction to leave the city. Some did: the bombed-out uninjured numbering over 2,600 were sent out by official transport to designated Rest Centres in the surrounding countryside. A large number of buses were provided to transport anyone who wished to leave Bath, although there were never enough to cope with the demand of well over 10,000 would-be trekkers. Some people climbed on to any bus, whatever its destination. There were a few examples of panic in the queues as it began to get dark and the last buses were preparing to leave. One family was so keen to get out of the city that they were even prepared to leave their aged and infirm mother alone in their house, arguing that as she was somewhat senile she did not know what was happening anyway.

Those that did stay felt even more than on the Sunday evening that they were very much on their own. Marjorie Horsell's husband stayed on in First Avenue but was quite conscious that many of the other Fire Watchers had left for the night. Only the most blasé made no preparations for a raid. One family spent the night asleep in deckchairs in their basement. Their billetees sat in the basement kitchen dressed in their outdoor clothes and clutching their handbags close to them. Kathleen Stainer and her parents did not intend leaving the city but, as the Monday wore on, they soon realised that there appeared to be only about three families left in the whole of the road. They, too, decided to go with the rest and packed up their bedding to go out into the countryside. They walked to just beyond the village of Englishcombe, half-a-mile or so outside the city. They spent the night lying on the grass verge alongside a lane with their heads covered, just in case the Germans saw their white faces and machine-gunned them; it would be hard to find a better example of the real fear that the bombers had inculcated than this attempted camouflage. There were dozens in the lanes, there were hun-

dreds sleeping rough on the hills around the city, although many did not actually sleep. The weather was at least dry, but it was also cold.

The luckier trekkers were able to find indoor shelter. Kathleen Stainer remembered that some went to village halls, many of which had been designated Rest Centres to cope with just such an emergency. The school and chapel in one nearby village were opened on the Monday night for sleeping accommodation and the village hall was prepared for the serving of meals. By nightfall some 150 men, women and children had arrived, many of them in a very tired state as they had mostly spent the previous night sleeping rough. Others were put up in private houses, although usually this was only for friends and relatives of the actual residents. And still they came; a farmer nearby found late on the Monday evening that as many as 200 people descended on him and all he had to give them was a little bread and a churn of milk. One observer felt that the trekkers in this village were 'marvellously composed and self-controlled'. Another onlooker in another part of the city took a very different view: 'Most depressing and most terrible of all was the unending stream of people pouring out of the town. Many were completely silent, many of them appeared stunned, incapable of any realisation.'

When most assessments were based on such simple methods as merely looking around at people in your immediate vicinity, then it is not surprising that two such contradictory opinions could be found. What cannot be disputed is that Bath had taken a hard knock, thanks to a lack of defences and a maximum effort by the Luftwaffe involving three raids over two nights. The Civil Defence headquarters had not always been able to work at peak efficiency but the personnel at individual incidents had done well and, with outside assistance, had restricted most fires and prevented widespread damage. The Fire Watchers, as an organised force, had collapsed on the second night but even this had not been disastrous. The spacious avenues of Georgian Bath with their stone-built houses were far less of a fire risk than the tightly packed medieval buildings in some of the other Baedeker cities. These large houses packed with sub-tenants had contributed to the heavy casualties attributable to a few bombs:

19 people killed in a couple of houses in New King Street; 17 in a road off Southgate Street; over 20 in the Regina Hotel. The failure to follow advice to stay indoors at home had also produced serious repercussions. At least 50 people had been killed in public shelters that had received direct hits. If some 400 or so people had been killed in total, then one in every eight of them had died as a result of not staying at home and of seeking supposed greater protection. If one also considers the two bombs at the start of the Saturday raid that demolished houses in Kingsmead Street then a mere eight bombs had accounted for 130 deaths. The other 300 or so bombs killed 270 people and even allowing for an estimated 10% that failed to explode, it became obvious that many of those that did go off fell without causing loss of life. Fourteen bombs landed in the open spaces of Victoria Park, for example.

How had people stood up to this bombardment? There had been isolated cases of panic on the first night but the most notable phenomenon connected with morale was the mass evacuation from the city over the next few evenings. In truth, no-one seemed to know quite what to make of mass trekking and this confusion did not just apply to Bath. Were the trekkers merely the 'useless mouths' who were quite rightly just getting out of trouble and merely showing a very commendable ability to adapt to new circumstances by making a nightly excursion? Or was it an admission of defeat, a failure to cope with bombing attacks that led many, including some essential personnel, to flee the city? It must be said that with a proportion of the Fire Watchers abandoning their duties and with so many houses temporarily deserted, a third night of bombing would have certainly set much of the city ablaze. Yet as a whole, it could be said that the population of Bath were dazed but not completely down. In respect of the general morale of the population, one might expect a third raid to be something of a make or break exercise: people were either beginning to positively adapt to this new routine or break under the continued strain. The point remains theoretical. The Luftwaffe did not return on the Monday night and the newly installed anti-aircraft guns on the hills around Bath waited in vain.

Left:
Local children play in a blitzed area between Harley Street and Northampton Street after the debris had been cleared. In the background are the houses of Rivers Street and Catharine Place.

Norwich:

Civilian Morale

If Hitler had wished to find a British city that had a great similarity to the recently devastated port of Lübeck, then in many ways he needed to look no further than Norwich. Both cities had achieved dominance in the Middle Ages, Lübeck as a port, Norwich as a centre of the cloth industry. Neither had managed to retain their lead and in succeeding centuries they were forced to watch other cities overtake them, both in terms of prosperity and of sheer size. This had one advantage of course: both cities continued to be famed for their medieval buildings that were never pulled down in the rush to expand into a new age. However, neither city had stagnated and in later centuries both had managed to attract more residents and new industry so that by the early 20th Century a medieval heart was surrounded by much more recent accretions. If there was a difference it was that the Old Town of Lübeck was perhaps a little more uniformly medieval, at least before Bomber Command wreaked havoc across it. The centre of Norwich did still possess buildings from the Middle Ages but their ancient monuments were scattered throughout the city, many beyond the limits of the old walls. The centre was also more of a mixture of architectural styles. The castle remained but with later additions. The City Hall was quite modern. It was also the case that the centre of Norwich was far less crowded with medieval buildings than had been the heart of Lübeck. Both the cathedral and castle stood in their own grounds. It was a minor – but important – difference between two cities that, in many other ways, were quite similar. At the start of the war, they even had roughly the same population, some 125,000 inhabitants or so.

As with most cities, the further you went from the centre of Norwich, the less crowded the housing became as you moved from the medieval heart through the Victorian terraces and out into the modern housing estates on the edge of town. Again, as was common, many of the industries that had grown up in the 18th and 19th Centuries had soon found that there was little room for expansion within the city itself and had also moved to the outer edges. But Norwich was not a major industrial city and some of its most important firms were able to remain in their original locations. Clarke's shoe factory stood a little way to the west of the medieval centre. St Mary's silk mills were closer still. Caley's chocolate factory had been built on one of the open patches of ground within the southwestern quarter of the old city. At the start of the war these three factories and many others turned much of their production over to the government. St Mary's received nearly all of its contracts for weaving from the government; Caley's handed over the bulk of its chocolate production to the Ministry of Food while it also found room for a small engineering shop with a sub-contract to produce tank sprockets. There were also some factories such as Barker's Engineering Works, more directly geared to war production, but at most some 8-9,000 of the city's population were involved in engineering. By far the most important firm in that respect was the Boulton & Paul Engineering Works that had some time before gone over to the making of military aircraft. The main production units had moved to new premises in Wolverhampton in the mid-1930s but there was still a factory at Riverside, nearby the railway station at Thorpe Road, although it was of marginal importance to the war effort.

Not that the Germans were to know that. As far as they were concerned, there were a number of military targets around Norwich – if none in the very centre – and the city had the further advantage of being eminently accessible. It was only a short flight from continental Europe and necessitated such a shallow penetration inland that the swift intruder could be in and out before most of the defences knew what was happening. Single aircraft might get through unnoticed and in the summer of 1940 Norwich was to be the unwilling recipient of a number of such hit and run raids, flying daylight missions in the attempt to drop a handful of bombs on a specific target. Limited raids against possible military targets with civilian casualties slowly mounted up as stray bombs failed to find their correct mark. Between July 1940 and August 1941, Norwich suffered some 27 raids that left 81 people dead.

It might be thought that as a result of all this action Norwich was well experienced in air-raids and quite ready for anything that the Germans might throw at them in the future. This is a false assumption: all that these raids had done was to confirm the belief that the city was a minor target. The local authorities expected such raids by single aircraft that caused isolated incidents which were easily dealt with. In consequence it was often the case that if the siren sounded at night, most people did not even bother to get up, let alone take shelter.

On the night of 27/28 April 1942 the first Baedeker raid was launched against the city of Norwich. It was another bright moonlit night although with a strong northeast wind. The air-raid sirens began to wail at 11.20pm but for some minutes nothing happened and most people paid no attention. Then at 11.40pm, some 20 minutes later, a lone German bomber was seen to come in low from the northwest and drop a series of incendiaries with some accuracy over the city's railway station. It was accurate, but possibly wrong. The German air crews had been briefed to attack any large factories which could be seen or, alternatively, the centre of the city. However, the greatest concentration of important businesses were clustered around Thorpe Road station which had already attracted the attention of lone bombers in the early part of the war. It appears that the first bomber might have just pinpointed the wrong station by mistake. He certainly

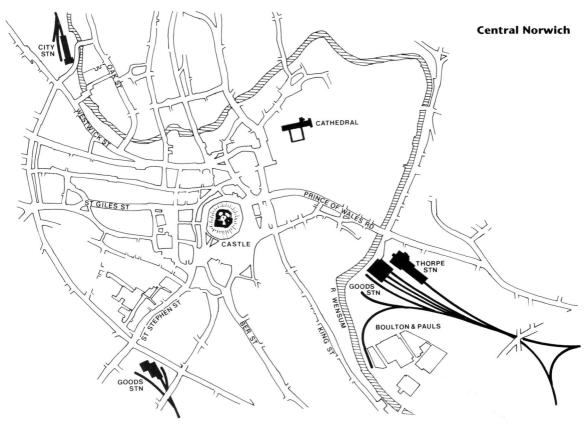

Central Norwich

Right:
Caley's factory fire crew in prewar days. *Rowntree Mackintosh*

Below:
Norwich City station, terminus of the Midland & Great Northern Joint Railway in the city, pictured on 28 April 1942 after the devastation of the previous night.

Bottom:
St Lawrence's Church is seen at the height of the raid on 27 April 1942. *Swain Collection*

did a good job, though: the station buildings consisted largely of felted wooden roofs lined with boarded ceilings on cast iron or timber posts. These inflammable materials were soon blazing away.

Five minutes after the first bombs had fallen, the main force arrived over the target. As in other cities, it was not a concentrated raid. It was rare to see more than one or two aircraft over the city at any one time but in the face of extremely light anti-aircraft fire from the surrounding area, most were able to take their time, to cruise around looking for a target and then dive down low for the attack. The raid lasted some 1½ hours with the final bombs falling at around 1.15am on the morning of 28 April. It does appear that the bulk of the force was attracted by the first marker incendiaries and as a result the main damage was inflicted on the west and northwest of the city. The City railway station itself was practically burnt out, along with a number of passenger coaches that were pulled into the platforms at the time. So was most of the goods station with the locomotive shed and a signalbox completely gutted. The Corporation Depot to the south was destroyed by fire and high explosives. There were not many factories within the vicinity of this station but one that did suffer serious damage was a shoe factory which took a number of incendiaries through its glass roof. Other fire bombs set light to the front part of St Mary's Silk Mills although its concrete floors prevented the fire from spreading too far. But the main part of this area of the city was residential with many congested patches of housing.

The Germans dropped at least 160 high explosive bombs that night and casualties were heavy. A minimum of 155 people were killed and the rescue services were kept busy in the crowded streets to the north of the city. The incidents make grim reading, as the would-be rescuers dug into demolished homes and crushed shelters. Stone Road: two casualties brought out alive by tunnelling through debris; Valpy Avenue: three bodies removed from debris, two unaccounted for but presumably in the heart of a fire there and impossible to reach; saddest of all, Millers Lane: nine adults and two children sheltering in an Anderson shelter designed to hold six at most. A bomb fell nearby sending debris into the shelter. All brought out alive except for one woman who was later found, under the debris. The others had thought she had already left the shelter and so a search was not made until two hours later when she was found, dead. In all, the rescue services were to extricate 84 people alive that night – but many more dead bodies.

Most aircraft dropped incendiaries as well but there was no great concentration and in many cases Fire Guards were able to deal with them quite promptly. Three incendiaries fell on the roof of one hospital and two were extinguished at once, but the third began to spread flames along the roof. Luckily the staff fire brigade arrived in time to put out the fire before it got any worse. Other bombs fell around the water works but this was open ground and they could be left to burn themselves out. There was no conflagration that night: fires were localised and were never allowed to join up thanks to the work of both the NFS and the Fire Guards. There was extensive damage to the north and west of the city but other parts got off far more lightly. There had been heavy casualties, but the situation had never threatened to get out of hand and as dawn approached on the morning of 28 April it could be seen

Norwich City Station and St Marys Silk Mill

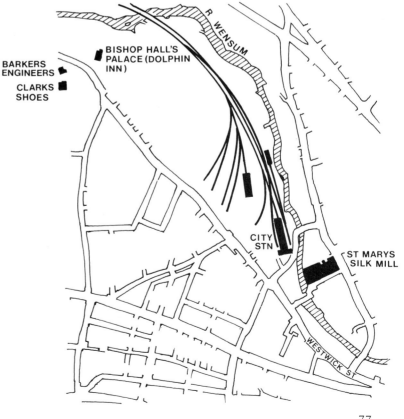

Right:
Severely damaged in the raid of 27 April was the Clover Leaf Milk Bar on St Giles.

Below right:
The Norwich Diocesan Teachers' Training College in College Road seen after damage received during the raid of 27 April.

Below:
The interior of the Teachers' Training College, showing the considerable damage inflicted. Nothing now remains of this particular building. *Swain Collection*

Bottom right:
The extent of the damage wrought on Rampant Horse Street during the raid of 29 April is clearly visible. *Swain Collection*

that Norwich had weathered its first real test quite well.

But the Germans had not yet finished with the city. There was a one night respite as the Luftwaffe went north to attack York but on the night of 29 April at 11.15pm the sirens sounded again to signal yet another raid on Norwich. By this time the city had been provided with some anti-aircraft guns of its own but, although these put in claims for hits, they did not seem to hinder the German bombing effort to any great extent. The first aircraft dropped a series of parachute flares which descended slowly and, coupled with the bright moonlight, lit the city up as if it was daytime. Some bombers then chose to dive under the anti-aircraft barrage to scatter their incendiaries in a large semi-circle across the city. There was a greater use of incendiary bombs in this raid but they were also interspersed with a number of heavy high explosive bombs designed to inflict maximum damage and to force the Fire Guards to take cover. As a result fires broke out once again across the north and west of the city but also, this time, in the centre.

There were immediate problems for the defenders on the ground. The high explosive bombs caused severe damage to the water mains and within a short time of the start of the raid, it was found that the mains supply could no longer be relied upon. As a result, it was relatively easy for the fires to get a hold and it was not long before the Civil Defence workers were faced by a whole series of small fires and worse still, a couple of spreading infernos that threatened to become true conflagrations. The first was in the area of the water pumping station which had already been singled out for attention during the previous raid when the vicinity had been hit by high explosives. Amongst the buildings nearby that went up in flames were Barker's Engineering Works, Bishop Hall's Palace and two laundries. Clarke's shoe factory in Northumberland Street took in yet more incendiary bombs through its partly glazed roof as well as through its windows. A strong wind then fanned the flames as they set alight to the wooden lasts, leather stocks and all the other inflammable material associated with shoe-making. The Fire

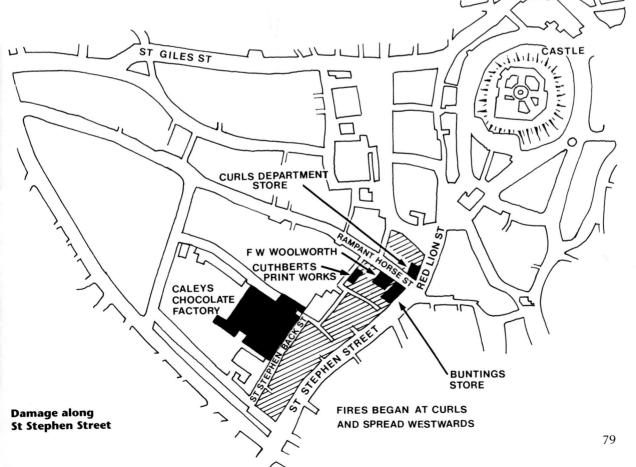

Damage along St Stephen Street

FIRES BEGAN AT CURLS AND SPREAD WESTWARDS

79

Watchers were unable to cope and tried to telephone the Fire Brigade but the lines were down and when the NFS did arrive some 1½ hours later there was little to save.

St Mary's Silk Mills had also received high explosive and some fire damage during the first raid. Now it was to suffer again. Incendiary bombs again hit the weaving section and this time, for good measure, set fire to the dyeing plant as well. Practically the whole factory was destroyed and it was estimated that only very few of the 260 looms could be repaired. It cannot have been a large firm for it did not possess its own Fire Brigade but arrangements had been made beforehand to set up a stationary pump with piping fitted into all of the shops; but no-one seems to have thought about who should be able to operate it. The Fire Watchers on duty during the raids did not know how to and had to call for assistance from the NFS which, because of commitments elsewhere and the sheer weight of incendiaries on the mills, arrived too late to be able to save them. The only water available by that time was that still held in the vats in the dyeing plants, a small volume and of no real use.

The second, and potentially more dangerous area of fire was in the south-western quarter of the very centre of the city. A shower of incendiaries fell across a mixture of shops and houses which had a series of steeply angled roofs that were themselves difficult to cross for the Fire Watchers on duty there. It was not long before fire had gained a good hold on Curl's Department Stores at the junction of Red Lion Street and Rampant Horse Street and, with the help of the strong west wind, flames began to spread through the adjoining buildings to the west. Woolworth's went up in flames despite the heroic efforts of the Fire Guards who held their posts until the very last moment. Bunting's caught fire although only the timber attic floor suffered serious damage as the concrete floors retarded further advance of the flames. Other old buildings went up as well, the Fire Guards being severely hampered not only by the rapid spread of the fire but also because of the negligible water pressure in the two mains which rendered all their hoses useless.

As the flames began to cross further and into Cuthbert's printing works, they started to come dangerously close to Caley's chocolate factory. Caley's

had independent water supplies as well as its own Fire Brigade. It possessed a deep well that gave 20,000gal/hr and was used to fill up supply tanks on the roof of the main factory building. As the flames spread towards the adjoining printing works, Caley's Fire Brigade took the decision to try and put the fire out on the works before it could spread to their own factory complex. They tried the mains water supply at first but, as elsewhere in the city, the water pressure was too low for it to be of any use. They therefore turned to their own supply in the roof water tanks. It was to no avail: they could not stop the printing works from being gutted. The situation got worse. The works' brigade had a powerful Mather & Platt booster pump which could produce 1,000gal of water per minute. It does not take much thought to work out that this meant they could use up to 60,000gal/hr, which was well beyond the productive capability of the well, giving a mere 20,000gal in the same time. Thus, having failed to extinguish the fires on the adjacent printing works, Caley's Fire Brigade then discovered that they had no water left to try and save their own buildings.

This was unfortunate. Caley's had escaped major damage during the Monday night raid but one high explosive bomb had fallen in the yard near the cycle sheds along with a further two bombs in nearby Chapel Field Gardens. These had broken about 75% of the windows of the main factory buildings and, as had been realised at the start of the war when blackouts had to be provided, there was a very large area of glass indeed. With the windows broken, the 30 or so Fire Guards were faced with an impossible task as burning debris was blown in at every level of the building. All floors were ablaze simultaneously and were aided by the inflammable nature of their contents, some 1,000 tons of finished chocolate as well as all the raw materials including cardboard packaging. The main two six-storied buildings were completely gutted, leaving just a smouldering twisted heap of steel and concrete. Flames also spread along a footbridge between the two buildings and through a subway to cause further damage, although the fire was finally stopped in the area of the stores, leaving a few outlying buildings intact at any rate.

The fire services were also able to stop the main fires from spreading that much further: Buntings Stores did not go completely up in flames, and fire was not allowed to go beyond the rear of Boots, but within this limited area near the centre of the city the damage was quite thorough. It did the staff of Caley's little good to see emergency mains being laid from the river to their works the next morning to provide a continual supply of water should another raid occur; there was not that much left to save of the factory if there were any further attacks.

The fires described here continued to burn for several hours; the raid itself was over much quicker. The last bomb landed at around midnight, meaning that the attack had finished within some 32-40 minutes. Casualties were also lower than in the previous raid, 67 dead and 86 seriously injured. This reflected the greater volume of incendiary bombs on the second night plus, it was felt, the fact that more people had been taken by surprise on the first night and had not been able to take shelter. It should also be noted, though, that the commercial parts of the city had also attracted more attention in the second raid rather than the residential quarters and so casualties were bound to be lighter. Even the commercial districts had not suffered too heavily. Fire had spread across buildings in two distinct areas but these had been brought under control and damage limited. There was no great acreage of total devastation: the raid had been sharp and concentrated, but less destructive of life than on the first night.

And still the Germans had not finished with Norwich, or so it seemed, when on the following night bombs fell yet again on the city. To be accurate, the attack took place at 1.35am on the morning of 1 May. This time it was a much more minor affair. The anti-aircraft defences claimed to have driven the attack away so successfully that only one aircraft penetrated the barrage to drop its bombs over the city. If it was just the one aircraft then it was carrying a great deal of bombs; either that or it was particularly lucky in where they fell. Incendiaries dropped across a series of roads including Heigham Street where they set light to buildings already damaged on the previous nights. Others set fire to Barnard Norfolk Works which produced wire netting for government contracts. The buildings were made of wood as were the bases of many of the machines. The resultant blaze was sufficient to close down the works for 10 days. The fire

with the most potential for damage, though, was the one that broke out at the rear of Garlands in London Street which crossed the centre of the city next to the castle. Continuing strong easterly winds threatened to spread the flames across the heart of the shopping centre but luckily the local Wardens and Fire Watchers were able to hold them in check until the NFS arrived to quickly extinguish the blaze. No-one was killed by this scattering of incendiaries in what was a very minor attack indeed.

There were no plans to attack Norwich and so quite why one aircraft turned up over the city remains a mystery. It was either very lost or more probably, designed to stir up worry in Norwich with the minimum of effort. In this it was surely quite successful although the question might be asked as to whether this was even necessary. Norwich had now received bombs on the city in three out of four nights. Even without taking into account this last, rather puny, effort it must be said that York apart, Norwich had not suffered as badly as the other Baedeker targets both before and after. No important industry had been destroyed. Boulton & Paul's had escaped serious damage. Some destruction had been inflicted on the shoe industry which on average lost three days of production but this would cause little harm to the war effort. Historic Norwich had got away quite lightly as well. The castle and cathedral were still intact. St Bartholomew's Church was burnt out but the major medieval loss was Bishop Hall's Palace which had been converted into the Dolphin Inn sometime ago. It was a sad loss, but it could have been much worse. However, no other city in this sequence of raids was to begin with one serious raid, followed by a gap of one night, then another heavy attack, then a light raid the following evening. There was no pattern to these raids, nothing to grow accustomed to; and as it was exactly this approach that had been suggested by British experts after the failure of the regular, German nightly blitz on London, it is worth looking at what effects this irregular approach had on the citizens of Norwich.

The frontline Civil Defence forces worked well if, admittedly, in conditions that did not fully stretch them other than during the second raid when the mains water supplies were severely restricted. The ARP Controller,

Bernard Storey, in his overview of the raids paid a glowing tribute to the work of the Civil Defence Services in Norwich. The Control Centre functioned well: indeed, it found that there were fewer incidents to cope with than had been predicted in previous mock exercises. The NFS received praise from Ellen Wilkinson, who worked for Morrison in the Ministry of Home Security, in her report to the War Cabinet. Wardens, and medical teams did good work as did the Rescue Parties despite having a great deal to do, especially on the first night when high explosives hit residential areas. There were only five parties on duty each night – a total of some 25 Rescue Party men – but another 140 were at home and 'on call' and when the sirens sounded for the first attack, 75% of these were able to make their way and reported for duty. The dedication and discipline of all these services, many of whose members had volunteered for duty at the very start of the war, were warmly congratulated.

The Fire Guards had not been in existence since the start of the war, nor were they all volunteers. The difficulties in the force, with particular relation to Norwich, have been noted in previous chapters although the city was no worse than many others in this respect. The Norwich system did look impressive. In a city with a population of at least 125,000 there were some 15,000 Fire Guards. Of these, some 12,000 had been registered to look after residential areas. These were attached to specific Wardens' posts and came under their supervision. Business premises came under the 'block scheme' whereby a whole business area would have a central rest room from which a team would operate. On paper it all seemed very impressive, but there were obvious weaknesses that later reports seized upon. There were so many Fire Guards that it seemed impossible to get around to training them all. At the time of the raids, many of those allocated to business premises had not even attended a lunchtime lecture on how to tackle fires and incendiary bombs. The organisation was also so large and relatively new that it lacked what might be called team spirit and a sense of purpose.

Where leadership was lacking, motivation was often low. Some were obviously more reluctant than others. Norwich was not lacking in volunteers to make up the bulk of its Fire Guards – even though some doubted the efficiency of a number of them if they

came under fire – and as many thousands did come forward, the local authorities found it necessary to send out a relatively few 2,500 compulsory enrolment notices. Here they seemed to hit a bedrock of those who had no desire to do more than they had to. Up to the time of the raids only 180 had bothered to return their notices and the Corporation seemed suspicious even of these. Such conscripts were detailed to watch over council and other public buildings, as if the council wanted to be able to watch over them at the same time.

The efficiency of the individual Fire Guard teams therefore depended on a number of factors, including each team's own discipline and the number of high explosives being dropped in the area. As a result, it is difficult to make a general statement about the workings of the Fire Guard organisation as a whole. Different witnesses reported different degrees of preparedness and efficiency. The senior Fire Guard Staff Officer was not particularly impressed. To hold that position he must have been quite an experienced figure and no doubt with a military background. On the first night of the Norwich raids he was working late in his office and so when the sirens sounded he did not take cover, decided to go out and see how well the Fire Guards were coping under actual raid conditions. He soon came across a major fire in a residential district that was being tackled by a Fire Guard party of some three or four people. Unfortunately, there should have been 15 of them but the rest had not turned up. A telephone call had to be made to the Fire Brigade for further assistance. The Staff Officer continued his impromptu inspection and came across a block of flats that were well ablaze as all the Fire Guards were found to have taken shelter. In the diplomatic language of the later report, they were 'encouraged' to come out by the Staff Officer to tackle the fire and after a while 'it was found that they had lost their temporary fear'. They then did quite a successful job of tackling the fire.

So it went on, the Staff Officer and others walking around and persuading Fire Guards to leave the safety of the shelters and do their duty. The residential areas were the worst. The Englishman's natural reticence meant that many street parties were not accustomed to working together. Isolated groups of individuals did valiant work but the Chief Warden noted that in many cases the single Fire Watcher decided to exercise his right to choose between life and possessions and chose the former. He stayed in his shelter while his house went up in flames. This put a greater strain on his neighbours in particular and the street Fire Guard parties in general as they frantically tried to prevent the fires from spreading. There was also a tendency to deal with the obvious bombs, those that fell in the road and gardens rather than those that landed on roofs which were much more difficult to see, harder to reach, but a much greater danger. Many refused to leave their shelters to tackle fires until after the all-clear had sounded by which time it was often too late.

It cannot be over-emphasised that such behaviour was perfectly understandable: the Germans deliberately dropped high explosives at intervals to disrupt the fire-fighting and as, in the darkness, they often aimed their bombs at areas which were already ablaze, standing around a fire armed only with a stirrup pump was not a particularly safe occupation. The aforementioned Fire Guard Staff Officer noted rather phlegmatically that even when the Fire Brigade did turn up to help the depleted Fire Guard team at the first incident he attended, matters were not helped as this fire was dive-bombed, machine-gunned and showered with 1kg incendiary bombs. A total of nine Fire Guards were killed in the first two raids, five in one building, three in another and one in the open road. It was noted that the first eight were all killed in shelters on business premises and only the last had actually been out doing his duty when he was hit. This seems a rather cruel observation, considering the other eight were all killed while at their places of work and in general the Fire Guards on duty at business premises were more effective than those in residential areas. It was pointed out that business teams were usually composed of men working in the same employment who knew one another and were accustomed to working together. They were also already on duty; there was not the additional mental strain of having to take the conscious step of walking out the house and leaving the family just as the bombs began to fall. The Fire Guards on the business premises were greatly praised for the work that they did and even if a building did go up in flames it

was usually seen as no reflection on the efficiency and bravery of the fire teams. On the second night it was said that the squads at Woolworths and Barclays Bank kept working to the last until compelled to leave by a major fire and a hit by a high explosive bomb which caused the buildings to collapse. The only complaint that the business premises fire teams did put forward to the Chief Warden was that they would be a lot happier if they felt that the Fire Guard groups guarding their homes were better organised.

The situation was generally less satisfactory on the second night of raiding when according to one report 'the Fire Watching system broke down completely'. This was an overstatement, if a pardonable one. Mention has already been made of the work done by Fire Watchers to prevent fire from spreading in the centre of the city. But it was discovered that in those areas of Norwich that had been particularly badly hit in the first raid, more than 50% of the Fire Guards had left the city or changed their residence. On the first night many had been on duty when the bombs had fallen; now some did not even bother to turn up for duty. A partial check revealed at least 50 defaulters and although some had understandable excuses such as the destruction of their houses or bereavement in the family, there were also cases of those who just did not wish to put their lives at risk (or, who often, blamed wives and families for being too upset to be left on their own). In such circumstances it was probably a good thing that the second raid was of a shorter duration than the first, and caused less damage to residential areas.

Of course, the failure of Fire Watchers to turn up for duty was not exactly a phenomenon exclusive to Norwich. The same was to occur, to a greater or lesser extent, in all the other cities attacked during the Baedeker blitz. Experienced officials in other branches of Civil Defence also tended to claim, with a certain degree of snobbery it must be said, that the Fire Guard was a relative newcomer with plenty of members and little discipline. What was more worrying to see was the tendency for some members of the established services to also show an increasing reluctance to turn up for duty as the days, and the raids, went on. Amongst the First Aid Centre personnel, for example, 137 reported in for the first raid, and only 110 during the second.

There was also the problem that members arrived for duty after the all-clear had sounded. This was understandable up to a point; while bombs were falling, it was easy to be delayed if you were forced to take shelter along the route. It was also the case that some Civil Defence workers had enough problems of their own as a result of the raids. Some 84 wardens were rendered homeless in these attacks though many continued to perform their duties. A number were actually reduced to sleeping at their posts and getting meals from wherever was possible.

However, some were not built of such stern stuff. At one post three wardens did not report for duty on the night of the second raid. It was not discovered for a number of days after that all three had taken their families into the country and intended staying there, at least in the short-term. One eventually did send in a note explaining that he was staying away until his house was made habitable again. Another indicated that as his place of work was out of action for another week, then there was no point in his coming back to Norwich at present. These excuses did not go down well as they merely put further strain on the wardens that did remain.

Those who failed to turn up for duty were only a small minority. As a whole, the morale of the Civil Defence forces stood up well. Less was expected of the supposedly undisciplined general population of the city. It is quite naturally difficult to recall how you feel some 40 years after an event, but in the case of Norwich there were a number of people who contributed to the work of Mass Observation and so we know how a handful at least did actually feel at the time.

At the time of the raids one woman was staying in an hotel in the city and was able to observe at first hand the reactions of other guests who had not been in an air-raid before. There was a variety of responses. One old lady of about 70 knelt on the floor with a cushion over her head and remained in that position for a good two hours. A younger girl was visibly shaking and clutched tightly on to her fiancé the whole time. A young person, a hearty rugby-playing type, was the first to sprint to the shelter. In the circumstances it was not surprising that the Mass Observation writer noted that her opening remarks about Norwich being a safe area were not exactly greeted with a great deal of amusement.

Another observer shared a hostel shelter with 10 girls from the Teacher Training College. The hostel keeper appeared to be very nervous but cheered up when her prospective son-in-law turned up as he was a soldier, with experience of combat in the previous war. The girls laughed and talked, and asked him questions. He reassured them that the bomb blasts were a lot further away than they were thinking although he also admitted that this experience was nothing like being in the trenches. There, at least, you had guaranteed protection he said, while looking meaningfully around him in the makeshift shelter which was no more than a kitchen room with added wooden supports. Most of the girls said they did not feel frightened — and wondered why. However, underneath the jollity and talk there was a good sense of real danger. The all-clear sounded at about 01.05am and the girls went upstairs, only to rush down again when they thought they heard the siren sound for another attack. In fact it was just a series of water pumps outside trying to deal with the fires.

Some people could not even bear to stay indoors. In their worry they fled to the public shelters but few people had used them up to this time and most had been locked up because of vandals. Each shelter had a note on the door explaining that the keys could be obtained from neighbouring houses but in the panic this arrangement was forgotten and many doors were broken in. There were even accounts of some people, at the height of the raid, making their way to shelters on the outskirts of the city. People continued to trek for a long time. One inhabitant noted 'whole streets and roads were deserted at nightfall for days and weeks afterwards. It was like living in a ghost town.' Exact numbers are harder to come by. As the Tuesday night, 28 April, was quiet it was difficult to accept the figures in one official report that suggest 40,000 left the city before the second attack, which indicates that a good one-third of the population had voluntarily evacuated themselves. The figures certainly ran into many thousands and the sight of trekkers making their way by any form of transport from about 5.00pm onwards every evening was a common one. One of the diarists for Mass Observation was struck by the fact that: 'There was a quiet spirit of acceptance; and as they tramped out of the city in their hun-

Right:
The interior of St Augustine's School. *Swain Collection*

Below:
St Benedict's Gates. *Swain Collection*

Below right:
The Avenues. *Swain Collection*

Bottom:
Brigg Street. *Swain Collection*

dreds in the evening — a few belongings, an old pram, tired dirty children, a setting sun — horrible, and suddenly one pictured people all over the world doing the same, out of Lashro, out of Mandalay, out of Rostock, everywhere; end in much worse circumstances than dry, springtime Norwich.'

This observer noted that there was no panic; and in truth, comments from both local and central government of the phenomenon of trekking at Norwich seemed to accept the fact that mass evacuation was not necessarily a sign of weakened morale. They tentatively accepted the idea that women and children would probably cause no danger if they left the city at night.

A check was made by the local authorities on the night of 5 May which revealed a number of gaps in the Fire Watching service. One man who was supposed to be on duty in the Cathedral Close failed to turn up because, he claimed, his mother and sister were still in a nervous state after the bombing. He also put forward the excuse that he had heard that some of the other Fire Watchers were not going to turn up either. In another case, all three Fire Watchers from the one post were absent on the same night, leaving their particular areas quite unprotected. Clearly, this state of affairs could not be left to continue and loudspeaker vans were sent out to warn that all able-bodied men should remain at their posts. This warning, which also seemed to imply that fathers and husbands should not accompany their families out of the city, produced some results although the council agreed that some prosecutions would have to be made. That this warning to men to stay in the city came a good week after the last serious raid also speaks volumes for the effects of the raids on Norwich.

Some, of course had no choice but to leave the city. It was estimated that 5,000 people had their houses totally demolished and a similar number had to temporarily vacate their homes because of the need for repairs or the danger of unexploded bombs. Some 10,000 people in total, therefore, needed other forms of accommodation but in this one area of Civil Defence there were a great many difficulties.

Investigators down from London were also to complain bitterly that the Rest Centres in Norwich were difficult to find as there were insufficient notice boards and direction signs. There appeared to be no list of Rest Centres

anywhere, nor were there notices telling people where they might obtain advice. Three Centres were in fact put out of action during the first raid and another three during the second, but this contingency had been catered for and reserve Centres were brought into action so that there were always 13 first-line Centres in use. What had not been predicted, though, was the poor turnout of helpers at the Centres. Most admitted to being understaffed. Worse was to come.

It was essential to deal with the homeless as quickly as possible and to find them alternative accommodation. Most Rest Centres were no more than church or school halls and if there was another raid while these unprotected buildings were still crammed full with people, then the casualties could be appalling. In theory the Billeting Officer could rely on a large team of helpers to go through the Centres and arrange temporary accommodation for each family there. The officer expected a staff of some 250 volunteers on the Tuesday after the first raid. In the event, a dozen turned up. It was perhaps not that surprising. An investigator from London noted rather archly that the city had had two years in which to establish an emergency billeting system but it was an unglamorous part of Civil Defence and it was not exactly the sort of organisation that could hold regular practice exercises. With few preparatory meetings and no sense of being a separate organisation the disparate volunteers just did not turn up on the one occasion when they were needed.

This put the Billeting Officer in a very difficult position although he did not make the situation any better for himself with his first pronouncement. There seemed to be a real fear that some who did not need help might try to use the system to get a safe billet well away from the city. According to one report, the Billeting Officer stated that no billeting would take place until those who had already made their own arrangements had left the Rest Centres. Perhaps 60% of the homeless were eventually to make their own plans for temporary accommodation. Further delays were caused by the authorities' natural refusal to billet able bodied men and any others whose houses were found to be still intact. Then the genuine homeless themselves could also cause problems. In the words of one local Civil Defence report, dealing with the morning after the first raid: 'It was found difficult to commence billeting first thing in the morning, because the state of mind of the people in the Rest Centre was not sufficiently settled to permit them to take a normal view. Very large numbers of people refused to be billeted in Norwich, and expressed a desire to be billeted in the county away from the possibility of a further attack.'

In other words, people would not do as they were told. Some must have hoped that if they did refuse to accept billets in the centre of the city, then they would be sent outside the boundaries and into the safety of the countryside. In the long-term this was true; all those who could not be found immediate billets were eventually sent by bus to the outlying County Rest Centres. But with some 1,200 people staying at the Centres after the first night's raid it proved impossible to deal with them all at once. Poor organisation plus a natural unwillingness to stay in the city actually produced the opposite result to what some people had wanted. Some 870 people had to sleep in Rest Centres on the next night, April 28, and if these were scattered across 13 Centres, it still meant dangerous concentrations of people in what were undefended buildings. Another rush of perhaps 2,000 people after the second night of raiding still caused problems; 416 of them had still not been found a billet on the following night and had to be bed down in the Rest Centres. It was not until the evening of 1 May that the Rest Centres were cleared. By this time it was estimated that the local authority had billeted some 8,000 people, 6,000 of these in the city and a further 2,000 in the country districts. Even so, this clearance of the Centres was only achieved at the cost of keeping open the County Rest Centres as well. On 3 May these were still playing host to 1,000 people, although the majority were nightly trekkers. It was also discovered that some of these were Fire Watchers who had no right at all to be there, and the council decided to prosecute 25 of them.

The fault did not just lie in the hands of those homeless people who turned up their noses at billets in what they perceived to be a danger area. As one report noted, the sheer scale of the attack upset any preconceived idea that one neighbour would automatically take in another from the same street. Norwich operated a Mutual Aid Good Neighbours Association (MAGNA) and

in some areas of the city this group did good work. But MAGNA worked best where there was a minimum of disruption; where its organisers were not bombed out themselves and so in areas which did suffer concentrated damage most people often had enough to do to look after their own problems, without having the time to consider those that were even worse off than themselves. It was noticeable that the greatest success of this Association was in an undamaged area which was able to accommodate some 400 homeless people. Others were not so immediately lucky. There were stories of people being refused by household after household. Some claimed that it was those who could offer the most help, those with the largest houses, that did the least. There may be some truth in this accusation. Attempts prior to the raids to draw up a list and set aside spare capacity for the homeless had met with very little success as many householders gave the impression that their houses were already full up. Immediately after the raid, the local authorities were forced to adopt a policy of 'blind billeting'. Billeting Officers went off in pairs with a bus full of homeless people. Then they would just pull up at a likely house, interrogate the owner, and return to the bus to fetch a family that would fit the accommodation that now turned out to be available. It was a rather rough and ready policy, but it was very successful.

Of course, most people were not reduced to such desperate measures and at least two-thirds of the population did not even trek out into the countryside each night but preferred to take their chances in the security of their own homes. Those that stayed were often more than a little contemptuous of those who did choose to trek: 'Well, we can't all run away'. Members of the Civil Defence services who were known to have left the city came in for particular criticism, not least the Fire Watchers who, by their selfishness, seemed to be endangering the lives and property of those who did stay. The sole topic of conversation seemed to be the air-raids and the damage they had caused. The local authorities had already been criticised for failing to provide adequate information after the raids; the local newspapers were not allowed to print specific details of damage; and people were very ready to talk.

Under these conditions it is no wonder that a lot of wild stories developed, many of these speakers seeming to take a morbid delight in exaggerating what had gone wrong. The women who contributed to Mass Observation noted down many of these stories. In one, NFS men were supposed to have handed their fire axes to passers-by and told them to deal with the fires, while they took shelter; others spoke of wild scenes of hysteria in public shelters; typhoid had broken out; the casualties were 10 times higher than the official figures; the Germans would continue to bomb the city until the City Hall had been destroyed. Most of these were patently untrue. The rest were usually of the 'friend of a friend told me' variety and noticeably lacking in any real detail. Such stories could hardly do much for morale. One of the Mass Observation contributors privately admitted that she became quite depressed as she travelled by bus each day with a colleague who regaled her with endless tales of gloom and despondency. Another of the diarists took comfort in the fact that some rumours were demonstrably wrong. She worked at the Teacher Training College which had been burnt down on the second night and knew it had suffered no casualties there. This was also announced in the newspaper the following day but it still did not stop one of her colleagues being told by a friend that they were still digging the students out of the college.

There were also stories about widespread looting, and organised looting at that. In one incident, a lorry was supposed to have stopped outside a house that was being pulled down and the occupants had asked the demolition workers to put the furniture into the lorry. The workers had assumed these were the owners of the house, had helped load the furniture on and then both lorry and furniture had driven off, never to be seen again. Leaving aside the fact that few workers would be that gullible – there was a very careful system in dealing with personal property in most cities – there is little actual evidence to suggest looting did occur on a large scale. The local newspapers over the next few months carried details of three trials for looting in which the defendants were found guilty. A soldier picked up cigarettes and other small items to the value of just over £2 which he found lying about the floor of a blitzed office; he was sentenced to three months in jail. A pensioner was given a one-month sentence for stealing a curtain and a lady's vest, total value five shillings, from a damaged and temporarily vacated house. The nearest thing to real crime was the case of a 35 year-old labourer who was given a six-month sentence for walking away with a gold watch, chains and other items that he claimed to have found outside the main gate of a badly damaged brewery, and he was only found out because his rooms were searched in connection with a totally separate charge. He turned out to have a long criminal record stretching back to 1923. Another two people were later charged with looting, but five cases were not exactly an epidemic. Either a lot of people got away with it or there was nowhere near as much looting as some people imagined.

There were few excessive optimists in Norwich after the raids, especially once the initial post-raid euphoria had evaporated. Most of those who remained in the city expected it to be raided again. There was little outright criticism of the Germans, more a simple resigned feeling that this sort of thing was bound to happen. A few blamed the British government. One gentleman on a bus got quite annoyed: he had fought for his country in the last war and had six children so why should the government allow this to happen? He was an exception but the interest in air-raids and all things military came dangerously close to becoming an obsession at times. One woman became so fed up of hearing about the raids that in desperation she took a friend to see the Walt Disney film *Dumbo*, an event only marred by the fact that they also had to see two government films that featured air-raids. Others felt the strain of trying to act normally while at the same time expecting another raid at any moment. Many made preparations for a swift exit from their homes. Few bothered to undress at night. Most kept their most valuable possessions close at hand: one woman kept her fur coat in a dust sheet, and a small case containing spare clothes, toothbrush, car registration book, insurance policy and a couple of poetry anthologies. Night-time was by far the worst and many slept fitfully. It was 'like waiting for death' as one put it. A week of disturbed sleep and another felt 'extremely depressed'. It was almost as if most people had resigned themselves to another raid, they would rather get it over with sooner than later. It was the anticipation that was hard to cope with, and the strain of putting on a smile in front of everyone else.

At the same time, as the days passed and no Germans returned, a cautious optimism began to develop that perhaps they were never coming back. Morale received a welcome boost with the arrival of further anti-aircraft guns and also the setting up of a balloon barrage. Even if these might not be particularly effective, at least they seemed to show that someone in central government cared for the well-being of Norwich. In truth, morale had never come even close to cracking. There had been no widespread panic. 'The people were frightened, but not cowardly', as one observer put it. They had not expected the raids and had been quite badly shocked at first; and the infrequent nature of the attacks had meant that the worry and fear had extended for a longer time than might have otherwise occurred. But fear and fright are a long way from mass panic and most people had acted sensibly or at least what they thought was in their best interests. By the evening of Monday 4 May there were signs that the mass trekking was at last beginning to die down. It was an unfortunate piece of timing.

Above right:
Whilst two small boys pick at the rubble of houses destroyed in Rupert Street, their elders start to assess the damage and complete the mopping up. Swain Collection

Right:
With two of Norwich's superb medieval churches as a backdrop, pedestrians pass the destroyed premises of the wine merchants Barwell & Sons on St Stephen's Street. Swain Collection

York:

A High Explosive Attack

York, a city with a population of some 100,000 at the start of the war, was what might be termed a natural target for a Baedeker attack. It had a long and well chronicled history from the Roman period onwards with its heyday in the Middle Ages when the present Minster had been built. Large lengths of its city walls still survived, along with the defensive position of Clifford's Tower, and within the walls remained some tightly packed rows of old shops and houses, the most famous being that known as the Shambles. Its 15th Century Guildhall was the oldest in the country at least since 1940 when the only more ancient one, that in London, had gone up in flames during the blitz.

In 1942 York had still to face the war directly. It had received some 780 alerts since the start of the war, but only four people had been killed by bombing and those on three separate occasions when stray bombs had been dropped, presumably, by the odd German aircraft wishing to lighten its load on its way home from another target. Few expected a raid directed specifically at York; it had a lack of military targets of any consequence.

The largest factory complex was that of Rowntree's the confectioners, but expansion over the years had led it to move to a site outside of the main city, in the outskirts to the northeast. Like many another factory complex it had turned over much of its production, or at least storage facilities, to war goods but fuse packing cases, optical instruments and the filling of fuses — in what used to be the 'Smarties' block — were scenes repeated in many cities. Chocolate and cocoa were still produced as well, some of the materials being stored in an old warehouse down by the river in the centre of the city.

There was also an airfield to the north of the city but this was not used

for nightfighters, and by 1940 it was a base for No 4 (Army Co-operation) Squadron, RAF, equipped with Lysander aircraft. They were certainly not capable of doubling up as fighters should the need arise. The one obvious military target might be the railway. York was an important railway junction, the headquarters of the London & North Eastern Railway Company with extensive passenger and goods lines, sidings and repair yards. The main passenger station stood just outside the old walls to the west of the city. It is worth noting that of the listed military, or possible military, targets the airfield and Rowntree's were quite a distance from the centre and the railway station slightly to the west. The relative lack of damage that York was to receive owed much to these fortuitous locations and to a good degree of accuracy by the Germans.

One of the best indications of York's immunity thus far in the war was the simple fact that the public shelters were hardly used at all. One example will suffice. Near the centre of the city stood a large shelter with two doors, each of which bore the rather confusing message 'Key on other door'. The key in fact, was in a small glass case at the end of the shelter with a notice asking people to break the glass to obtain the key. The glass was unbroken. What is more remarkable is that this fact was noted some days after the city sustained its own direct Baedeker raid.

On the night of 28/29 April there was no specific reason to expect a raid on York. True, a pattern was beginning to emerge over previous nights with the attacks on Exeter, Bath and Norwich, so that anyone living in an old, non-military cathedral city might have some cause for concern, but there were quite a number of such cities scattered throughout England. British intelli-

Right:
A view of prewar York, with the Minster visible at the top centre.
Reproduced from The York Blitz 1942 *courtesy of the co-authors Leo Kessler and Eric Taylor and of the Publishers Sessions of York, England*

Below:
York Minster, pictured from the southeast, in prewar days. *York Library*

gence still had no specific names of any towns to be raided. Some inhabitants of York later recalled a premonition that York was to be raided; Peter Barton who worked at the York Telephone Exchange at Lendal in the city centre picked up a rumour he thought came from the Royal Observer Corps which worked from nearby wooden huts. On the evening of the raid he went home and told his mother, 'It's York's turn tonight', but there appears no good basis in fact for this, it merely proved to be a lucky guess. The Observer Corps itself had no forewarning as one of its personnel, Albert Cooke, remembered a year after the raid. But they were quite expecting York to be raided and so when they plotted some 40 aircraft, 30 miles out to sea in the early morning of 29 April and then noted them turn sharply to the west and come in over Flamborough Head, they had no doubt that York was the target. The city's worst night of the war was about to begin.

Even this might be construed as being wise after the event. As in other previously neglected cities, the warning sirens had sounded frequently in the past without any bombs coming their way. Two developments had taken place as a result. Local authorities tended to delay sounding the warning sirens until it was obvious that the city was being attacked, and not just being flown over, or buzzed by the stray aircraft. Many people had adapted quite well to the idea of sleeping through sirens until wakened by something a little more dangerous. It is notoriously difficult to give a completely accurate chronology of events when a great deal is going on and some areas are being attacked, others untouched, and one should be wary of all timings. But it does appear that the air-raid siren actually began to sound at 2.42am, although the Germans already had been over the city for some 10min or so.

As had been the case in the other Baedeker attacks, the raid began with a series of sticks of flares and incendiary bombs which fell across the west of the city. The Wardens' reports after the raids emphasised the large number of incendiary bombs dropped, although it must be added that they may have seemed more because they were concentrated in a few parts of the city. Incendiaries were dropped across Pickering Terrace, Bootham Terrace, Queen Anne's Road. Some landed in Burton Stone Lane but these were near Lumley Barracks and the soldiers there immediately turned out to extinguish the fire bombs. Indeed at this early stage of the raid the fire-fighting was excellent. Wardens, Fire Watchers and householders all gave a hand to put out the incendiaries before the fires they created could take a hold.

Peter Barton, the Post Office worker, was with his father Bernard in Bootham Crescent when they were awoken by 'a combination of air-raid warnings and strange street noises'. Looking out of the bedroom window Bernard Barton found that the street was brilliantly lit. There seemed to be incendiary bombs everywhere, exploding on the road, bouncing off the roofs, landing in the gardens. Dressing quickly and taking the two youngest children downstairs, Bernard, his wife and Peter dashed into the street to deal with the nearest bombs. The immediate ones were easily put out with shovels of soil or sand to starve them of oxygen. Even dustbin lids proved an asset. Peter Barton found that they did not appear frightening at all. Indeed, those on the ground were easy to deal with and were no danger to those who tackled them. However, there were also a number of incendiary bombs that had landed on roofs or had rolled down and lodged in gutters. Peter went along the road to one house where flames were visible on the upper floors of two of the terraced houses. There were already helpers dealing with this blaze and stirrup pumps and water buckets were used to douse it. At present, it all seemed rather exciting and merely putting into practice what had long been known in theory; and incendiary bombs, on their own, were no threat to life.

There was another more worrying problem. It was widely realised that the incendiary bombs were only a prelude to the main attack and were used to illuminate further targets. It was therefore a matter of some urgency to extinguish incendiaries before high explosive bombs were dropped on them. It was a calculated risk whether to stand and try to put out the fire or risk being hit by a bomb if the fire could not be extinguished in time, for on most occasions it was the high explosive bombs that were the real killers. Unless trapped, one could run from an incendiary. A handful of people across all the cities that were attacked were machinegunned to death. It was the blast effect of a high explosive bomb going off that caused almost all the casualties. When the air-raid siren was activated at 2.42am, some high explosives had already fallen. Peter Barton was attempting to deal with another house fire when the first high explosives started to drop nearby and he took the sensible step of running back down the road to his own house to take shelter. Others were not so lucky. In Bootham Terrace, the NFS had quickly arrived on the scene to deal with a fire. Now a stick of bombs landed on the Terrace, killing a fireman, two of the Fire Guards, the Deputy Ward Head Warden, a soldier and some civilians. One of the Fire Guards, a Mr Ord, was apparently blown apart.

It is noticeable that a fair number of casualties were inflicted in the open and it is obvious that many Civil Defence personnel remained at their work, regardless of the dangers. Time

and again, high explosive killed. It was not only the effect of the blast but also the deadly fragments of bomb casing that scythed through the air from the centre of an explosion. At the junction of Chatsworth Terrace and Winchester Road, a bomb fell some 25yds from a group of three Wardens, killing two outright and leaving the third in a state of severe shock. In another street two Wardens were walking towards a shelter when they heard a bomb falling. They lay on the ground but the bomb fragments ripped into their legs. One of the wardens later had to have his right leg amputated.

There is little doubt that once again the Luftwaffe was somewhat confused as to the action it should take. York was to be bombed in revenge for Lübeck because it was a beautiful city, but when the Germans looked at their aerial reconnaissance photographs

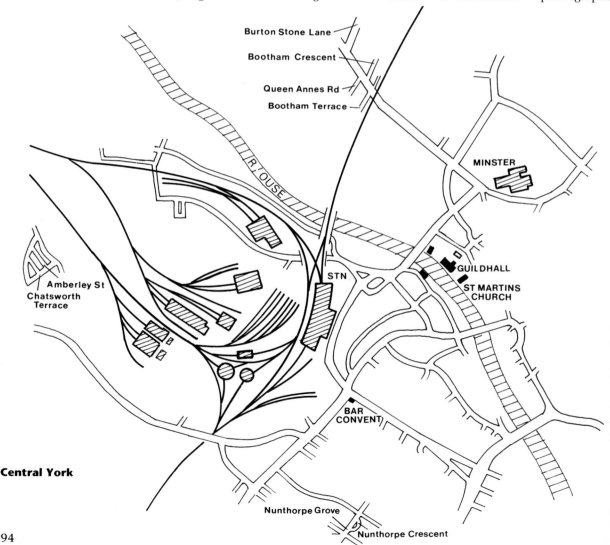

Central York

taken earlier in the war, it was the railway workings that were marked out; and it was these that the aircraft were aiming for. One member of a Ju88 crew, Hans Fruehauf, later recalled that his primary target was the railway station and that at their briefing the crews had been told that a successful attack would help stop supplies being sent via Hull to help the Russians on the Eastern Front. This was a rather exaggerated view of the consequences of any success. Other postwar reports confirm that the railway was the main target although, in radio broadcasts of the time, the Germans also claimed to have destroyed a gasworks but to have deliberately spared York Minster. The gasworks are doubtful, the Minster story possibly true. Once again it was a clear and moonlit night. The Germans still took no chances; at least 37 illuminated flares were counted at the beginning of the raid and the Minster would have been a highly visible target, yet it suffered no real damage. The propaganda victory for the Allies if it had been destroyed would have been immense and the Germans no doubt realised this.

The bombers approached from two separate directions, from Flamborough and from Hornsea, on their own or, at most, in pairs. They came at anything from 4-12,000ft, then dived down to 1,000ft and below to drop their bombs. By all accounts it was the most accurate of all the Baedeker raids, some 54% of bombs dropped landing on the target. Yet it was also one of the lightest main raids. The Germans claimed to have sent 74 bombers on the raid; the British estimated that some 30-40 actually hit the city. Whether this was the usual underestimate by the defending forces or not, even the Germans admitted on the radio that York had been less heavily hit than either Bath or Norwich. The figure of 70-80 bombers was standard for many of these raids and so one must assume that a higher proportion than usual failed to find the target. Those that did reach York partly made up for this by their undoubted accuracy, but this could not make up for sheer lack of numbers. The raid was precise but not heavy. Of course, this was hardly consoling for York at the time and in particular for those areas which were to bear the brunt of this new found accuracy.

The 10.15pm King's Cross to Edinburgh train was approaching York as the bombs began to fall. One of the passengers was Petty Officer Jacques who was travelling with a naval party of two Leading Hands and 15 Ratings on their way to Hexham. PO Jacques wrote an account of his experiences soon after the raid, for reasons that will soon become apparent. Just outside York, while sitting in their compartments, the party heard bombs beginning to fall. As the officer in charge, Jacques went out into the corridor and as the train crawled along in the darkness he could see two fires close by, presumably started by incendiaries. The train pulled into No 9 platform at 2.53am, some 10 or so minutes after the raid siren had been sounded. The Assistant Station Manager announced that all passengers should leave the train and take shelter but a number, concerned about their luggage or just unwilling to move, stayed put. Jacques later claimed that he and his party did not even hear this message. Others just stood about on the platform. The naval party and many others remained on the train. They could hear high explosive bombs falling in the distance, cannon and machine gun fire. A bomb fell, close by it seemed. In fact it fell on the Leeman Road coal depots, blowing rails out of the sidings so that they fell across the main passenger lines at some distance from the station. Then as a guard came along the train to switch off the lighting in the carriages, Jacques saw a series of flares coming down over the top of the station, followed almost immediately by a number of high explosive bombs.

Jacques fell flat on the floor of the corridor as all the windows were blown in, along with the side of the carriage. He got up to check that his party was safe and having confirmed this he sent most of them off to the shelter under the platform. Then with one of his Leading Hands he tried to make his way through a number of wrecked carriages to search for anyone who might need assistance. Eventually they came across a Naval Commander who was badly hurt and they carried him onto the platform. Meanwhile there was now an added danger. A large number of incendiaries had also been dropped. As Jacques and his Leading Hand carried the injured Commander back down the platform they could see that the wrecked coaches, as well as various offices and the whole after part of the station roof, were well ablaze. Jacques was later to criticise the station staff for their failure to deal with these fires

Above:
The Rowntree ARP patrol in 1940, pictured at the cocoa works.
Rowntree Mackintosh

Above right:
Amongst the buildings severely damaged during the attack on York of 28 April was the railway station, where the graceful curved trainshed lost its glazing and the booking hall and other offices were burnt out.

Centre right:
Destroyed beyond repair in the raid on York's railway network was one of Sir Nigel Gresley's immortal 'A4' Pacifics, No 4469 *Sir Ralph Wedgwood*. Although the locomotive was subsequently scrapped the name was transferred to another of the class.
National Railway Museum (Don 42/56)

Right:
The bay platforms at the south end of York station showing the destruction resulting from the raid on 29 April.
Reproduced from The York Blitz 1942 *courtesy of the co-authors Leo Kessler and Eric Taylor and of the Publishers Sessions of York, England*

before they took a firm hold, but in truth the staff had been faced with an impossible task.

In the event of an air-raid warning all railway staff on duty at the station were deemed to be on duty as fire-fighters, so there were staff available. But the simple truth was that too many incendiary bombs had hit the station for any group to deal with them successfully. The high explosive bombs had landed near the south end of the station, wrecking part of the roof and a number of nearby buildings. The incendiaries in the roof and elsewhere had spread the fire. Some of them had then fallen through the roof and landed on various platforms and departments as well as the King's Cross train. As members of the railway fire fighting teams arrived it was a case of choosing priorities. There was a further problem. It was soon discovered that the main hydrants could not supply enough pressure of water because of the overall demand across the city. The first hydrant they tried was damaged and would not work. Jacques found a number of military personnel holding two hoses but they were flat and when he traced them back he found they were not even connected to a hydrant. Jacques himself took one hose across the rails to a hydrant on a neighbouring platform but an adapting piece was missing and it could not be connected (the piece was found some minutes later). Another hose was carried across a number of lines of track but then some trains had to be moved and so the hose could not be connected. A station fire crew abandoned the hunt for a hydrant and running water and tried to connect up their own pumps to the nearest static water supply, a 15,000gal tank, but the connecting piping was not available and their own hoses would not stretch nearly that far.

By now, the ticket office was well ablaze but some dashed in to rescue ticket racks, desks and money. Others kicked incendiaries off platforms onto the rails. Still others dealt with the casualties from the train; at least seven had to be taken to hospital. A number of railway workers divided up the King's Cross train and pulled 14 coaches away from the six that were already on fire and left the latter to burn themselves out. With a lack of working hydrants, the station crews had to concentrate on limiting the damage. This meant allowing certain of the rolling stock and some less impor-

tant buildings to burn, a fact that was later criticised by uninformed onlookers. The NFS had arrived by 4.00am but by that time the fires had taken a very firm hold. It was not for another five hours that all the fires could be said to be under control, relay pumps being run in from the river as the water supply finally became adequate. Mains pressure improved as well.

The railway station was the major incident of the night; indeed, at another incident at the GPO garage, a passing fireman informed the desperate Fire Watchers that no assistance could be given as all available pumps were at the railway station. Harold Webster, travelling through York in the early morning, saw a large number of fire engines there, the streets covered with fire hoses and the roof pouring with water from the hoses playing on it. The damage appeared serious; a large part of the roof was destroyed, the booking hall and records office gutted, a train of some 30 trucks burnt out. There were some complaints that buildings had been left to burn, fire services slow to react and yet this criticism appears unfair. The fires had been so widespread and so immediate that no-one can be blamed for having to

1 CIVIL DEFENCE HQ ABANDONED
2 MANSION HOUSE SAVED
3 GUILDHALL BURNT OUT
4 ST MARTINS CHURCH GUTTED
5 ROWNTREES WAREHOUSE BURNT OUT

MINSTER

MUSEUM ST
LENDAL BRIDGE
STATION
CONEY ST
R OUSE
BRIDGE ST
MICKLEGATE
BAR CONVENT HIT BY HIGH EXPLOSIVES
NUNNERY LANE

Damge in central York

choose which buildings to save, or for the failure of the water supplies. Nor was the damage as extensive as it first appeared. Incendiary bombs could do little damage to railway lines and in a few days the trains would be running on time again. The worst incident seemed to have been caused by a high explosive bomb which landed in an engine repair shed, housing 30 locomotives. Three engines took the brunt of the explosion and shielded the others from serious damage.

Not all of the bombs directed at the railway actually hit it and a series of near misses caused havoc in the nearby terraced street. A Mr Goodhall who lived close to the railway in Leeman Road later counted some 11 high explosive bombs that landed within 300yds of his house. He was sheltering downstairs, having judged it was too dangerous to try and reach the shelter in the back yard. The windows of his home were blown out by a near miss and his elder brother was burnt on the hand by a fragment of bomb which landed close to him. The house lost all its windows, doors, blackout curtains and slates as the blast effect of the bomb ripped through the less robust parts of the house, but the home remained standing. Others would not be so lucky.

Some bombs were not so straightforward. The Bar Convent in Nunnery Lane, also not far from the station, received a fair amount of publicity after the raids, no doubt partly because any incident that involved nuns and the girls they taught obviously had no military value and could only serve to portray the Nazis in an even worse light. On the night of the raid, the nuns and some 15-30 pupils went down to the cellars to take shelter. However there had never been a serious raid before and at least one nun, Mother Bernard, was not accustomed to take shelter. She preferred to stay in her own room. It soon became obvious to those in the cellar as they heard the explosions and machine-gunning in the distance that this was the real thing and Mother Agnes accompanied by Mother Andrew decided to go and bring the other nun down into the cellar. It was a large building and in near darkness while the raid was on, but the two nuns made it along the corridors to the East Wing without any difficulty and roused Mother Bernard. While Mother Andrew went back along the corridor to retrieve something, suddenly there came an agonising cry from the corridor.

Mother Andrew immediately rushed out of the room to run down the passageway when, luckily, Mother Agnes stopped screaming. She shouted to Mother Andrew to stop: there was a hole in the floor and she had fallen through it. Mother Andrew told her to flash her torch and, guided by this light, she crept carefully along the pitch-dark corridor until she found herself peering over the edge of a hole in the middle of the passageway. Through the hole she could see Mother Agnes lying below her on the laundry floor. There was now another source of light: looking up, Mother Andrew saw that there was a hole in the roof directly above her and that through it she could intermittently see a number of the German aircraft illuminated by flames from the station. She turned back again and suggested that she jump down the hole and help Mother Agnes up the stairs of the laundry. But Mother Agnes said this would be impossible; she was too heavy, her leg felt as if it was broken and Mother Andrew must go and get further assistance.

What, possibly, neither nun had contemplated at that moment was how the holes in both roof and floor had appeared in the first place. There was no fire, as if an incendiary had burned its way through; there was no severe blast damage. In fact it was just as if a large chunk of metal had smashed its way through roof and floor – and in a sense this was the case. But this metal was a delayed action bomb, liable to go off at any moment. Mother Andrew was overlooking it, Mother Agnes was in the hole alongside it. Perhaps it was a good thing that neither woman realised just how much danger they were in.

Mother Andrew ran back to Mother Bernard's room and to give her as much protection as possible she helped to push her under the bed. Then she ran back to the hole, very carefully crawled around the edge of it and then sprinted down a number of passageways to the cellar steps. Here she found a number of other nuns, including Mother Patricia and the Headmistress of the school, Mother Vincent. They were just approaching the laundry steps when time ran out and there was a large report as the delayed action bomb went off.

Dust filled the cellar, temporarily blinding eyes and clogging mouths. There was a terrible noise of falling bricks. It was impossible to see and a smell of gas filled the cellar. In such a moment of crisis, most of those in the cellar seemed to be stunned, or as Mother Andrew described of herself, 'so dazed and yet so wide-awake'. The nuns staggered around automatically and without thinking, dusting down the children who appeared for the most part to be equally stunned. Few cried. Mother Andrew could see Mother Patricia nearby and thought she looked like a man as she was so dusty and her torn habit looked like trousers. She could not really comprehend that Mother Patricia was dead.

At this point a number of Civil Defence workers arrived from the street, at first by climbing through a coal hole, and began to carry out the casualties. Mother Andrew allowed herself to be led out still unaware that her own veil and habit had been blown off, but she held on to her original task and told the Civil Defence personnel who now came running across in large numbers that Mother Agnes was still in the laundry and could they dig her out?

It was soon realised this was a hopeless task. Mother Agnes must have been killed instantly. A roll call was taken to ascertain how many others were unaccounted for. Four other nuns, including

the two that had been beside Mother Andrew, Mother Patricia and Mother Vincent had been killed. Working through a mass of collapsed brickwork and having to use oxy-acetylene cutters to get through the smashed and tangled heating pipes, it was not until the Sunday that all the five bodies were recovered. The rest of the Convent tried to continue with their routine as far as possible, a standard response to sudden shock. There was Holy Communion and Mass early the morning after the raid. Tidying up, picking up glass, sweeping – anything was done just to keep going and to take one's mind off recent events. Mother Andrew felt no emotion at all until about 9.00am when the body of Mother Vincent was brought out of the cellar and then she and a number of the nuns broke down.

Elsewhere, in the centre of the city the main danger to buildings was that of incendiary bombs and fire. George Metcalfe was in the Fire Service and when the sirens sounded he cycled the five minutes from his house to his post on the fireboat moored near the King's Staith on the River Ouse. From here he had a clear view of the bombing and saw a number of incendiary bombs land on top of the Guildhall. Once

Damage around York station

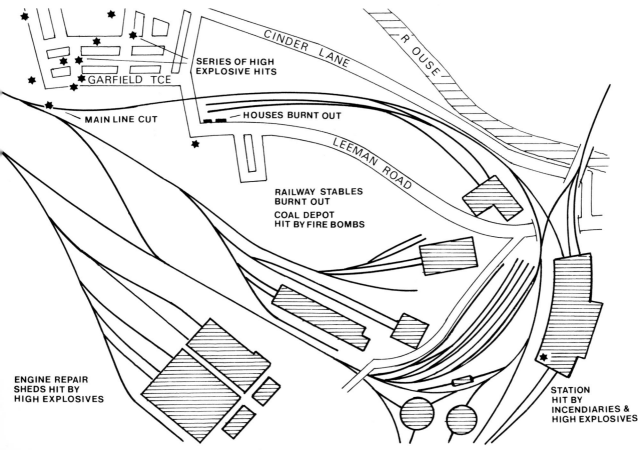

CINDER LANE

R OUSE

SERIES OF HIGH EXPLOSIVE HITS

GARFIELD TCE

MAIN LINE CUT

HOUSES BURNT OUT

LEEMAN ROAD

RAILWAY STABLES BURNT OUT

COAL DEPOT HIT BY FIRE BOMBS

ENGINE REPAIR SHEDS HIT BY HIGH EXPLOSIVES

STATION HIT BY INCENDIARIES & HIGH EXPLOSIVES

again as the Germans dived low they were dropping incendiaries so close to the ground that they landed in a very concentrated pattern. One complete container of incendiaries had landed just before 3.00am in the grounds of a nursing home some 65yds from York Minster. It then exploded, scattering incendiary bombs everywhere.

Amongst other targets, incendiaries landed on two shops, the Guildhall and St Martin's Church. This was of more consequence than might first appear. The Civil Defence Control Centre was located in a two-roomed basement office to one side of the Guildhall. Some of the personnel had expected that York might be raided and in preparation half of them had been sent to get some rest upstairs on camp beds in the Council Chambers. One was Eileen Chapman who was woken up at the start of the raid by the sound of the others rushing down the stairs. She followed them, albeit in a rather dazed state, and at the bottom of the stairs she was met by the duty policeman who was glad to discover that she was the last one out as the roof was already well ablaze. The staff began to take messages in and to issue instructions out to the Civil Defence services but this did not go on for very long.

The main telephone exchange was not far away in the Lendal area of the city and it, too, was suffering the unwelcome attention of incendiary bombs. Two Fire Watchers on duty were taking shelter in an upstairs room when they noticed an incendiary on the floor, amongst the equipment. They put two sandbags on top of it but the racks had already caught fire. The watchers ran for the nearest hand extinguisher but each time it appeared to be winning the extinguisher then ran out and as they went for another the fire would flare up again. Having exhausted four extinguishers in this manner, they rang for assistance from the NFS who arrived in 10 minutes, but by this time there was so much smoke that they had to wear breathing equipment. The NFS put the fire out with their water hoses. Then another fire broke out. This was also extinguished. The NFS then left, and the fire burst out again. Then another fire started up. The Fire Watchers equipped with stirrup pumps put them both out but a combination of fire, foam and water had created havoc amongst the telephone equipment and by 3.30am the telephones in the Con-

trol Centre, and throughout most of York, went dead.

They had already been causing intermittent trouble. Wardens had noted just after 3.00am that both the Guildhall and St Martin's Church were on fire and that when they tried to report these, their telephones were already out of action. George Metcalfe on the fireboat found that it took some 6-8 minutes before a messenger arrived from the Fire Station with verbal instructions to move upstream alongside the rear of the Guildhall, and by this time it was well alight. Fire Watchers had tried to extinguish the incendiary bombs on the timbered roof but were to report that there were far too many of them, although a later report was to criticise some watchers for appearing not to have used a nearby hose. The fireboat pulled alongside and directed its powerful jets onto the roof but, as the lead began to melt, it was forced to withdraw. Despite all efforts, the wooden roof and ancient massive oak pillars were set alight. The stone walls alone stood intact in the morning. The Guildhall had just been nearing completion of a three-year restoration scheme to rid it of, amongst others, death watch beetle.

The fireboat now started to pump water to supply pumps in Coney Street in an attempt to extinguish the fire in St Martin's Church, but incendiaries landed first in the belfry, the fire spreading rapidly to the roof. The building was gutted although the church registers were saved by the verger who lived nearby and dashed in to rescue them. The NFS and Fire Watchers now turned their attention to trying to prevent any further spread of the flames and by dint of hard work the 18th Century Assembly Rooms as well as the Mansion House were saved.

However, conditions rapidly became intolerable in the Control Centre as the adjacent Guildhall blazed away. They had already lost their telephones, the building was shaking and full of choking dust as high explosive bombs fell nearby, and all messages were being taken by despatch riders and cyclists. Some control had been lost as, with the telephones down, not all incidents were being reported. It was now decided to evacuate the Control Centre which involved making one's way down a narrow passageway, 4-5ft wide, between the municipal offices above the Control Centre on the one side and the windows of the Guildhall on the other, with melting lead, bursting windows and flames belching out 10-15ft from the resulting gaps. But this was achieved without any difficulty or panic. However, it was then found that the secondary Control Centre in St Peter's Church was also on fire and the Control Room staff eventually took refuge in the undamaged Mansion House. Here the army initially provided them with one field telephone. In the circumstances it was not surprising that Wardens were unsure where to send details of incidents and that the Civil Defence leaders in the Control Centre, at least for a short while, did not have a complete picture of what was happening in the city. This was not a fatal problem. Local Civil Defence services proved easily capable of dealing with most incidents although they were perhaps helped by the limited nature of the attack.

Even so, it had become obvious very early on in the raid that York's Fire Services on their own would not be able to cope with all the fires they were being called to deal with. York was well provided with water supplies. Thirty-three of its static water tanks were full and by the evening prior to the raid some 75% of the planned surface lines had been laid. There were also plentiful water supplies available from the two rivers that crossed the city, the Ouse and the Foss. The Fire Watchers had been most efficient at the start of the raid in putting out incendiary bombs and preventing many fires from spreading, and the mains had also suffered very little damage. Later reports commented that of 55 fires, only nine were even classified as medium and that it might have been quite expected that fire damage in medieval York, aided by a particularly strong wind, could have been far worse. However there were still problems. There was so much demand for water that the pressure in the mains became so low as to be almost useless and it took fireboat pumps, relay lines and static supplies to put out many of the fires. This lack of pressure had enabled the fire to get a very good hold on the station; the early failure of the telephones may have prevented the making of speedy contact with reinforcements from other cities. The first NFS reinforcements arrived at 4.30am from Hull and this was on the initiative of the Area Fire Force Commander who had lost all telephone contact with York. For a while, therefore, the Fire Services in York were on their own.

With the telephones down, each engine was potentially on its own as well and decisions had to be taken as to which fires deserved priority and this meant, reluctantly, leaving some to burn.

It seems obvious that the industrial and business sectors of the city, the railway station in particular, received most assistance. This made sense, although it would be harder to understand if it was your own home that had to be sacrificed for the greater good. One official visitor a few days later reported the consequences. He found that in one badly damaged working class district feeling against the NFS was quite bitter. Houses had been burning from soon after the start of the raid and yet no fire appliance had appeared until half-an-hour after the all-clear. Even when appliances did come to one area, they concentrated on two houses at the end of a street which were obviously beyond saving and facing open fields so that there was no danger of the fires spreading. Residents of other burning houses pleaded in vain with them to direct their attentions to their houses, but largely to no avail.

Large factories were expected to provide their own Fire Brigade but in York this really meant Rowntree's and even here there was a twist of fate which rendered careful preparations quite useless. The main factory complex to the north of the city had 20 Fire Brigade members on duty each night as well as Rescue and First Aid Squads and over 140 Fire Watchers. As it was on the outskirts it suffered no serious damage at all. However in the centre of the city, beside the River Ouse and on the opposite bank to the ill-fated Guildhall stood an old warehouse belonging to Rowntree's and used to store cocoa beans, sugar and other raw materials. This had only two Fire Watchers on duty on the night of the raid. At 3.00am they made a tour of the whole building and found no problems. At 3.10am they again went to the top floor and found an incendiary bomb burning and spluttering on the floor. One warden tackled it with a carbon dioxide extinguisher while the other ran downstairs to get a stirrup pump which he had forgotten to carry with him. He put a bin of water in a hoist to send up with the pump but he then found that it would not work as the electricity supply had stopped. More fires were found in the top floor and the Fire Watchers retreated. Their first thought was of the Works Fire

Brigade but the telephones were not working. One of the watchers then cycled the one mile to the main works but the Brigade there, no doubt correctly, refused to help as long as the raid continued and there was still the possibility that their buildings might sustain damage. Luckily the York Fire Services were working on other fires near the warehouse and when they saw flames coming up through its roof they immediately detached two pumps to work on the building but it was too late by then. The roof collapsed soon after, the inside being largely burnt out. However, they did manage to prevent the flames from spreading across to nearby buildings, no mean achievement when the gap was only some 6ft or so. It is perhaps worth noting at this point that in all the fires described here – the warehouse, the Guildhall, St Martin's Church – not one person lost their life. Incendiary bombs were very definitely only dangerous to buildings rather than people.

It was in the residential areas of the city that most people were killed, and these almost always by high explosive bombs. What is also worthy of note is how many bombs wasted themselves in open ground, in York as elsewhere. Conversely, even where there was damage to housing, and this could be very widespread indeed, there might be relatively few casualties. A direct hit on an Anderson or street shelter could cause terrible casualties but time and again a near miss could plough up gardens, wreck walls, tip shelters and still the occupants might emerge relatively unscathed.

The Nunthorpe Estate had been built in the 1930s, on the former site of some allotments. A pond had also existed there at the time so the ground was prone to be somewhat damp. Nunthorpe Grove consisted of a series of semi-detached houses with all the even numbers on one side, and the odd numbers on the other. Behind the Grove stood Nunthorpe Crescent. As the raid began the inhabitants of the Grove had begun to take cover. David Thomas, a young child at the time, lived at No 41 Nunthorpe Grove with his parents and a younger brother. The two children were awoken by their parents who rushed them into the garden and down to their Anderson shelter at the back of the house. Sparks and tracer bullets could be seen across the sky, coupled with the sound of explosions. As they sat in the shelter they could still hear these sounds, sometimes loud, sometimes in the distance. Two doors down, at No 37 lived the Moses family — mother, father and three children. They also went to their Anderson shelter as the bombs began to fall.

Not everyone had a shelter at the end of their garden. No 19 Nunthorpe Grove was built near the old pond and the garden was so water-logged that an Anderson shelter was inappropriate. Here lived Frank and Edna Blakeborough and their three year-old child Anne. On the evening of the raid Frank Blakeborough was at work on the night shift at York Carriage Works. There was also another young woman in the house, Mary Tedham, who was an ATS girl and billeted in the house. Edna was awoken by the sound of bombs falling; she heard no siren. Her first thought was of her sleeping child. She arose, picked up and wrapped a shawl around

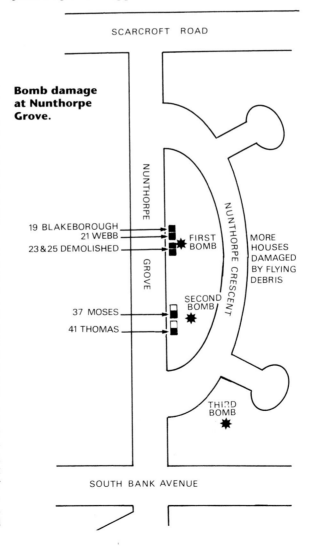

Bomb damage at Nunthorpe Grove.

SCARCROFT ROAD

NUNTHORPE GROVE

NUNTHORPE CRESCENT

19 BLAKEBOROUGH
21 WEBB
23 & 25 DEMOLISHED

FIRST BOMB

MORE HOUSES DAMAGED BY FLYING DEBRIS

SECOND BOMB

37 MOSES
41 THOMAS

THIRD BOMB

SOUTH BANK AVENUE

Anne and then went to wake Mary Tedham. Mary wanted to get dressed but Edna said there was no time and so Mary followed her downstairs clad only in her army issue vest and a greatcoat. They went into the living room but immediately there were machine-gun bullets coming in through the window, embedding themselves in the corner of the room. All was confusion. The baby was screaming, the two women were quite naturally frightened. They turned the settee upside down to hide underneath it but the baby continued to cry and so all three went into the pantry under the stairs. At that moment there was a knock on the door; it was a Major Larkham who was billeted next door at No 21 with Edna's neighbour, Lillian Webb. They, too, had an ATS billettee, a girl by the name of Dorothy Thompson. The Major took the baby and told the two women Edna and Mary to follow him to No 21 but as they made their way between the houses Edna heard an aircraft above and saw it open fire. She panicked and ran around the house twice before going in.

There were now six people in the house: Mary, Edna and her baby Anne from No 19 and Mrs Webb, Major Larkham and Dorothy from No 21. They all sat huddled in the corner of No 21, apart from Dorothy who appeared to be the calmest as she insisted on cleaning her shoes for parade the following day. They sat for some time until the Major announced that the raid must be over soon and that he was going to make some tea. This he did and just as he handed out the tea the bomb landed.

There was a sudden, terrible noise and at the same time the window blew in and the ceiling light began to swing. It seems probable, on the basis of later bomb surveys, that this was the result of a bomb landing a short distance away. In seconds the household reacted. The explosions had dislodged the black out curtain and Mary sprang forward to pull it across again. Edna thought of putting off the light. Dorothy ran to the door into the kitchen to turn off the gas and thus was out of the room when a bomb landed on Nos 23-25 Nunthorpe Grove, next door, destroying both houses as well as Nos 19-21. The blast wave tore through No 21, temporarily concussing those in the house as the building fell around them.

Mary Tedham did not remember being literally blown up, but became conscious again just before she fell back to the ground and as debris rained down found herself buried up to her waist in rubble. Civil Defence men immediately came running over to get her out, despite further machine-gunning by a German aircraft. The debris must have been relatively loose for she was quickly pulled out, even though she noticed that her right foot was hanging as if it would fall off. Both her ankles were later found to be fractured.

Edna remembered even less. She came to for a few seconds to hear a man's voice calling, 'We can see where you are, for God's sake don't move!' and the next thing was that she was in an ambulance. Blood was pouring down her face and into her mouth and as she put her hand to her head she found there was a hole there, one so big that Mary felt she could have put her hand in it. Edna's child, Anne, was pulled out by a Civil Defence helper, Mr Popeley, even though he thought she was dead. But she was still alive, as were Major Larkham and Mrs Webb. Only Dorothy Thompson, was unaccounted for.

Another bomb in this stick landed further up the road near where the Thomas' and Moses' were sheltering, each family in their own Anderson shelters. At No 41, David Thomas' father had just decided to return to the house for some reason when the shelter shook and David felt soil fall onto his head. In fact the shelter roof had been ripped apart by blast as a bomb landed nearby. David got out of the shelter to see that the wall of sleepers across the front of the door were in disarray and in the full moonlight he could see the net curtains in the house calmly blowing outwards through what remained of the window. There was debris everywhere and the rear wall of No 39 and 41 was bulging outwards. This was all caused by the blast. (As the bomb had ripped through the house it removed windows and doors but, as the pressure wave passed, the house had then filled with high pressure air. When the pressure wave had passed over it, it was replaced by a low pressure area. As a result the pressure inside the house was, temporarily, higher than the outside, so as high pressure air rushed back out again the walls were pushed out as well.) It was obvious that a bomb had landed somewhere close, but where? In fact it was not until several days later that David realised how lucky he had been. There was a massive crater a few feet behind their shelter at the bottom of the garden, and spanning a number of other gardens as well.

Nearby, at No 37, one of the Moses family had also thought briefly of leaving the shelter, just before the bomb fell. The eldest son had run back into the house to fetch his black labrador dog but it had been so scared by the noise that it refused to move. He had run back down the garden, had heard the sound of an aircraft diving down, glanced up, saw it, and made a dive for the shelter door as he heard the bomb come whistling down. The blast blew him from one end of the shelter to the other, leaving him with a nasty lump on his head but otherwise intact.

The Anderson shelters had certainly proved their worth; no-one lost their life in either the Thomas or Moses family. But the direct and indirect effects of these few bombs were widespread. The sheer force of the blast meant that it was not just bomb fragments which constituted the only danger. To the back of Nunthorpe Grove was Nunthorpe Crescent and in one of the houses lived Anne Holliday with her parents. At the start of the raid they had come downstairs, the father to sit in his usual chair by the fireside, the mother and daughter opposite him on the settee. As the raid continued the mother decided to shelter under the table. Anne stepped on to the floor beside the settee. Then they all heard a whistling noise and realised it was a bomb, but it was one of those that landed in Nunthorpe Grove, possibly that which fell behind Nos 39-41. The bomb threw up a large amount of debris and it seems that a heavy boulder shot up from one of the gardens and came crashing through the roof and brought Anne's bedroom and everything above down on top of the family. She blacked out momentarily to find herself with her legs under the floorboards and a wooden beam across her back. She called to her father but there was no reply. Her mother, the only one who had taken shelter under the table, spoke instead. Anne asked her whether she could get out and seek help as she could not move and thought her legs were broken.

The house was still intact, if badly damaged, and the mother managed to crawl out and then hobble to the front door to call for assistance. As elsewhere in this area neighbours and Civil Defence workers were quick to respond. A warden, Jack Hudson, came in and began to remove the debris. Anne asked after her father: he was in the corner, was he alright? Mr Hudson replied that he would get her out first. The warden had avoided the question and Anne knew that her father must be dead, killed instantly as part of the house had collapsed on top of him. Anne was eventually lifted out and taken to hospital, her back and legs hurting greatly and her left leg in particular hanging at an odd angle. A neighbour named Mr Judges was put in the same ambulance, in great pain and suffering with a severely crushed leg.

The all-clear sounded just after 4.00am. In many areas neighbours helped, especially if their own houses were still intact. The Barton family were once again out and about soon after the raid had finished. In Bootham Terrace itself there were houses destroyed, houses with their fronts off, almost all the houses with at least their windows blown out. The Barton's home became an unofficial First Aid Post. An elderly couple, only partly dressed, appeared on the doorstep and came into the hall in a dazed condition, carrying the remainder of their clothes. The bodies of two elderly ladies still in their night attire were brought in and laid out on the lounge carpet.

They had been killed by blast although they had no visible signs of injury. Another woman was brought in and put on the kitchen floor. She was thought to have suffered a broken jaw and so despite her cries she was not allowed any water to drink. The fallen lounge door became a temporary stretcher and was used for at least one man who had been killed by blast while lying on the ground. His face was almost unrecognisable.

As the day wore on, the casualties went off to first aid posts and to hospital and the rescue workers continued to look for those that were still missing. In Crosslands Road a bomb had fallen in a back yard, demolishing Nos 8 and 9. The occupants of No 9 had taken cover in an Anderson shelter which was badly damaged, but all three inside — mother and two children — were pulled out uninjured and taken to a Rest Centre. However the three occupants of No 8 were reported to be still under the debris that used to be their house. Here it was a relatively simple case of getting more assistance and with hands and shovels working from the top down through the rubble. After removing some 4ft in depth of debris they

Business goes on. With the ruined remains of St Martin le Grand in Coney Street behind it, the Jersey Dairy continues to trade from the doorway of its demolished shop.
Reproduced from The York Blitz 1942 *courtesy of the co-authors Leo Kessler and Eric Taylor and of the Publishers Sessions of York, England*

reached the first occupant, a young WAAF girl who was fine except for a superficial cut to the base of her skull. She was able to provide the information that the other two occupants, Betty Smith and her two year-old son Michael, had been near her when the bomb fell. More debris was removed, a great deal of it, until at last they exposed the lower limbs of Mrs Smith. She was conscious and could help direct her would-be rescuers, but there was still a great deal of rubble to be excavated. Tackle had to be brought up but luckily at the same time a proper Rescue Party arrived and soon after Mrs Smith and her son were released. But Michael, the two year-old boy, was found to be dead and a doctor recommended that Mrs Smith be immediately admitted to hospital.

Most deaths appear to have occurred at the moment of the bomb exploding. Some might linger on. Joan Whitehead, then aged 17, lived in Winchester Grove and around the corner from her grandmother and aunt in Chatsworth Terrace. She and her father had been amongst the first on the scene in the Terrace but her grandmother's house had been demolished and her father had to give advice to the Rescue Party leader as to where he thought the two women might have been sheltering. As the morning wore on and the Rescue Parties sifted carefully through the rubble of a number of houses, a four year-old girl was heard to call out. She was with her parents trapped somewhere under the debris. Then the site caught fire, possibly from a gas escape or perhaps from a smouldering coal fire that had finally set alight to flammable materials that had fallen on top of it. The rescuers and onlookers formed a bucket chain, taking water from a nearby crater which had filled up thanks to a burst pipe, but it was to no avail. Mrs Whitehead remembered that the girl and her parents were brought out dead, as were her own aunt and grandmother. It would be preferable to hope that they finally succumbed to injuries inflicted by blast, or indirectly by being crushed when the house collapsed, rather than the alternative of being burnt alive while trapped in the remains of their houses. Crushed and torn bodies were a terrible sight and Rescue Parties often tried to spare relatives further grief. Joan Whitehead's father was not allowed to see the body of his sister when she was brought out, but was assured that she was 'all there'.

Some people took longer to track down. At No 21 Nunthorpe Grove, five people including Edna Blakeborough had been pulled out alive but that still left the young ATS girl Dorothy Thompson unaccounted for. A first Rescue Party looked all day around the site but only found some pieces of ATS clothing. Joan Stanhope who regularly walked with Dorothy to work, informed her superior who sent some soldiers from the office to help look for her. Days passed, as rescue party succeeded rescue party, searching everywhere around the crater, sifting through the rubble. A Rescue Leader followed up one report that a Dorothy Thompson had been taken to another mortuary outside York but, on checking, this proved to be a 50 year-old woman who just happened to have the same name. It was not until the late afternoon of Thursday 7 May that Dorothy Thompson's body was found. The Blakeborough's house had been built near the old pond and so the bomb crater had filled up rapidly with water. The rescue services had finally to borrow a trailer pump from the NFS to cope with the water and when they finally drained it, there at the bottom of the crater entirely covered with mud and clay was the body of Dorothy Thompson. She was only 24 years old and had recently become engaged.

The others involved in that incident were to spend much time in hospital. Mary Tedham eventually had 13 pieces of bone removed from her left ankle and was finally discharged from hospital in April 1943. Edna Blakeborough's husband, Frank, was told that she would not live or, if she did, would have none of her faculties left as she had a compound fracture of the skull and multiple injuries, but she was eventually to make a full recovery. Anne Holliday, pulled out of her house in Nunthorpe Crescent remembered on her first night in hospital that nursing staff were tending a dying woman who had lost nearly all her family during the raid. Anne was later taken to an operating theatre where her leg was put in plaster up to the hip. After a week she was moved to a hospital in Wakefield with other casualties, including a couple who both had broken backs. One died just under a year later. The other survived as a paraplegic for another seven years.

The majority of the 52 casualties admitted to the New General Hospital in York were as a result of blast. Some

Centre left:
The site of Nos 19 and 21 Nunthorpe Grove, partially cleared after the raid.
Reproduced from The York Blitz 1942 *courtesy of the co-authors Leo Kessler and Eric Taylor and of the Publishers Sessions of York, England*

Centre right:
Surrounded by damaged and destroyed houses the heart-rending task of salvaging property begins.

Left:
On the morning of 30 April, rubble and rescue vehicles block the entrance to Queen Anne Road as the clearing-up progresses.
Reproduced from The York Blitz 1942 *courtesy of the co-authors Leo Kessler and Eric Taylor and of the Publishers Sessions of York, England*

had fractured limbs and fractured pelvics, some had been crushed by falling buildings. A number were suffering from wounds and cuts from bomb splinters; a fair number had multiple wounds due to glass splinters. There was a strong suggestion that these might have been reduced if people had kept below window level when bombs fell causing glass to be sent flying across rooms. Some people certainly did have miraculous escapes; this was a feature of many a newspaper article of the time. It is also a basic truism that accounts then and reminiscences since dwell largely on those that survive. Yet in some 80 or so cases there were no stories of miraculous escapes, there were just 80 or so deaths. Blast killed almost all of them. They died by being blown apart, by having internal organs shattered. Some had bones fractured, or heads crushed as houses collapsed on top of them. They died as shell fragments, glass and rocks smashed through windows and into houses. Some succumbed to injuries while trapped in the rubble of their houses, alone or surrounded by other relatives, already dead. A very few may have been machine-gunned, or even burnt while trapped under rubble. Some reports claim that one couple in York were burnt to a cinder when Wellyn House Flats collapsed in Queen Anne's Road. They were reported to have been very nervous of fire and always had water and towels available for emergencies. Some died of related problems; one at least had a heart attack. Some survived for several weeks in hospital before finally surrendering to their injuries. There was nothing heroic about these deaths.

It is not difficult to find numbers of those who died; unfortunately differing sources give different numbers. Home Office personnel who visited York and then reported back to London gave a figure of 76 dead. Figures from various groups within York are slightly higher from 79-82, with a top figure of 86 although this appears to include those killed in the rural district adjacent to York. Even if one works from the highest figure however, compared to the other cities attacked in this series of raids York got off relatively lightly. Bath had two nights of raids and four times the casualties. This followed on from the fact that York had received a smaller percentage of bombs than other cities, although it had been one of the most accurate of this series of raids. But

no doubt because of the relative lack of bombs the raid had never really got out of control. Fire damage was mostly confined to the west of the city. Incendiary bombs had been concentrated in one particular area, gutting the Guildhall, St Martin's Church and Rowntree's warehouse. The railway station had also been badly damaged but after these initial German successes, no advantage had been pressed home. The station had been hit early in the raid but then there was little or no further bombing into the flames and the Fire Watchers were able to leave their shelters to tackle the fires. It seems the Germans peaked early and were not able to stoke up the accurate first bombing. The York Fire Brigade had been troubled by the initial number of fires, lack of communications and lack of water pressure from the mains at the start of the raid but most later reports agreed that, perhaps with the exception of the station, concentrated incendiary bombs had doomed most buildings from the start; and many others such as the Mansion House, Assembly Rooms and Railway Hotel had been saved. Outside help had then arrived to put down fires, already largely contained.

In the residential areas the initial crop of incendiary bombs had been tackled by Wardens and locals with enthusiasm and courage. Single houses had been burnt out, rather than whole roads, and the main damage had been caused by high explosives in areas such as Bootham, Clifton and Leeman Road, once again mostly to the west and north of the city. Even so there were still relatively few bombs and their effects were localised. A number of Warden posts in the east of the city had nothing at all to report the next day; there were no incidents there. Of 27,000 houses in the city, possibly 579 were rendered uninhabitable and a further 2,500 damaged to some extent. Again this compares favourably to the widespread damage in other cities. Individual bombs or sticks of bombs could cause great devastation, though. The two or three bombs that landed in Chatsworth Terrace and Amberley Street had accounted for over one quarter of the deaths.

It was generally felt that the York Civil Defence services had acquitted themselves well. The senior personnel had experienced the most trouble of those in any city. Most Baedeker cities had lost telephone links early in their raid; most had their main Control Centre put out of action. Only York lost all that, plus the use of its second, emergency, Control Centre. Messages could still be relayed by motorbike or bicycle when the telephones went dead, but it was more difficult when the Control Centre moved and messengers were unsure of where to go. But the local services seemed to cope well, even with a certain lack of central direction. Local troops and civilians gave much assistance and outside help arrived promptly from experienced blitzed cities such as Hull. Whether these breakdowns in communications would have been worse if more damage had been caused, it is difficult to say.

At the Handley Page factory which was not damaged in the raid, the day shift should have numbered some 625 employees. In fact 200 did not turn up on the morning after the raid and more went missing in the afternoon, so it appeared that some had come in merely to discuss the night's events. There were certainly some cases of shock. The factory officer noted that those who had never been bombed before were much more disturbed than those who had come to York from other blitzed towns. There were a few cases in which workers suddenly burst into tears, men included.

There was certainly a belief, or fear, that the city would be attacked again. The BBC broadcast a radio report which mentioned the fact that York Minster had not been hit. It was not common to announce that specific buildings had been hit, or missed, but the BBC could argue that even the Germans must have known the Minster was still intact. However, the Mayor of York immediately sent a telegram to the BBC criticising them for this broadcast considering Germany's supposed avowed intention to bomb places of historic interest. In other words as long as they knew the Minster was still standing, the Germans might come back. Certainly a fair number of people appear to have believed this, a not unnatural assumption considering the form of the raids so far with double attacks on Exeter and Bath, and a certain amount of trekking out into the countryside did take place. This again was limited; fewer trekked from York than from any other Baedeker city and fewer days were lost per worker.

The wartime newspapers were notoriously optimistic in their assessment of public feelings and bad news was often skimmed over, but general indications were of a fair degree of self-satisfaction. Most people had coped well, the Civil Defence services had performed adequately, personal shelters had proved to have worked in all cases. Trekking hardly merited a mention. Problems raised in other cities such as mass trekking, looting and failures of Fire Watchers received hardly a comment. York was either particularly well organised or it had not been tested as much as other cities; and the York raid was certainly a relatively light one. This remains an academic point as on the next night the Luftwaffe moved their attentions back to Norwich, and York was not to suffer a major attack again for the rest of the war.

Below:
Firemen working in the charred remains of Leopard Arcade gradually search the remains for any injured.
Reproduced from The York Blitz 1942 *courtesy of the co-authors Leo Kessler and Eric Taylor and of the Publishers Sessions of York, England*

Canterbury:

Decline

Exeter had been the last real success for the Luftwaffe. However, the Baedeker raids had not finished yet. After a brief lull, and then a more traditional raid on Cowes, on the following night of 8/9 May some 76 German bombers took off for another attack on the city of Norwich. The warning sirens sounded at 12.38am but what happened next was quite different from what the Germans had planned. After the first raid on the city on 27 April, a number of anti-aircraft guns had been rushed to the city although they had little effect when Norwich was raided some two nights later. But they now benefited from a good week to improve their defences and the time had not been wasted.

As the Germans approached Norwich, barrage balloons prevented the lead aircraft from unloading their marker flares at a low level. Then the guns opened fire and continued to do so for at least the next half-an-hour. They were not particularly deadly but they certainly seemed to have the desired effect and barely an aircraft dared to brave the barrage. One that did try swiftly came to grief. A Dornier Do217 hit the cable of one of the balloons. The aircraft was fitted with cable cutters but these failed to work and the impact tossed it into the balloon which proceeded to burst into flames. The Dornier then dived towards the ground, straightened out at a mere 200ft, was hit by anti-aircraft fire and finally crashed into the ground at Stokes Holy Cross. Three bodies were found in the wreckage next morning.

It is quite possible that this lack-lustre performance was intended to be the end of the Baedeker raids. The British defences could claim some credit for this although not as much as they would have liked. In April 1942, 783 RAF nightfighter sorties by AI-equipped aircraft claimed 16 German aircraft destroyed out of a total of 975 enemy sorties. In May, 547 fighters could still only claim 14 destroyed, out of 791 enemy sorties.

Another claim that has been put forward is for the success of those groups that were set up to jam the German navigational devices. Mention has already been made of the fact that operator error had led to a failure to detect a new ultrasonic frequency being used in operation of the German beams in the early Baedeker raids. As a result these beams were not blocked effectively until late May, and well after the Luftwaffe's most successful raid on Exeter. With the beams blocked, it would seem obvious that the Germans would have much more difficulty in finding their targets. There is some evidence to suggest that the work of No 80 Wing on the night of 8/9 May was of some use in confusing the Germans and getting them to waste their bombs on the open country and decoy 'Starfish' sites. A number of points ought to be considered, however. Firstly, a good three weeks were to elapse between this Baedeker raid and the next which naturally makes it difficult to assess the success or otherwise of the jamming techniques. Secondly, the next raid when it finally came, was on Canterbury and achieved a 50% degree of accuracy, well up to previous standards and marginally better than the second raid on Bath when the jamming was still ineffective. Canterbury was an ideal target for several reasons: it was near to the continent and only a short distance inland; it could be located without the use of radio navigational devices. These factors were similar to those which had helped Bomber Command to find Lübeck, although it was beyond the range of Gee.

Mid-May saw a lull in the attacks; but the main reason for this lay with the motives of the German forces themselves. The Luftwaffe was losing on average only one or two aircraft each night out of a bombing force of perhaps 70 or more, but it was by and large the same 70 aircraft that were going out on each raid, and the losses were beginning to bite hard. It was also the case that it tended to be the inexperienced crews of the *Gruppe* that made up the largest proportion of the casualties. Furthermore, launching an attack on perhaps seven successive nights was bound to put an intolerable strain on the air crews. There are some suggestions that the Luftwaffe senior staff had already recognised these problems before the raids actually started. Two *Gruppen* of German bombers, some 90-100 aircraft, were withdrawn from Sicily and sent to support Luftflotte III in Western Europe; their first task may have been the bombing of Exeter on 3/4 May. If this was the case, and the Luftwaffe units facing Britain did receive a new injection of help, then it might seem strange that after the next raid on Norwich, the German attacks came to a complete halt. Between 9-18 May they launched not a single attack against a British city. This was the longest continual break since before the whole series of Baedeker raids had begun on 23 April with the largely ineffective raid on Exeter. There was a good reason for German inactivity.

All bomber forces at this period still preferred to attack in good visibility and at the time of a full moon. Thus during a period of greater darkness, the Luftwaffe ceased raiding. When the weather began to improve they did not immediately return to the bombing of historic cities but instead to their long established attacks on Britain's sea communications: Hull (19/20 May); Poole (24/25 May); and Grimsby (29/30 May). The Luftwaffe had returned to its attacks on British ports. General Pile began to think of withdrawing some of his guns from the Baedeker cities in order to use them more profitably elsewhere in the defence of real military targets. On reflection, he decided to wait for just a few more days until the next full moon had come and gone.

It was perhaps not such a prescient move as it now appears with hindsight; it is quite possible that in the very last days of May 1942 Hitler had no more plans to continue with the Baedeker raids. If his word was law it was also one that could be rapidly rescinded. Hitler's original decision for the raids had been in response to Bomber Command's attack on Lübeck. In the succeeding weeks, while Hitler was planning his raids on Britain, 'Bomber' Harris continued to be very busy indeed launching further bombing raids on targets in Germany that only served to enrage the Nazi leader still further. The Commander-in-Chief of Bomber Command remained keen to show what his forces were capable of and hoped to capitalise on his success at Lübeck.

Repeated night attacks failed to recapture the success achieved at Lübeck. Bomber Command returned to Essen, then tried Dortmund and Cologne, but with few obvious results. Apart from the problem of the ever-present industrial haze over the Ruhr, it was obvious that these cities were too large to be effectively raided by a force that barely reached 250 aircraft. Either Harris had to find more aircraft or he had to go for smaller cities.

His initial reaction was to try the latter option. Another of the 'alternative industrial areas' listed in Directive 22 was the city of Rostock. Like Lübeck, it was a port close to the Baltic sea with a large number of medieval buildings and a certain amount of industry. It had a population of some 123,000. Rostock was at least more of a military target than Lübeck as it possessed important aircraft factories belonging to Heinkel and Arado. Unfortunately the Heinkel factory, which was by far the more important, was situated in the southern suburb of Marienehe. This did not bother Harris: he merely prescribed two aiming points for the attack, the main force attacking the centre of the town while a smaller force went for the Heinkel factory. Once again it was beyond the range of Gee but being close to the coast it should be quite easy to find. In fact, two raids on 23/24 and 24/25 April failed to achieve any real degree of concentration, but Harris was determined not to give up. He persevered for another two successive nights, achieving a much greater impact. After the fourth raid on 26/27 April Harris declared himself satisfied. Both the Arado and Heinkel works were seriously damaged (although the former was back to full production in a matter of days and even the latter recovered in time). At the same time 70% of the old town had been destroyed including the three main churches, and the majority of the population had temporarily fled the city.

It was more bad news for Hitler and he did not take it well. His original order for the Baedeker raids of 14 April had talked of considering attacks likely to have the 'greatest possible effect on civilian life' when targets were being chosen. This still appeared rather vague and when Hitler had lunch with his Propaganda Minister Joseph Goebbels at noon on 27 April, the talk was of the devastation at Rostock and the need for continued raids against Britain. It was at this point that Hitler made the already quoted comment that the British could only be brought to their senses by hitting them hard. He also began to look further ahead. As Goebbels noted, 'The Fuhrer has already given orders for preparing and working out such a plan of attack on a long-range schedule'. The Propaganda Minister now agreed with the same policy: the raids should continue.

Tempers can cool and Hitler could be a realist. The Baedeker raids on Britain could achieve no long term military results and were wearing down the German forces, especially after the stiff reception they met over Norwich on 8/9 May. Also, it seemed their deterrent value had proved itself: after Rostock, Harris appeared to abandon attacks on historic German cities. It seems a valid explanation for the return to attacks on ports such as Hull and Grimsby after a lull in mid-May. But Harris had no self-imposed limitations and was still looking for a further victory to prove the worth of Bomber Command to detractors at home. Small forces could devastate small and accessible towns, but what if he could scrape together a much larger force for a one-off raid on a major city in Germany? He went further. At the height of the blitz on Britain in 1940-41 the Luftwaffe had sometimes managed to send over a force of 500 aircraft or more. Harris wanted to do even better, and to launch an attack with the magical figure of 1,000 bombers which would surely not only wipe out a major German industrial city but should also capture the imagination of the British public and put an end to the calls for Bomber Command's disbandment by some politicians and senior commanders. Now all that was required was a target commensurate with the resources he had available. Cologne featured in the February directive because of its 'transportation and general industries'

and on the night of 30/31 May some 1,046 bombers headed towards the city.

As could only be expected with such a sizeable force the results were quite spectacular. Some 600 acres of the city were completely destroyed, half of that being in the the centre of the city. This was only a little under the total estimated area of destruction achieved throughout the whole of Germany up to that point in the war. That apart, other statistics eventually proved less impressive. The British estimated a death toll of between 1-6,000. In fact only 474 were killed, a number that no doubt reflected the fact that two-thirds of the tonnage dropped was incendiary rather than high explosive. Within two weeks the life of the city was functioning almost as normal and, on average, only a month's industrial production had been lost. Despite Harris' assertion to Churchill, Cologne had not been 'practically destroyed'.

The 600 acres of devastation was wonderfully photogenic, however, and no-one could deny the propaganda value of the first ever 1,000-bomber raid.

Leading Nazis could not believe it. The only crumb of comfort that Goebbels could find was the assumption that the British did not have the capacity to maintain attacks on such a level, although a similar but less successful raid was mounted against Essen on 1/2 June. No-one could argue with the acreage destroyed, though, and Hitler came to another snap decision: there should be another reprisal raid against Britain. It says something for the rapid move in events over the previous few months that Cologne should merit a German reprisal. It was not a beautiful and unspoilt city like Lübeck but a large, industrial centre. Indeed, its most historic landmark, Cologne cathedral, had been spared by Bomber Command. Hitler had not got upset on any of the 70 previous occasions that the British had bombed the city. Thanks to Bomber Command's use of incendiaries, the death toll was not even as high as in certain raids on London and Coventry, for example. But Cologne had been hit hard and by a large attack force and, whatever the merits of it as a military target, all Hitler wanted to do was to show that Germany could still strike back whenever it was attacked.

The Baedeker raids were back on again. Unfortunately for Hitler, his resources on the Western Front were now so limited that any idea of launching a raid commensurate with that which had hit Cologne was quite impossible. Some 1,046 British bombers had attacked a large city. *Luftflotte III* could now muster perhaps 80 bombers on any one night and so Hitler was reduced to finding a suitable target for this force. He found one, but by no stretch of the imagination could Canterbury, population 24,000, be seen as of equal importance to Cologne. It had practically no industry and very little at all going for it in terms of military value, apart from being a defensive position in the unlikely event that Hitler might still be contemplating the invasion of England. It was an unashamedly soft target. It had all the historic sites – the premier cathedral in England, assorted monastic remains, a castle, city walls, medieval housing and a congested town centre – crowded within an area small enough to be devastated by a limited attack force, and all within a very short distance of the French coast. The British had recognised its vulnerability of course and Canterbury had been one of the first cities to be provided with anti-aircraft guns at the start of the Baedeker raids. It also appears to have received at least part of a balloon barrage only a matter of days before it was attacked.

Like all other towns and cities in England, Canterbury also had its own Civil Defence services. Its Fire Services appear to have been more than adequate for the size of the city: some 12 pumps on duty at any one time, with a further 16 in reserve. The Fire Guards had received some training although there were some problems in terms of manpower. As central government had take the decision to reduce the numbers of Civil Defence personnel during the first part of 1942, the local authorities found that this put an increasing strain on their manpower resources. The Fire Guard and Home Guard in Canterbury found themselves at loggerheads with each other, trying to preserve their numbers. The Home Guard appeared to be the favoured group, and there was a fear that some key personnel in the Fire Guard might be directed into the other force. This lack of manpower did not just apply to the lower ranks of Civil Defence: even the local authorities found that numbers were sometimes lacking and in consequence a number of officials doubled up in a number of duties. This was to have important consequences in the forthcoming raids but up to May 1942 it seems to have caused

no worry at all. As in Norwich and elsewhere, Canterbury spent the first few years of the war receiving the odd bomb that was presumably intended for elsewhere. There was an obvious danger during the Battle of Britain in the summer of 1940 and considering Canterbury's position it is no surprise that it should begin to suffer some damage at that time. These casualties, and others caused by stray bombs, were easy to deal with, and put no strain on the Civil Defence services. A few bombs hit the city on both 21 August and 9 September of that year, killing a total of 14 people. On the very next evening after the RAF attack on Cologne, on 31 May/June 1942 a force of 77 German bombers was sent to attack the city of Canterbury.

It was no great distance and most seem to have found the target. The main attack was concentrated in the centre of the city and as the bombing was accurate and the fires widespread late arrivals had no difficulty in finding their way. Canterbury's guns claimed one bomber destroyed, Hornchurch claimed two others and a Beaufighter of No 219 Squadron claimed to have shot down a Junkers Ju88 into the sea off Winchelsea. The Germans admitted to no losses and certainly those that did reach Canterbury do not to appear to have been put off by the defences. Local witnesses agreed that the aircraft did come low so any balloon defences appeared to cause little trouble. But there were far fewer reports of dive-bombing and machine-gunning the streets as compared to other cities and so perhaps the crews were forced to exercise some caution.

It would be overstating the case to say that Canterbury expected a raid, but after the other Baedeker raids it might be said that some were not surprised at it. Ever since Exeter and Bath had been first raided, some inhabitants of Canterbury had taken to getting up and seeking shelter if and when the siren sounded. All historic cities seemed to be under threat: on 30 April, the Regional Commissioner had warned Canterbury to keep its Civil Defence forces fully on the alert. On the day before the raid, a further message was sent from the Commissioner to emphasise caution as a heavy attack might be expected. This was more supposition. It was a clear night, a full moon and Hitler had not yet publicly rescinded his Baedeker directive. British Intelligence still had no definite advanced

136. Cathedral from Westgate.

warning of which city was going to be attacked next. The air-raid sirens sounded at 12.42am although there appeared to have been no aircraft over the city until some 10 minutes later. Like many cities, Canterbury had been frequently disturbed by aircraft passing overhead on their way elsewhere. They had their own system for indicating that on occasion the Germans seemed rather too close and that a raid on the city might be imminent. This was 'Tugboat Annie', a nickname given to a steam hooter on the local gasworks. When this sounded, soon after the ordinary sirens, it gave notice to many people that Canterbury itself was about to be hit. It soon became apparent that this was another raid in which the Germans were endeavouring to set fire to as much of the centre of a city as possible.

Thousands of incendiaries fell over the area although they were interspersed, as ever, with a number of high explosive bombs to discomfort the fire-fighters. A concentrated attack seemed to develop on the eastern side of the old city, within the walls, an area which took in both shops and residential streets. Within a short time the whole area from Watling Street to Burgate Street and Rose Lane and Butchery Lane to Lower and Upper Bridge Streets seemed to be ablaze. The narrow and congested streets with their old and combustible buildings were very like the centre of Exeter: 'Canterbury itself is probably a fire-raiser's dream' as one later report put it. A Mr Keates was fire watching at premises in the shopping centre. He was lucky and there were no incendiaries on his particular building but fire bombs did fall further up the street and he saw shop after shop burst into flames until the premises on the opposite side of the road were also ablaze and the Fire Watchers were eventually driven out as the walls began to collapse. Through the centre of this area ran the main thoroughfare of St George's Street. Various stores

Left:
Viewed from the west, Canterbury Cathedral rises majestically above the surrounding buildings.
Paul Crampton: The Fisk-Moore Collection

Bottom left:
Wooden-framed buildings at the southern end of Burgate prior to the raids.
Paul Crampton: The Fisk-Moore Collection

Bottom right:
Burgate on 1 June: firemen damp down the last of the flames.
Paul Crampton: The Fisk-Moore Collection

Central Canterbury

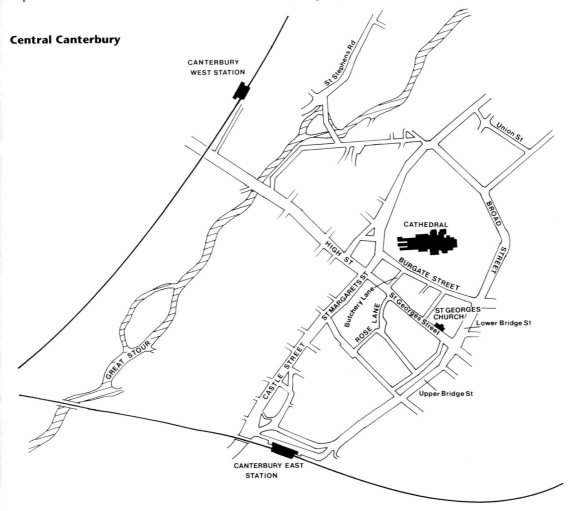

Right:
Some months after the raids, the widespread destruction is all too evident in this view of the Burgate area taken in the summer of 1942. Of interest is evidence of the city's balloon barrage. *Paul Crampton The Fisk-Moore Collection*

Below:
The gutted shell of the church of St George the Martyr stands open to the elements.

Bottom left:
The Cathedral Close suffered severe damage during the raid.

Bottom right:
With the Cathedral's crossing tower in the background, the damage to the Cathedral's library is all too evident.

116

went up in flames including Woolworth and Martin's. Incendiaries soon fell onto the Church of St George the Martyr. There were a number of Fire Guards based there but so many fire bombs landed on the building that, as one put it, even with a dozen people on duty they would still have been unable to save it. High explosives nearby added to their problems and the church was gutted although the rector, Father Geoffrey Keable, was able to get into the church to snatch the Blessed Sacrament from a tabernacle surrounded by fire and smoke.

In nearby Upper Bridge Street lived the Holmes family. They were awoken by the air-raid siren followed soon after by 'Tugboat Annie'. At least 16 marker, chandelier flares could be seen as the raid began and within a short time there were enormous fires all around the area. Across from the Holmes' house, a large residence went up in flames. Just down the road Twyman's sack and rope factory was ablaze, as was the roof of the Canterbury Motor Company. Behind Upper Bridge Street, and some 30ft above it on top of the old city walls, stood St George's Terrace with a mixture of Victorian and Edwardian houses. Most of this row was also ablaze but luckily the wind was blowing the sparks and other burning material away from the Holmes' house. They were also fortunate in the fact that their road was not too close to other built-up parts. Between the blazing St George's Terrace and Upper Bridge Street stood the cattle market, and to one side was the open space of Dane John Gardens. The Holmes' house did not catch fire.

On the other side of St George Street which bisected the main area of fire, stood the Cathedral. As in other cities this was partly protected by the fact that it stood in its own grounds, the Precinct. But if there was little chance of fire spreading from other buildings, there was still the danger of damage from high explosives and especially from incendiaries. Like Exeter, there seemed to be so much going on around the Cathedral that some felt that the Germans had chosen it as a deliberate target.

A number of people lived in the houses scattered around the Precinct. One such was Lois Lang-Sims who heard the blasts from 'Tugboat Annie' but did not bother to get up at first yet she remained awake and then heard a single aircraft flying high overhead. The most worrying aspect, though, was

that she gradually realised that the room was getting lighter and this at a time of what was meant to be a complete blackout. She went to the window and instead of darkness, saw the Cathedral bathed in 'a rose-coloured-radiance'; a single marker flare was drifting down and across the Precinct. Lois did not have long to think about this. A few moments later a high explosive bomb fell nearby cracking the windows and sending plaster falling from the ceilings. It was only the first of many.

Peter Shirley also lived in the Precinct, with his parents and sister at the SPCK bookshop where his father was the manager. The latter had been on Fire Watch duty on the previous evening but now on the Sunday night it was Peter's turn. There were four of them on duty in the Precinct based at a post in Canon Crumb's house. When the sirens sounded Peter immediately went to the crypt of the Cathedral, by the south door, and used the field telephone to talk to the three Fire Watchers who slept on the roof of the Cathedral above. Having informed them of what was happening, he ran across to the bookshop to rouse his parents and sister. Incendiaries were already falling across the Precinct as he did so, but he

Damge in central Canterbury

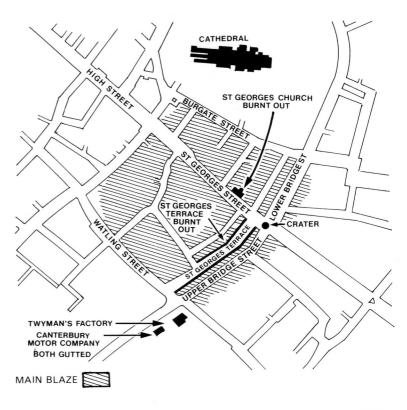

managed to get over to the shop and to direct the rest of his family to the Christ Church Gateway where they always took shelter. By this time the first high explosives were beginning to land, forcing Peter to take cover, first beside the wall of one house and then near to his actual post at Canon Crumb's house where he sheltered with another of the Fire Watchers on duty. Here they stayed until it all quietened down.

Meanwhile, the Fire Guards on the roof of the Cathedral were being kept busy. Even while the raid was still on they were crawling around the parapets to get hold of the incendiary bombs before they could set alight to the building. At least 11 of them did threaten to start major fires but in all cases the Fire Watchers got to them in time. Most were tossed off the roof to burn themselves out on the grass below. Just to add to their already considerable problems, a number of high explosive bombs fell perilously close to the Cathedral itself. One landed some 20yds from the entrance to the Warrior's Chapel and blew out most of the windows of the building. Further near misses had the added effect of lifting incendiaries burning away on the lawns up and through the broken windows of the nave. Luckily the stone floors proved no more flammable than did the grass outside and they were easily put out. Another high explosive bomb struck the Cathedral library which was completely wrecked.

Incendiaries set fire to a number of the other buildings in the Precinct. Peter Shirley managed to put a sand bag over one incendiary that had landed on the pathway to the south door but then found that his own post, Canon Crumb's house, was on fire. The Fire Watchers went round to the Dean and Chapter yard to get hold of their fire truck and connected up the hose to a nearby hydrant. Peter was then able to climb up some scaffolding at the side of the house, which had been put there to effect some repairs, and directed the hose through the window. Unfortunately this had little effect as only a trickle of water came out: if was assumed that there was so much demand for water across the city that the mains pressure was very low.

Other buildings were more fortunate. One inhabitant of the Close found that an incendiary bomb had burnt through his roof and landed on a bed. Undaunted, he picked up both bedding

and bomb and threw them out of the window. In another case, the elderly occupant donned his gas mask to help cope with the effects of smoke as he went into a room to dispose of incendiary bombs. But fire had already spread to the furniture and it was by luck that the archibishop's chaplain and chauffeur both saw the flames coming out of the window. They dashed into the house and threw out a burning chesterfield and bed. Then they smothered the flames on other pieces of furniture and thus saved the house.

As the raid ended Lois Lang-Sims was able to emerge from the cupboard in which she had taken cover along with her mother. The porter's wife, a Mrs Gill, came running to tell them that they should leave the house immediately as the whole row could go up in flames. Lois went to the front door and looked out. It was still night-time but now the Cathedral was bathed neither in silver moonlight, nor the pale pink of the first marker flare: there were so many fires in the vicinity that it was 'dyed blood red from end to end'. She got dressed and went out into the Precinct. One house was an open shell with a huge vertical flame shooting upwards. The green was pock-marked with craters and the burnt-out remains of incendiaries. To others, watching from further away, it seemed the the Cathedral could not survive. Some saw it ringed by fire, silhouetted against the flames just like the famous photograph of St Paul's taken during the severe raid on London of 29 December 1940. At times the flames even reached so high that the Cathedral could not be seen. Catherine Williamson looked on from a friend's garden and when the fires obscured their view her colleague asserted that one particularly loud crash must be the collapse of the Bell Harry Tower of the Cathedral. In fact this was not the case and the danger was more apparent than real; apart from the library, the building took no really serious hits from high explosive and it was premises nearby that were burning rather than the Cathedral itself. It had still been a close-run thing. A few hundred incendiary bomb cases were to be collected from the Precinct grounds after the raid.

At the start of the raid the Civil Defence staff had problems of their own. The Town Clerk ARP Controller, George Marks, had spent the day prior to the raid checking on the preparations in the event of an attack but when it actually began he was at home off duty and having a rest. It appears that when the sirens sounded he looked out of his window, saw the marker flares and realised that an attack was taking place. He therefore put a telephone call through to the Control Centre at Dane John to ask what orders had been received from Regional Headquarters, but when a bomb fell in the Post Office area the telephone lines were knocked out. Marks then decided to drive his car to the alternate Control at St Laurence Cricket Ground, but as he left the house to get into the car a bomb fell nearby. Obviously shocked, he retreated back indoors to wait for a more suitable moment, but this never came for soon afterwards another bomb scored a direct hit on the house and buried both him and his wife in the rubble. They were trapped but still alive and on hearing the all-clear some time later Mr Marks mused aloud to his wife and wondered how long it would be before they were dug out; but he died before the rescue workers could arrive and only his wife survived.

This could only cause further problems for the Civil Defence personnel. Catherine Williamson noted that 'I entered the Control Room to find that the Staff were in a state of consternation as they had heard news that the Controller had been trapped in his house'. This was no doubt an understatement: not only was their leader missing, but also the Centre was working in almost total darkness. The city's telephone and lighting had broken down early in the raid and the Control Centre's emergency lighting system had also failed to operate. The staff were reduced to working by the light of hurricane lamps but as the telephones were not working either there was a limit to what they could do. As had happened in other towns, the Civil Defence forces on the streets were left very much to their own devices.

Opinions differed as to their efficiency. As in Exeter there was some criticism of the fact that a sizeable portion of the eastern part of the medieval city was burnt out. It was all on a much smaller scale, as befitted a smaller city, with perhaps some six acres suffering widespread devastation. But it was also a very easy area to set alight and one in which flames could easily spread and, as the Emergency Committee reported afterwards, some credit should be given for what the NFS managed to save rather than just bemoan what went up

in flames. Later reports noted that while there were some areas where there was a shortage of water, for the most part the NFS 'must have done some excellent work'.

The Fire Guards received more mixed reviews. 'If the Fire Guards were enough and efficient enough, the majority of the damage might have been prevented' claimed the Kent County ARP Officer. There was a suggestion that some Fire Watchers had taken shelter for rather too long and that more than one hotel had been destroyed because it had taken no fire prevention measures; and, of course, the usual problem of there being too few Fire Watchers.

The Emergency Committee reported that some people looked after their own properties but did nothing to help others who were in difficulty. On the other hand, Mr Holmes saw many people rushing out to help neighbours with fires in the Upper Bridge Street area and certain Fire Watching teams did splendid work: the Cathedral staff have already been mentioned in this context. Even if a building did burn down, this was not always a reflection on the ability of a particular Fire Guard squad. The team of St George's Church were beaten by the sheer numbers of incendiary bombs. With an estimated 6,000 incendiaries falling over the city, some being dropped at very low heights, then perhaps 20 incendiaries could fall on a single building and totally overwhelm a Fire Watching team.

With such a concentrated attack on such a small city, it was quite imperative that outside reinforcements should arrive quickly. The Control Centre had informed Regional Command at 1.02am that an attack was taking place, but the telephone links were destroyed 15 minutes later and little further information could be obtained from Canterbury. It was obvious that help would be required, however, and by the time the raid had ended at around 2.15am, assistance was already on its way.

Unfortunately there were further difficulties. It was the responsibility of the police to direct incoming squads who often had no knowledge of the city and were further perplexed by the destruction that had blocked many of the main streets, particularly to the east of the city. There was some criticism that the police as a whole failed to perform this task. Special Constable Whitteridge went out immediately at the end of the bombing to report for duty. His post was at the Britannic Insurance Company's office in St George's Place, but when he reported there soon after 2.15am the door was open but no-one was there. Whitteridge soon found the heat from the burning buildings opposite so intense that he decided to move and took up a position at the important cross-roads beside the Cattle Market. As there were no other police in evidence, he took control and directed the heavy traffic of ambulances and fire services, and answered many enquiries for directions, for the next five hours until he handed over to Special Constable Naylor at 7.00am. It was an eventful period. While talking to an outside-county Inspector at 3.00am, a delayed action bomb exploded nearby; and an hour later Whitteridge found a still intact incendiary bomb and deposited it in a convenient water trough. Throughout the whole period of his self-imposed duty he did not see one Canterbury policeman above the rank of constable.

In another part of the city Daphne Hillier and her brother stood in their night-clothes, directing soldiers from a neighbouring barracks to a number of houses which had received a direct hit. Other reinforcements came from further afield. Hank Evans was a Section Leader in the NFS in charge of fire pumps at Margate. They had 'stood to' as soon as the sirens had sounded and could both hear the thump of explosions and see the flashes in the sky over Canterbury, some 16 miles to the west. It came as no surprise, therefore, when Divisional Headquarters sent through orders for Evans to bring his pumps to a pre-determined rendezvous point to meet up with other fire-fighting appliances and head on to Canterbury. There was soon a stream of fire engines along the road to the city: 'the reddish glare in the sky ahead was outlined by occasional flashes as exploding bombs lit up the clouds of dense smoke rising in the sky, and as we came to the top of a hill at Sturry which overlooks the old city, the scene was horrific, with flame rising into the sky to a great height and seeming to envelop the Cathedral'. As Evans got nearer to Canterbury he realised that it was not, in fact, in such danger and that it was buildings around the Cathedral that were alight; but he also became conscious of the numbers of people coming in the opposite direction, away from the city, some clad only in nightwear, slippers and coat.

'Fortunately for us, by this time, the bombing had largely ceased, although we could occasionally see the odd incendiary bomb spluttering – some embedded in roads, and lighting up the old buildings in the narrow streets. We began to have extreme difficulty in getting towards the centre of the city because of the debris and the fires raging in some buildings. Our target was to assemble for instructions in Broad Street, but we never quite got there because of the obstructions, and I went on foot, with others in charge of various sections to receive orders.

'The scene around us was awful – whole buildings demolished or burning fiercely, water gushing up from fractured water mains, spouts of flame from gas mains, and as we came towards the Burgate, where there were rows of shops and living accommodation over, the whole lot was burning with an intensity of heat which I never did experience again during 30 years of fire-fighting. The flames from each side of the road converged towards each other and met in an upward flare of roaring intense heat, sucking up loose debris from the road and shooting burning brands into the sky. It was impossible to get near the Street, let alone pass along it, and we turned back towards the High Street, where – because the fallen debris and heat from burning buildings was less concentrated than in the Burgate – it was at least possible to clamber over the ruins to find someone in command'.

Evans and his men moved from incident to incident, taking their orders and helping where they could. They continued to work through the night until relieved by crews from London and elsewhere in the early morning.

As the raids came to an end, more people had come out into the streets. Some had little choice. The Sharpe family managed the MacFisheries shop in St George's Street. When they emerged after the raid it was to find the shop on fire. The family scrambled over a high wall into the Simon Langton Grammar School grounds at the back but the one son, Brian, had had his leg amputated a few months earlier and was unable to climb over. He was helped by his brother who led him through the shop, past the intense heat of what remained of W. H. Smith and hence to the school shelter. Here they were greeted by the Chief ARP Warden with the words 'Where the hell have you been?'

Left:
The recovering of casualties was potentially a hazardous operation for both the rescuee and the rescuers. With ropes being used to guide a 'stretcher', the body of one victim of the raid is gently removed from the first storey of a damaged house. *Kentish Gazette*

Below left:
The back-breaking job of clearing the roads and eliminating the most dangerous of the ruins involved the efforts of a large number of people.

Bottom left:
As if emphasising the arbitrariness of war, houses in the foreground have been competely demolished whilst those beyond have suffered only slight damage. *Kentish Gazette*

Right:

In amongst the rubble of terraced houses soldiers start the process of clearing the debris. *Kentish Gazette*

Below right:

Showing clearly the results of a direct hit from a high explosive bomb, the destruction of these houses affected numerous others in the surrounding area. *Kentish Gazette*

Bottom right:

With many of the spectators' eyes turned towards the camera, the firemen continue to damp down the raging fires.

Catherine Williamson was making her way along to the Control Centre when she had to pass the main fire around St. George's Gate. Many of the houses on the City Walls in the area were on fire, their frontages leaning out at very dangerous angles. Mr Holmes of Upper Bridge Street walked along the cattle market intending to check that his grandparents, who lived in Burgate, were alright. But he found the way ahead blocked by a large bomb crater and a huge fire burning on two sides of the crossroads. St George's Church was well alight and in St George's Place he could see four rescue workers pick up what appeared to be a body and put it on a stretcher. Yet, all things considered, the death toll was surprisingly low. Some 43 people had been killed by the bombing and almost all of these as the result of high explosive bombs. Incendiaries had been dropped in larger numbers and had created some conspicuous areas of devastation but it was the high explosive that caused the deaths. Even these were limited in effect. Once again, many bombs fell on open ground and a mere handful caused severe casualties: 11 dead in Northgate Street including a two year-old child; seven dead in Lower Bridge Street, two with multiple injuries after being crushed by falling masonry; another seven killed in Victoria Row, and six people – all from the same family – in Union Street, the youngest a mere two months old. Thirty one out of 43 deaths, caused by a mere four bombs.

More extensive damage was caused to housing in Canterbury and within a short time the after-care services had at least 700 homeless to deal with. Unfortunately these services almost immediately broke under the strain. This was no reflection on the ability of a Mr Phillips who was in charge of billeting for he was also supposed to be responsible for the Rest Centres, Emergency Feeding Centres and Registration of Civilian Dead as well. It was far too much for any single person, a fact that the Regional Commissioner realised at once and his deputy, a Mr Bottomley, was despatched to the city immediately.

On the afternoon of 1 June he called a conference of the senior staff in Canterbury in order to try and make some sense of the situation. There were at least 2-3,000 homeless, and doubtless more would be found by nightfall. Buses were laid on to try and move as many as possible out of the city. A further meeting took place the following day with Bottomley trying to be as diplomatic as possible. He realised, he said, that Regional assistance was usually sent only when the local authority's organisation had broken down, but of course this was not the case here: Canterbury had merely asked for help and advice. It was a carefully phrased comment, but in the course of the meeting Bottomley found he could not avoid some trouble. He followed on his work of the previous night by asserting that the buses would continue to be used for two categories of trekker: those who were still in Rest Centres and had not yet found a billet; and those who were not homeless but wanted to leave the city to stay with friends in the surrounding districts on a temporary basis.

This acceptance of a second group appeared to give official approval for everyone to trek out each night and was roundly condemned by another at the meeting, a Mr Saunders, who represented Kent Public Assistance Committee. He stated quite categorically that he would only deal with those who were homeless, were still in Rest Centres and could not do anything for themselves. He would not help those who still had accommodation and just wanted to get away from the city, although he had heard that the army had done just that on the previous night by providing buses to take some 200 people to hutments near Chilham. The army representative excused himself by claiming that he thought he had official approval from the Canterbury ARP Control Centre. The Dean of Canterbury tried to explain that the people involved may have had homes but were still deserving cases. They had been ignorant of the facilities that were available and had failed to make arrangements for themselves in the hours of daylight. Saunders still stuck to his guns and Bottomley was forced to change tack. He stated 'most definitely' that there would be no official sanctions for such arrangements in the future and that as far as possible people should 'remain put!'. Trekking by those with homes still intact was not to be encouraged and more billets should be found within the city for those who were homeless.

It says little for the post-raid services that even after being called in as outside help, the Deputy Regional Commissioner should have to change his mind over such an important topic as trekking after only one full day in the city. Catherine Williamson who, immediately after the raid of 31 May/1 June, went to work at the Information Depot, wrote her account in 1949, and a diplomatic account it was too. But even she was prepared to admit that she and her colleagues were snowed under by requests from the public, and that a proper Central Information Bureau was desperately needed. These existed in other cities, but not in Canterbury. Some local newspapers were quite ready to put the blame on the local population for not having taken the trouble to acquaint themselves with the workings of the Civil Defence services before the raids. An editorial in the *Kentish Observer and Canterbury Chronicle* claimed that the majority of people had 'ridiculed the possibility of a blitz' and that 'the spirit of complacency was far too prevalent!'. As a result, continued a further editorial, 'there are many people who are going around in circles' despite the fact that there were a number of centres where they could go for advice. The point that after a sudden shock, like an air-raid, some people might be confused and unable to take the initiative seems to have been lost on this particular newspaper, although the Dean of Canterbury had made a similar comment at the meeting with the Regional Commissioner on 2 June. If some of the public did not expect Canterbury to be raided and made inadequate preparations then the same could be said of certain aspects of the Civil Defence services themselves and in particular those services designed to hand out advice after a raid. At a later meeting on the workings of the Rest Centres a Mr Crookshanks, General Inspector for the Ministry of Health, declared that two-thirds of Canterbury's provisions had been rendered obsolete by the raids and on 1 July the city's Rest Centres were handed over to the responsibility of Kent Public Assistance Authority.

Despite a certain amount of confusion, most in authority felt that public morale had held up well. There had been relatively few deaths. Destruction had been largely limited to the north and east of the city and although historic buildings had been hit, most were damaged rather than destroyed: the Cathedral, St Martin's Church (the earliest in England), the Norman staircase of the King's School and St Augustine's College. A number of old buildings had been burnt to the ground, but some

were more famous by association rather than for their own intrinsic worth. The Elizabethan dramatist Christopher Marlowe came out of it badly: both his birthplace (57 St George's Street) and the church where he was baptised (St George's) were destroyed. So, too, was a house in Lower Chantry Lane, the reputed home of Dickens' mythical character Uriah Heep. Various war memorials also suffered damage, along with more modern shops, churches and schools. The most noticeable feature was the widespread destruction to either side of the eastern end of the High Street, where it merged with St George's Street. One of the few parts left standing was the shop occupied by Marks & Spencer, a relatively new building with a fire resistant roof. As daylight appeared, areas were still on fire, buildings leaning over at dangerous angles and collapsing into the street. In some parts people had to climb over great mountains or rubble spread across the road. A few people could be seen, dirty and exhausted, attempting to salvage what they could from half-demolished homes, but the general damage was not too widespread and only a very few people spread the rumour that the Cathedral should be blown up by the British authorities to ensure that the Germans did not have to return again.

Trekking was widespread. This was not surprising for even without the stories of 'A German promise to finish the job off' the confusion in the post-raid services (and even in the mind of the Deputy Regional Commissioner on the morning of 2 June), meant that there appeared to be no firm announcement made to discourage people from leaving the city on successive nights. The failure of the Rest Centre organisation did not help matters either. As billets were not found, people voted with their feet and left the city. Violet Brand went with her family and others to stay with her aunt who lived outside of the city. Catherine Williamson and her family went to stay with friends as well. Others were not so fortunate and slept rough in the open fields, hay stacks and woods. The Holmes family first went to a fruit orchard near the city and then on subsequent nights joined with the large number of people who were sheltering in a long railway tunnel on the Whitstable line. It was some days before the Emergency Committee at Canterbury thought to publicly remind Fire Watchers that they should not

Left:
The gaunt remains of St George's Place. *Paul Crampton: The Fisk-Moore Collection*

Below left:
Damage in a side street.

Bottom left:
In the aftermath of the raid, civilians and soldiers sift through the remains of a street of houses. *Kentish Gazette*

Above:
Civilians and members of the rescue services gingerly examine the remains of a devastated house. *Kentish Gazette*

Above right:
Viewed from The Parade, firemen damp down the flames of the Longmarket and Corn Exchange. *Paul Crampton: The Fisk-Moore Collection*

Right:
Emphasising the destruction of the city's historic core, this shows the High Street after the raid. Traffic, including a horse-drawn cart, makes use of the now-cleared road.

Below right:
With a foreground a mass of interwoven hose pipes, firemen attempt to dowse the flames amongst the ruins of St George's Street. *Paul Crampton: The Fisk-Collection*

leave the city at night, but then they also found that it was extremely difficult to make some Fire Guards turn up for duty even if they did remain. Rather than prosecute, they decided merely to put up posters reminding people of their duties. This might have been a costly mistake for without Fire Watchers the city was quite vulnerable; and as circumstances proved, the trekkers were quite correct and there were to be further raids on Canterbury.

A rocket battery arrived at the school playing fields on the corner of Giles Lane during the daytime of 1 June. An effective balloon barrage was moved into the town as well, but on the night of 1/2 June the Germans struck at the East Anglian town of Ipswich instead. They maintained their new tactic of trying to worry cities recently attacked, however, and in the early hours of 2 June the sirens sounded over Canterbury again. It was only a lone aircraft and it dropped a stick of six incendiary containers. Some fell across the Sturry Road area but caused no trouble and nobody was hurt.

On the following night, 2/3 June, the Germans did launch another attack on the city of Canterbury with some 58 bombers but it was a curious affair that did not go as planned and was somewhat reminiscent of the abortive attack on Norwich of 8/9 May. The air-raid sirens first sounded at 1.45am but nothing further seemed to happen and the all-clear was announced some 25 minutes later at 2.10am. Then a mere 15 minutes later the sirens sounded again at 2.25am and this time an aircraft was seen to fly over the city and drop a couple of high explosive bombs. For the next half-an-hour or so aircraft came over at fairly regular intervals of some five minutes and dropped what appeared to be a large number of flares and incendiaries – perhaps 1-2,000 – but they did not appear to drop anything else. All the time the 'Z' batteries were firing their rockets and the anti-aircraft guns were blazing away. The balloon barrage also helped to keep the enemy aircraft high. At 3.00am there was a lull and the defences went quiet. Twenty minutes later another handful of aircraft appeared over the city and the defences opened up again, the Germans disappearing soon afterwards. Two RAF officers who had been sent to the city to do a bomb census after the first raid on 31 May/1 June and who now observed this raid were quite perplexed:

'The most curious feature of the whole attack was the fact that a very large number of flares were dropped and the planes seemed to be finding the target. All the time we were expecting the real attack to develop but it never came to anything. After the lull we were sure that we were going to get a good attack of high explosives, but after dropping some flares the planes appeared to go away again without dropping anything'.

The damage was decidedly limited. Incendiaries did set fire to a number of buildings including the Congregational Church in Watling Street. A possible six high explosive bombs fell on the city, too. One caused a large crater in Burgate Street. Another landed on the outskirts of the city in Old Park Avenue, close to the barracks. Janet Laing lived there with her mother. On the first night their house was undamaged and they did not have to leave. During this second raid, however, the two of them took cover in their Morrison table shelter along with a woman next door and her small child. This time they were not so lucky. Having heard a number of bombs drop nearby a final one scored a direct hit on their house. The Morrison shelter held and some time later they heard a rescue squad arrive. Janet and her mother called out but no-one seemed to hear until her mother used a whistle that she had had the foresight to tie previously to the side of the shelter. This alerted the rescuers who were then able to dig a tunnel for them to crawl through. They were lucky: there were no deaths in the house. The only people that were killed that night lived nearer the centre at Oaten Hill Place. A direct hit killed five people although it appears the casualty rate could have been much higher. a Mr Skam owned a garage in the area and sent his six cars out of the city for safety each evening. These took the rest of the inhabitants of Oaten Hill Place as passengers and so many of the houses were empty when the bomb fell.

The Germans tried again. After an attack on Poole on the night of 3/4 June, they returned with another 52 bombers to Canterbury on the evening of 6/7 June. This was the least effective raid of all. The anti-aircraft guns put up another heavy barrage – and this time the Germans did not even seem to make the effort to get close to the city. Some 17 bombs fell in the outlying areas but only one fell in the city itself.

Right:
As a result of a number of high explosive bombs falling near to the Assembly Rooms in Bath, half the Regina Hotel (to the right) was destroyed with the loss of many lives. *Wessex Newspapers*

Below:
Surrounded by debris in Stour Street, a remarkably clean Austin van of the emergency services waits for its next duty.
Paul Crampton: The Fisk-Moore Collection

This hit the only five houses that had been left standing in St George's Terrace after the first fires. As a result, there was no-one in them and the entire raid caused no losses within the city itself. The only death occurred on a dark road outside the city, and that was by accident. A fire engine was driving along at 1.35am past several incendiaries, when the driver noticed that he was going over a number of small stones and debris. Because of the aircraft overhead he had no lights on and it was very dark, making it difficult to see clearly. He braked sharply, but it was too late: the fire engine went into a bomb crater and over-turned, crushing one of the fire crew beneath it. It was a very deep crater and by the time they had been able to extricate him, he was dead.

It was the final raid on Canterbury, and hardly a glorious victory for the German bombers. Harris had continued to hammer away at Rostock until he achieved the results that he required. Hitler appears to have tried to do the same with Canterbury, but with far less successful results. It was not that Canterbury was a particularly difficult target: the guns and rockets and balloons claimed very few aircraft destroyed. Nor did the Germans come in mere handfuls: at least 50 aircraft were sent to the city each night. It can only be assumed that the effort just proved too much for the Luftwaffe crews involved, attacking night after night against defences that were becoming visibly stronger. The guns might not be deadly, but few had the energy to test them. So the Germans flew around the city and dropped their bombs outside its limits and headed for home and safety. It was a very inconclusive end to the Baedeker raids.

THE
AFTERMATH

Propaganda

The series of air-raids in the Baedeker blitz posed a number of problems. Both Britain and Germany wished to boast of their success against cities such as Lübeck and Cologne on the one side, Bath and Exeter on the other, but these claims were based on the simple destruction of large areas of these towns, which had to be put forward as a valid, military objective. In the first place, the two countries had to assure public opinion both at home and abroad that the cities they were attacking were legitimate military targets — troublesome in the case of Lübeck, near-impossible with the example of Canterbury. Secondly, they had to stress that within these cities the bomber crews were given strict instruction to avoid unnecessary civilian casualties by aiming their bombs at obvious targets of a military nature such as railway stations and factories. The British had to explain how pin-point bombing could be equated with widespread destruction of residential areas; and the Germans had to find a good excuse for the bombing of obvious non-military cities such as York and Canterbury. Neither country was to be totally convincing.

The British opened the propaganda war of 1942 with their accounts of Lübeck. Newspaper reports stressed the pin-point bombing of military targets in Lübeck, Rostock and Cologne although they could not resist publishing photographs that also revealed the widespread — and thus imprecise — damage inflicted as well. There were few dissenting voices but on 29 April in the House of Commons, the MP the Rt Hon Rhys Davies asked a pertinent question: Had the greatly intensified bombing raids over Germany, including that on Lübeck, involved a departure from the principle that all operations should be confined to military

objectives? The Secretary of State for Air, Sir Archibald Sinclair, gave the stock answer: there was still no change in government policy. He went on to give a long list of the legitimate targets to be found in Lübeck and Rostock, their port facilities, submarine and aircraft factories.

Davies refused to give up: had 'the Right Honourable gentleman seen the pictures in the Press, presumably permitted by our Ministry of Information and Propaganda, of the very terrible sights in Lübeck, apart from any military objective?' It was a good question, but as Davies spoke he was interrupted by cries of 'What about Bath?'. Davies was clearly flustered. He quickly added 'Has he (Sinclair) also seen what was done in Bath and in Norwich and can he do something to prevent all this destruction?'.

It was a poor retort to the interruption. In his attempt to show that he was by no means a supporter of Germany, Davies had diluted the power of his question. It was no longer a matter of Lübeck in particular, but of the bomber offensive in general, over both Britain and Germany. Sinclair did not even make an immediate reply.

Another MP, a Mr Logan, stood up to criticise Davies: 'Has the Honourable Member not heard of the pictures we have of the damage in our great cities, and does he know how the morale of our people is inspired when they see that something similar is being done elsewhere?' As the Commons was obviously in little sympathy with Davies, Sinclair was able to follow up with the comment: 'The best way to prevent this destruction is to win the war as quickly as possible'. It was a bland comment that did not even begin to answer the critic. Not that this really mattered for at almost the same time the Germans managed to hand the British a propaganda victory of a plate.

The German Foreign Office held one of its daily press conferences at lunchtime on 27 April. The assembled newspaper correspondents were addressed by one Baron Gustav Braun von Stumm, Deputy Head of the Information and the Press Division of the Foreign Office. In the course of the briefing he came round to the topic of the new series of air-raids on Britain. It seems he was looking for a good phrase to describe them, one that would show they were something a little out of the ordinary and one designed to instil a certain amount of fear into British civilians. He found one. 'Now', he said, 'the Luftwaffe will go for every building which is marked with three stars in *Baedeker*'. It was certainly a good phrase: the travel guides published by the firm of Karl Baedeker had been widely used before the war and included special reference to places of particular historic or artistic interest. There is no evidence at all to suggest the the Luftwaffe High Command was using a particular firm's guide books as a source of inspiration, but it was certainly a good way to worry the British population. *Baedeker* had been freely available in England before the war and listed many places in that country. Unfortunately, telling the truth by the use of a clever phrase, admitting that the Luftwaffe were bombing cultural and historic targets, was just what the Nazi leaders did not want to do. Goebbels was furious with von Stumm and took steps to make sure that such a mistake could not be made again. He told his own staff that 'it is totally wrong to boast of the destruction and it remains, as such, an extremely regrettable act'. He might have added that it was not only regrettable, but also rather difficult to explain.

Anyway, it was all too late. One of the foreign correspondents who attended von Stumm's briefing session was a neutral Swedish reporter by the name of Svahnstöm who worked for the *Stockholm Tidningen*. His story appeared in the newspaper the following day, 28 April and *The Times* immediately picked up on it. On the very next day the newspaper ran an article under the twin headings of 'German threat of new targets' and 'Three Star buildings in Baedeker'. Fleshed out with some accounts from German newspapers concerning the historic buildings destroyed in Exeter and Bath, the article quoted von Stumm and then went on to say that the Germans were trying to excuse their behaviour by claiming that the British had deliberately gone for historic monuments and civilian morale in their attacks on Lübeck. The Baedeker appellation was turned back on the Germans; they were now admitting the bombing of non-military targets.

The Times was quite accurate: von Stumm had used the word 'Baedeker'. But the British newspapers only referred to 'German officials' and their identities remained unclear. It was only a small step from this situation to ascribing the 'Baedeker blitz' to the one Nazi that everyone knew, Adolf Hitler himself. Quite when this took place is a little unclear, but it does seem certain that by the end of the war many people appear to have believed that Hitler had invented the phrase. The occasion when he was supposed to have first mentioned it can be pin-pointed. On the afternoon of 26 April Hitler addressed the German parliament, the Reichstag, and during the course of his speech he was supposed to have declared that he would use a copy of Baedeker's guidebook to England and cross off the cities in there one by one as they were destroyed. In fact, he did nothing of the sort.

He complained that the British had adopted 'new methods' of air warfare against the 'civilian population' and said that if these continued he would 'make a reply that will bring great grief'; and that was all. *The Times* reported this speech correctly and there seems no reference at the time to Hitler talking of crossing off the entries in his personal copy of the guidebook. However, people did believe this to be the case, an official summary of the aerial fighting over Britain mentioned it after the war, and historians have accepted this accusation ever since.

Faced with what appeared to be an honest admission of Nazi brutality, Goebbels' propaganda ministry was immediately fighting a losing battle. Even without von Stumm's slip, the Germans were hard-put to try and find valid reasons for bombing Exeter and the other target cities. Military objectives were few and far between, but the Nazis still had a go at stressing them. York was a major railway junction; so was Exeter. (It was just a pity that Exeter's railway stations were not in the very centre of the city which helped them escape the brunt of the bombing.)

Above:
With the scaffolding still surrounding the tower of St George the Martyr and Canterbury Cathedral, the area of bomb damage in St George's Lane remains weed-strewn even in the late 1940s. The tower of St George was eventually to be tidied up and preserved.
Paul Crampton: The Fisk-Moore Collection

Centre right:
The site of the Exeter branch of Marks & Spencer is cleared after its destruction during the raid. *Marks & Spencer*

Below right:
A new Marks & Spencer store opened in Exeter in 1951. *Marks & Spencer*

Norwich had many military targets: it was another important railway junction, a centre of the British aircraft industry, it had steel and ironworks and produced submarine engines. All of this was announced on German radio on 29 April. However, when the Luftwaffe raided the city again in late June, Norwich was supposed to be a well-known wheat market and producer of electrical goods. Consistency does not appear to have been a hallmark of the German propaganda ministry. The destruction of the gasworks was a persistent claim; German aircrew talked on the radio of seeing eruptions of flame from exploding gasholders at Bath, York and Norwich. Some, at least, appear to have been cases of wishful thinking. A number of military targets were straightforwardly odd: Norwich was the 'capital' of Norfolk; Canterbury was the home of an archbishop who was 'notorious for his incitement campaign against Germany'. Such claims were not only oblique, they also showed the desperate straits to which the Nazi propaganda ministry was reduced in trying to find military targets in cities chosen, primarily because they did not have any.

The one success that the Germans did achieve was that the Baedeker raids received a great deal of publicity in a way that further raids against oftbombed targets such as London and Liverpool would not. King George V felt that the attacks were 'outrageous'. Rumours abounded: that the Roman remains in Bath had been destroyed, that 6,000 were dead in Exeter and 17,000 in Bath. In particular, these raids reintroduced the belief that everywhere in Britain, and not just obvious military targets, was liable to attack. The Ministry of Information received scores of letters from worried radio listeners who had been told by friends that Lord Haw-Haw had promised raids on places as far afield as Salisbury, Harrogate and Exmouth.

Not everyone felt sympathy for those who had been attacked. There was a certain amount of feeling in parts of the country that the Baedeker cities had been lucky to avoid trouble and did not know how terrible war could be. There was also a belief held by some that people had gone to Bath, in particular, to find a safe refuge which was, again, seen as rather unfair: 'I think it was about time they had something to make them realise there's a war on' wrote one woman who had experienced the blitz on Merseyside and was

living in Norwich when the raids occurred there.

The Ministry of Information's summary of the reports from the Regional Commissioners noted that 'in a few working class areas, the belief that rich evacuees are now getting their fair share' is expressed. There were complaints from Hull when it was raided on 19 May that this received very little publicity, and even the suggestion that some of Hull's anti-aircraft guns had been sent away to defend more newsworthy cities. Many of the Baedeker towns were also invaded by 'tourists' in places as far apart as York and Bath. In the latter city people became so upset that the local authorities sharply reduced the number of buses travelling from Bristol to Bath to deter the morbid visitors.

The newspapers' reactions to the Baedeker blitz were rather mixed. Some were quite critical. Bath and Exeter seemed to be singled out for criticism from the more popular of the national newspapers. On 1 May a meeting of the Emergency Committee at Bath discussed a recent editorial in the *Daily Mail* which claimed that the local Civil Defence services had not operated as well as they might. The War Cabinet was told that there were newspaper reports of people starving in Bath, based on 'entirely inadequate evidence': in fact, there had been only a temporary shortage of bread in some districts of the city. The War Cabinet became worried about giving such information in newspapers which the Germans would be able to read. Bath's Emergency Committee was far more concerned with local pride. They went as far as to ask the Chief Constable to see if he could prosecute at least one reporter for libel. When he reported back that this seemed impossible they decided to take the matter up with the Home Office.

Exeter faced similar criticisms of inefficiency and disorganisation. The Mayor was even prepared to make a statement to the local newspaper, the Exeter *Express and Echo*, in which he hit out at the critics. One story in particular caused problems. In the inevitable confusion of an air-raid, some children could become separated from their families and Exeter found itself with 15 such youngsters in their Rest Centres, their parents presumably elsewhere or, in rare cases, possibly dead. These children had been taken to a residential nursery to give them temporary accommodation and in the course of the next few weeks most of them were identified and reunited with their families. In order to speed up this process, the local authorities had taken photographs of the children and circulated them to the police and the various post-raid bodies.

The *London Evening News* heard of this and ran a brief article. The *Daily Mail* followed up the story on 18 May and managed to obtain photographs of the three children who had still not been identified. These were published in the newspaper. The *Mail* claimed they were included so that if they were not residents of Exeter, and were perhaps evacuees, their parents might be living in another part of the country and would only recognise them in a national newspaper. It also made a very good story, of course, and some of the *Mail*'s readers came to the wrong conclusion.

As a result, Exeter Council receive a number of enquiries from people offering to adopt one or other of the children. The children were, in fact, all identified in the end but the story continued to run and to gain further momentum. The Exeter *Express and Echo* reported that some London newspapers were continuing to print tales of children being torn from their parents and found wandering the streets in forlorn attempts to search the rubble for their parents. It made no difference, of course, that Exeter City Council announced this story to be completely untrue.

Below:
The human consequences of the Baedeker raids: victims of the blitz on Bath are buried in a mass grave at Haycombe Cemetery.
Wessex Newspapers

Effects

There was one last raid in the Baedeker sequence. Harris scraped together a final 1,000-bomber force and on the night of 25/26 June he launched it against the city of Bremen. The attack was not a great success but it appears to have triggered off the last of the Baedeker raids for on the following night, 26/27 June, some 60 Luftwaffe bombers headed once more for the city of Norwich. It was another night of good visibility with almost a full moon. However, the defences were ready and the raiders received an enthusiastic welcome. At 2.05am the warning sirens began to sound and five minutes later the first aircraft started to drop marker flares over the northwest.

A number of bombers penetrated the anti-aircraft barrage and showered thousands of incendiary bombs across the city. Some 33 high explosive bombs also fell within the city limits but this was a comparatively low number and it was not enough to extinguish many of the incendiaries before they could cause any damage. Some 117 houses were still gutted plus a number of shops and public buildings. For the first time, the Cathedral also seemed to be marked out for special attention although it had its fair share of luck. Some 1,000 incendiary bombs fell in the precincts but half of these came down in two canisters that failed to open, rather than being scattered across the whole area and bursting into flames. Approximately 60 incendiary bombs landed on the Cathedral itself. The bulk of these were in another unopened canister which smashed through the roof of the transept and then appears to have burst open. Once again, stone floors and stone vaulting hindered the spread of most fires. The greatest danger was of incendiaries lodging in the supporting timbers of the roof, between the inner and outer walls, but Fire Watchers were able to get into these spaces to extinguish the flames before they could spread and cause serious damage. One Fire Guard team even lowered a rope to the Cathedral floor for a fire hose to be attached and lifted up to the roof. The Cathedral did not suffer serious damage.

It was only a minor raid and casualties were light. Perhaps 14 people were killed in all. These included at least three individuals who were performing Civil Defence duties. A fireman who had already rescued a number of horses from burning premises was killed when high explosives began to drop nearby; only his helmet could be found later. A part-time warden, Thomas Bright, was also killed by high explosives. He was dealing with an incendiary outside the Maternity Home when a bomb fell, demolishing a building nearby and burying him under the rubble. An 18 year-old Fire Watcher, Neville Muirhead, was last seen in the doorway of a school that was totally destroyed shortly afterwards. Two other Fire Guards had a lucky escape when a near miss shook the ARP post that they were sheltering in but the bomb did kill a couple of women who lived nearby and had often provided them with cups of tea. The Fire Guards were called upon to identify the bodies. The final death toll was very low, however, and Norwich could count itself lucky that its defences had once more discouraged the majority of the bombers from pressing home their attack.

This was quite definitely the last of the Baedeker raids, but not the complete cessation of all attacks. Bath was to lose no further lives but both Norwich and Exeter were still to receive the occasional 'tip and run' attack that inflicted some casualties. Canterbury suffered the most; a low-level daytime raid in 31 October 1942 killed 32 civilians. Two more died in a follow-up attack the same night. York had the most unlikely damage. In 1945 a Royal Canadian Air Force Handley Page Halifax bomber crashed soon after take-off and landed on Nunthorpe Grove. Another five houses in this much damaged street were destroyed although the only casualties were amongst the air crew.

The dying, as a direct result of the Baedeker raids, continued for some time after. There was those who were rescued alive from demolished buildings only to succumb to their wounds. Mr Poole's parents of Stanley Road, Bath, were pulled out of the wreckage of a street shelter. The mother died soon after, the father in hospital, within the week. One person injured in the second raid on Canterbury (3 June) survived for over three months before finally dying.

Some had the trauma of having to trace and identify the bodies of their relatives. Leslie Nott was the despatch rider who had narrowly avoided death in the Scala shelter at Bath. After the raid he had tried to find his colleague Wally Angus who had been with him just before the first bomb had landed nearby. When there was a lull in clearing up, Nott went back to the spot he had last seen him. Angus' motorbike was still there, but of Angus himself there was no sign. Nott tried the nearest mortuary, and the next and the one after that. At the fourth mortuary, and after pulling back the sheets on at least 150 bodies, he found the body of Wally Angus. A piece of shrapnel had pierced his helmet and killed him instantly.

Then there were those that could not be identified. The explosion at the Scala shelter took place in such an enclosed space that the blast effects were greatly enhanced: some people were literally torn apart and in the clearing up operations biscuit tins were used to collect the pieces. All that could be written on one identification card was 'small pieces of remains only – cannot be identified'. On another card, the words Male/Female were crossed out and above was written the one word 'indistinguishable'. It is no wonder that in some cases remains could not be identified and some people just seemed to have totally disappeared. As Mr Poole, recovering in hospital, wrote to Bath City Council: 'I have neither seen nor heard from my wife since the tragic night, and it must be presumed that she was fatally injured at the time and

unidentified, as were so many other unfortunate victims'.

Others were not found for many weeks although the case of one man in Canterbury was quite peculiar. Alec Chilcott lived at St George's Place, Canterbury, in the heart of the area worst hit on the raid of 31 May/1 June 1942. During the night of the raid he had been alone in the house, his wife being on duty at a canteen elsewhere in the city. A young boy had seen Chilcott that evening at about 9.45pm when they had talked for an hour or so. When the raid began, Chilcott's house took a direct hit and it was assumed he had been killed. Yet next morning , his sister who lived at Okehampton, Devon, received a telegram that read 'Chilcott seen this morning in the street'. It was unsigned. As the weeks went by, however, no trace of him could be found. The rescue parties systematically worked through the rubble but there was a good deal of it in Canterbury and it took a long time. Some remains were found at Chilcott's home but these were later identified as being of one of his two dogs. Then on 20 July at 9,40am, one Richard Smith was part of the rescue squad clearing the debris at the site of the house where Mr C. Marks, the ARP controller, was killed on the first night of the bombing. Smith put a hand down a hole and felt hair so he cleared away more debris, found a felt hat, lifted it up and found a head underneath. After all these weeks the body was badly decomposed but a watch and a ring were taken away and used to identify it as that of Alec Chilcott. Perhaps when the raid started he had decided to leave his house to go and join his wife. St Augustine's Road was on his route; perhaps when bombs began to fall nearby, he took shelter near Mr Marks' house and was killed when it took a direct hit. The provenance of the telegram, however, remains a complete mystery. Looking for bodies was hardly a pleasant task in the first place but when they had lain undiscovered for weeks or even months, the natural decomposition made it all the worse.

It must be stressed that death directly affected relatively few people. Many more were shocked and surprised by the novelty of air-raids, but as the days and weeks wore on after the attacks, it was general discomfort that affected most. The spring of 1942 was dry and warm and so there was less difficulty in living with some of the problems; and when at least 90% of the houses in Bath lost their windows, then the temperature in late April and early May certainly mattered. For some days after an attack, households in most towns might be without water, gas or electricity. Coal fires provided the only source for cooking. Water had to be boiled. Toilets could not be flushed. There was further inconvenience, disruption to public transport, difficulty in getting along blocked roads. Some had to arrange for council workmen to come around to make emergency repairs: tarpaulins on roofs, frosted glass substitute on windows, temporary ceilings. Many spent days clearing up the mess, with shattered glass to be picked up and dust absolutely everywhere. Each town also had its quota of unexploded bombs, high explosives that still might go off. Most were removed without causing further injury, although it is possible that some became inaccessible and had to be left where they were. The bomb disposal teams had the most dangerous job of all. Clearing up was not dangerous in itself, but it was a further source of inconvenience that only served to prolong the misery of the raids.

Workmen did emergency repairs to housing but there was also the vexed question of what should be done about houses, and areas of building, that had been totally destroyed. This problem was of particular relevance to the question of historic buildings damaged and devastated. Most local authorities seemed uncertain as to how much they should restore and what they should replace and if Hitler was aiming to destroy cultural targets then some towns seemed to have helped him to score some posthumous victories.

The historic part of Norwich largely escaped damage. York saw localised destruction: the stone walls of the Guildhall remained intact but the wooden supporting beams and roof had to be largely replaced. The gutted church of St Mary-le-Grand was tidied up and left as a shell. In Bath there was rather more damage in what was both a heavier raid and on a larger city with a great deal of historic architecture. As this dated mainly from the 18th Century, though, replacement was not so difficult. It was relatively easy to rebuild the odd house in a long Georgian terrace where all the houses looked the same. In-filling took place throughout the city and very successfully too: few would realise today that houses in both

the Circus and the Royal Crescent had been gutted by fire. Even the Abbey Church House, one of the few substantial pre-Georgian houses in the city, was rebuilt as before having had its frontage sliced off by a high explosive bomb. The greatest architectural loss had been the gutting of the Assembly Rooms, but after some delay, this too was rebuilt.

In Canterbury and, in particular, Exeter, the problem was exacerbated by the fact that these cities suffered destruction over a complete area, rather than just the odd house or public building. Reconstruction of historic buildings was obviously expensive and there was always a temptation to level the site and start anew if the present remains were not thought of as sufficiently important. Unfortunately, in the clearing up, mistakes were made. Exeter Council commissioned a report from a Mr O'Neil, an Inspector of Ancient Monuments. Of the demolition of the Old Black Lions in South Street, a building he felt might once have been a medieval guildhall, he wrote: 'I can say definitely that in my experience that this is the worst case of vandalism which I have known to be perpetrated after a raid anywhere in Britain under the aegis of a local authority'. O'Neil failed to preserve what was left of Bedford Circus as well, arguing in vain that the sinuous outline of the facade was due less to the bombing and more to the original builder's failure to invest in expensive foundations. In 1946 the council published Thomas Sharpe's plan for the rebuilding of the city under the title 'Exeter Phoenix'. The council wished Sharpe to rebuild with 'particular reference to the historical and architectural character of the city'. The planner did not agree: 'To attempt to rebuild 20th Century Exeter with medieval forms would be the work of a generation that is visually blind and spiritually half-dead'. Not all of Sharpe's plans were put into practice, but the city of Exeter was substantially rebuilt in a modern style.

In Canterbury there was also general rather than particular devastation, although over a smaller area than at Exeter. Within weeks of the raids, a letter appeared in a local newspaper asking that St George's Church should not be rebuilt as it constituted a bottleneck in the road network in the centre of the city. In fact the main body of the church was eventually demolished but the tower was reinforced and allowed to stand. The destruction of the eastern end of the main street had been quite comprehensive but most of the buildings that had been destroyed were not of great historic significance. A new bus station was built, and modern shops; like Exeter, there was little concession to the medieval past in the design of new buildings. The worst hit area also still contains a number of car parks, one of the earliest uses of blitzed and cleared sites of World War 2.

It was only in Bath that the planners appeared to over-reach themselves. Sir Patrick Abercrombie published his 'Plan for Bath' in 1945. It included suggestions not only for the blitz-damaged areas of Kingsmead and Southgate but for the whole of the city – including the Georgian centre. There was no question that the Royal Crescent should survive, but Abercrombie did propose gutting the central section of this most famous of terraces, adding an extension to the rear and converting it into a new Guildhall. Luckily there seems little evidence to suggest that Bath City Council ever took this proposal at all seriously; nor did they implement many of his less controversial ideas. The whole plan was ferociously expensive and development, when it came, was far more piecemeal. Kingsmead Square was still being rebuilt in the mid-1980s.

As the cities were rebuilt, so did memories of the raids begin to fade. Most local newspapers produced booklets of the raids. As befitted wartime publications, these had to be vague as to detail and largely uncritical. The second wave of published accounts came in the late 1970s to coincide with the release of official documents to the Public Record Office in London. Most newspaper articles still tended to be rather uncritical and readers' letters helped to build up a number of specious rumours. One concerned casualties and the idea that any number of people had been killed and their bodies never found.

The letters page of the Exeter *Express and Echo* in 1979 had a whole series of such stories. One woman claimed that a number of girls had been fire watching at Marks & Spencer, had taken shelter and had then been entombed when the building took a direct hit. The rescue parties had dug for a week but had failed to reach them and were forced to abandon the attempt. Marks & Spencer have no records of such deaths but other contributors suggested new loca-

tions for this tragedy such as Singer's, or Wreford's the drapers. It is possible that the story had some basis in truth in the death of a number of Fire Watchers at the Devon and Exeter Savings Bank in Bedford Circus, but all their bodies were recovered.

In Bath there was a similar story, or variants thereof. When the air-raid shelter opposite the Scala cinema received a direct hit one rumour had it that a body was thrown onto the roof of the cinema where it remained until someone noticed birds circling overhead. Another story had it that some bodies were so badly mutilated that they were left where they were and a layer of lime put over the site. Each person who mentioned this rumour had not actually seen the body on the cinema or even the lime on the site: it was always a colleague who knew someone. Yet the Rescue Party leader in charge of the Scala incident and one of the ambulance drivers who collected bodies, and pieces of bodies, are adamant that both stories are untrue. This still did not stop them being raised again when the grass area where the shelter stood was put forward as a possible site for a new library in the mid-1980s. The 'abandoned bodies' story remains strong, as indeed it might for it has a long pedigree. Both Coventry and London produced tales of those given up for dead in shelters that received direct hits. It is a tradition that goes back at least as far as World War 1.

The second rumour concerned the reasoning behind the Baedeker raids. Again, readers' letters put forward many a theory. Some were wildly inaccurate: Exeter had been raided because of the presence of the Admiralty Chart Establishment or the firm of Willey & Co; the Cathedral bells had to be silenced before they gave warning of an invasion. More accurate writers did at least tie the Baedeker blitz in with the idea of revenge raids. Hitler had launched them in retaliation for attacks on either Hamburg or Dresden; and Coventry was hit during the sequence of cathedral raids as well. None of these suggestions are correct although it is interesting to note they tie in the Baedeker attacks with all the major raids, on both sides, in World War 2.

In this way, the unique nature of the Baedeker air-raids is forgotten. The raids were the first to be aimed directly at destroying the morale of the civilian population; true terror raids in fact. This was perhaps not realised at once because both Britain and Germany had routinely accused the other of already doing this and Bomber Command, at least, had been attempting area bombing for many months from 1941 onwards. The destruction of Lübeck should have handed the Nazis a major propaganda victory; the British were now launching terror raids. Instead, the destruction of Exeter and the other cities, plus von Stumm's unfortunate reference to Baedeker, took all attention away from Harris' motives in attacking Lübeck. The British bomber offensive thus achieved its first major success without having to answer any embarrassing questions about what exactly it had succeeded in doing in the first place. By the time Cologne was raided, the continued Baedeker offensive had given Germany very little scope in which to argue from a position of injured innocence. The Nazis were quite blatantly the worst offenders in the air war. Harris was able to continue with his experiments with gradual, but increasing, effect until the destruction of Dresden made anything achieved at Lübeck and Cologne pale into insignificance. It is no exaggeration to say Hitler's response to Lübeck's destruction enabled Harris to divert attention from his increasingly destructive policy of area bombing.

The war moved on, and most people forgot the Baedeker blitz. It was not a prolonged offensive like that against London, there were few German aircraft involved and no chance of major success for the cities were provincial. When a roll of honour was prepared for the civilian war dead of World War 2 the preamble even managed to get it wrong as far as the Baedeker cities were concerned, adding Cambridge to the five cities that actually were attacked. Stranger to relate, the cities themselves chose to forget the raids as well. In 1943 the City of Bath Girls' School asked for articles on the blitz for its magazine. The response was exceedingly poor. At the end of the war most councils threw out the vast bulk of their wartime documentation. A few asked departmental heads to write a brief summary of their wartime activities. Exeter Council raised the idea some years later of getting each senior official to write a longer account to put together as a proper survey of their achievements in the war. The redoubtable Mr Whiteside wrote an excellent summary of the work of his Emergency Information Office but

nobody else even bothered to reply and the whole idea foundered. The Dean of York Minster suggested a war memorial to the civilian dead. None was built. The gutted church of St Martin-le-Grand was left as a reminder and it was suggested that the clock should be left stopped at the time when it was halted during the raid. It is now ticking again. The church tower of St George's in Canterbury still stands but, as no plaque is attached to it, there is no reason to remember why it now remains in isolation. In Bath the residents of Queen Square handed over the ownership of the private park in the centre of the square to the City Council on the condition that it became a memorial to the civilian dead of Bath in World War 2. No memorial was put up.

The idea of destruction and sudden death does not fit in well with the image put over by these tourist towns. Few buildings carry plaques to commemorate the damage; it does not look good to admit that this or that historic building is in part a mere 40 year-old replica. York station is one of the few places to carry a plaque commemorating the bravery, and sacrifice, of its employees. The Baedeker cities are not unique in this respect. It seems a general conclusion that soldiers who make the conscious decision – or who are drafted – to go overseas and fight the enemy deserve their own memorial. Civilians who stay at home and are killed do not. Even Civil Defence workers on active duty while the bombs were falling received little recognition. The tragedy of the Baedeker blitz is that, in the simplest sense, the death of perhaps 1,000 civilians served no purpose whatsoever. Hitler's decision to launch these raids was based on a simple desire to be shown he would not take the British attacks lying down. He knew they could not be maintained. His hope that they would deter Britain from further raids was a vain one and so he continued the offensive out of sheer spite. If all war is hell, then some sacrifices are at least inevitable if the 'good' are to prevail.

The Baedeker dead did not help to shorten the war by one second. They were a product of Hitler's anger, a knee-jerk response of no importance to global strategy. Yet the suffering of the civilian war dead deserves commemoration. If this account has dwelled at times on instances of panic, inadequacy and inefficiency then this surely only emphasises the many acts of bravery and heroism as well as the suffering. Most of the wartime leaders are dead. The Civil Defence workers have retired. You talk to people in their homes and hear how they drove this vehicle through the streets as the bombs fell or tunnelled their way into a demolished house in a vain attempt to rescue those trapped inside. You chat with a middle-aged woman in her terraced home and, as her story emerges, you realise that it was this self-same house that was demolished by a bomb 40 years ago, and that this woman, then a child, was trapped in the debris alongside her dead mother: ordinary people, who did extraordinary things.

Then you read the official records, the death certificates of those killed in Bath, each with a photograph attached taken after death, faces in agony or just sheer astonishment. There are the notes about identification of bodies: 'Mrs P.

Marsh identified by husband, by clothing only. Cause of death: high explosive bomb and fire'. Also daughter Mary Elizabeth, aged 4, identified by 'found in mother's arms'. You may walk the streets of these cities and marvel at the sheer incongruity of what exists now and what happened then: new department stores where Fire Watchers worked and died in Exeter; a new branch of Woolworth's in Bath on the site of St James' Church, where the recent dead floated in the water sprayed onto the building in a vain attempt to prevent it from burning down. The most unreal sites of all are the houses in every city, rebuilt after destruction, rebuilt after the dead had been removed. You would not know that many of the Baedeker cities had even been hit by bombs let alone that so many died. They deserve better than this.

Below:
The work of rebuilding the High Street in Canterbury progresses during the 1950s. The tower of St George the Martyr, with its damaged clock face, remains shrouded in scaffolding. Kentish Gazette

Appendices

Appendix (1): A Summary of Principal Baedeker Raids

City	Date raided	Times raided	Nos of bombers	Weight of attack (tons)	Deaths	Remarks
Exeter	23/24 April	10.44pm-11.40pm	?	2	5	Minor raid
	24/25 April	12.10am-1.55am	44	26½	73	Severe damage to west and east of city
	25/26 April	12.00am-2.00am	few	½	4	Nuisance raid
	3/4 May	1.36am-1.55am	90	51	164	Severe raid. Much damage by fire
Bath	25/26 April	10.59pm-12.11am 12.46am-1.10am 4.35am-6.02am	163		400	Two nights of heavy raids. More high explosives on first night and more incendiaries on second
	26/27 April	1.15am-2.45am	83			
Norwich	27/28 April	11.40pm-1.15am	73	96		As Bath high explosive first night, more incendiaries on second. Heavy but localised, damage
	29/30 April	11.15pm-12.00am	70		67	
	8/9 May	12.38am-1.10am	76	Minimal	0	Ineffectual
	26/27 June	2.10am-3.15am	60		14	Mostly incendiaries. Little damage
York	28/29 April	2.42am-4.04am	74	49	79	Limited damage
Canterbury	31 May/1 June	12.55am-2.30am	77	40	43	Fire damage to east of centre
	2/3 June	2.25am-3.30am	58	5	5	Attack not pressed home
	6/7 June	Early morning	52	6	1	Attack not pressed home. One death, by accident

Note (1) *Times are based on the period when bombs were dropping; the all-clear often did not sound until some time afterwards*

Note (2) *As mentioned previously, all definite figures for deaths should be treated with some suspicion*

Appendix (2): A Note on Sources

There are abundant sources on the Baedeker blitz, the only problem for the researcher is trying to find them. This account has tried, as far as possible, to rely on contemporary documents, those written without the benefit of hindsight. Both local and national archives possess much information relating to the Baedeker raids but it is not always easy to track them down. It seems to have been a purely arbitrary decision at the end of the war for each Council to decide what they should and should not keep. Some culled their Civil Defence papers dramatically and produced summaries of the work done by each department. Some did not even bother to make summaries. Others kept huge volumes of duplicated materials for one department and nothing for others so it is almost impossible to predict what a local archive will still possess. Most do have the following: Wardens' reports; details of damage; lists of dead; Rescue Party reports; overview of Civil Defence work. Exeter's overview now only exists as a copy in the Public Record Office. The situation is further complicated by the fact that every local archive operates its own cataloguing system and some of these can be quite general, with all Civil Defence and related material put into the same box.

The Public Record Office at Kew holds reports on most cities, written by investigators who visited the cities soon after they were bombed. Some cities are better served than others. Most reports are in the Home Office (HO) series and include reports on morale, shelters and the efficiency of the Civil Defence services. All are based on a one or two-day inspection of the cities raided and are necessarily impressionistic.

This book has made use of other contemporary records as well, in particular those relating to buildings such as the cathedrals and certain shops. The relevant archivists have been kindness itself. All that does vary greatly is the amount of information that has survived.

The more obvious sources are contemporary newspapers and present day recall by people who experienced the raids. The newspapers have obvious limitations: those produced immediately after the raids are necessarily vague and optimistic. Accurate details of destruction usually took at least a month to appear, and numbers of dead perhaps some two years. The natural limitations of relying on 40 year-old reminiscences have already been mentioned. Wherever possible, the accounts used in this book have been checked by reference to contemporary records or other witnesses to the same events

EXETER

LETTERS AND INTERVIEWS
Lt-Col Peter Aggett, R. H. Alford, Alfred Bowden, W. H. Cherry, Wilfred Dymond, S. Gordon Ford, Walter Hill, Miss A. Mundell, Maurice J. R. Pike, Reg Vincent.

DEVON RECORD OFFICE
The Devonian Year Book 1943 (article);
City Engineer's Department — Box 76: includes Rescue Party Reports, NFS Report, Rowsell Report on Fire Guards, Handbook of Emergency Information;
Town Clerk's Office:
Box 3: Group L 40 Fire Watching,
  42 NFS;
Box 9: Group M 92-95 War Damage;
Box 12: Group N 132 Enemy Attack on Exeter;
Box 16: Group O 187 Civilian Deaths;
  188 ARP Control and Report Centre;
Box 25: Group O 301 CD Air-raids on the City;
  303 Damaged Properties;
  307 Children.

PUBLIC RECORD OFFICE
HO 186 861	HO 198 57
HO 188 456	HO 198 194
HO 191 183	HO 199 139
HO 192 868	HO 199 456
HO 192 1649	HO 207 1163

PAPERS
Minutes of Exeter and Co-operative Industrial Society;
Exeter Cathedral: Appeal Brochure 1946;
Marks & Spencer: records.

NEWSPAPERS
Exeter Express and Echo: 1942, 1944, 1973, 1979.

CONTEMPORARY PUBLICATIONS
Green, S. M. *The Story of the Exeter Blitz* (A. Wheaton & Co Ltd, Exeter, n.d.)
Hart, Edward *The Fairest Jewel in the West* (n.d.)
Hoare, M. C. B. *This Jewel remains — an illustrated record of the German Baedeker raid on Exeter* (n.d.)

Sharp, Thomas *Exeter Phoenix* (Exeter City Council, 1946)

SECONDARY SOURCES
Davies, D. P. *The Bombing of Exeter* (Regional Resources Centre, Institute of Education, University of Exeter, 1973)
Worrall, G. *Target Exeter* (Jaine Heap Ltd, Stoke-on-Trent, 1980)

BATH

INTERVIEWS
Dr Bernard Astley-Weston, Herbert Bath, William Burden, Jill Clayton, Albert Davies, Eric Davies, Faith Dolman, Tom Gale, Henry Hamlin, Marjorie Horsell, Sam Hayward, Bernard Humphries, Edwin Hurford, Winifred Hurford, Hubert Jackson, Dr Frederick Kohn, Maj Geoffrey Locke, Anne Marks, Myrtle Meredith, Leslie Nott, Frank Selwin, Grace Selwin, Ron Shearn, Fred Short, Mrs Smith, Edwin Stainer, Kathleen Stainer, Walter Sweetenham, Don Tuddenham, Mary Warne, James Webster, Mark Whiteley.

BATH ARCHIVES
General: Records of air-raids on Bath; Civil Defence 1939-45.
Particular: ARP Precautions — Official Guides 1941, 1944; Civil Defence Reports of Heads of Services; Air-raid Incidents; St Peter's Mortuary; St James' Mortuary; Civil Defence Overview; Bomb Census; Damage Reports; Death Records; Notifications of Death; Watch Committee; Emergency Committee.

PUBLIC RECORD OFFICE
ADM 1 10740   HO 198 57
HO 186 861   HO 198 138
HO 192 862   HO 197 194
HO 192 863   MH 101 18
HO 192 1651

MASS OBSERVATION
MO Fr1285 (Baedeker raids)

PAPERS
Alec Clifton-Taylor (unpublished notes);
Stothert & Pitt: archives;
City of Bath Girl's School Magazine, 1943.

NEWSPAPERS
Bath Weekly Chronicle 1942, 1944;
Bath and Wilts Evening Chronicle April-May 1982.

CONTEMPORARY PUBLICATIONS
Abercrombie, *P. A Plan for Bath* (Pitman, Bath, 1945)
Wimhurst, C. *The Bombardment of Bath* (Mendip Press, 1942)
Underdown, T. H. *Bristol under Blitz* (Arrowsmith, Bristol, 1942)

SECONDARY SOURCES
MacInnes, C. M. *Bristol at War* (Museum Press, 1962)
Rothnie, N. *The Bombing of Bath* (Ashgrove Press, Bath, 1983)

NORWICH

LETTERS
N. Bacon, Sid Cudlington, A. Hammond, Clifford Temple, Eric Thompson.

NORFOLK RECORD OFFICE
MS 21495
N EN 1 39
N EN 2 18
N EN 2 19

PUBLIC RECORD OFFICE
CAB 73 10   HO 192 205
HO 191 98   HO 192 1648
HO 191 184   HO 199 63
HO 192 200   HO 199 98
HO 192 201   HO 199 456

MASS OBSERVATION
MO Fr1285 (Baedeker raids)
Report (A); diary (a); Report (B); diary (b); Report (C); Report (D).

PAPERS
Rowntree Mackintosh: Log book, photographs;
Norwich Cathedral: assorted notes.

NEWSPAPERS
The Times, Eastern Daily News, Eastern Evening News.

CONTEMPORARY PUBLICATIONS
Grice, E. *Norwich — The Ordeal of 1942* (Saman-Wherry Press Ltd, Norwich, n.d.)
Mottram, R. H. *Assault upon Norwich* (Saman-Wherry Press Ltd, Norwich, n.d.)
Swain, George *Norwich under Fire* (Jarrold and Sons Ltd, Norwich, n.d.)

SECONDARY SOURCES
Banger, J. *Norwich at War* (Wensum Books, Norwich 1974)
Bowyer, Michael J. F. *Air Raid: The*

enemy air offensive against East Anglia, 1939-45 (Patrick Stephens Ltd, Wellingborough, 1986)
Mackintosh, E. D. *Norwich Adventure* (private print, n.d.)
Mottram, R. H. *The Glories of Norwich Cathedral* (Norwich, 1948)
Thoresby, P. *The Story of Norwich Cathedral* (Norwich, n.d.)

YORK

LETTERS
Bernard Barton, Peter Barron, Tom Bashford, Edna Blakeborough, Ron Chapman, Eileen Chapman, Joy Crawshaw, Alice Eaves, Donald Fiddeman, Gwen Gledhill, C. R. Goodhall, Mrs M. Hall, Mrs L. Harper, Steven Herbert, Anne Holliday, Marjorie Leng, Chris Marshall, George Metcalfe, Mr D. L. Morgan, Mr R. D. Moses, Mrs K. Moss, Iris Reynolds, Joan Stanhope, Eric Taylor, Mary Tedham, David Thomas, Harold Webster.

YORK CITY ARCHIVES DEPARTMENT
Acc.89.38: In particular — Wardens' Report; Rescue Parties; Hospitals; Heads of Civil Defence.

YORK REFERENCE LIBRARY
City of York, Civil Defence, 1939-45.

PUBLIC RECORD OFFICE
AIR 41 49   HO 192 1656
HO 188 456   HO 198 5
HO 192 129   HO 199 46
HO 192 130   HO 207 1045

PAPERS
Rowntrees Mackintosh: Archive Department;
Bar Convent Museum: Letter from Mother Andrew.

CAVERSHAM PARK
German radio intercepts, 30 April 1942.

NEWSPAPERS
Daily Mail, The Guardian, Yorkshire Evening Press, Yorkshire Evening Post, Yorkshire Gazette.

CONTEMPORARY PUBLICATIONS
Rowntree & Co Ltd, *The Cocoa Works in Wartime* (York, n.d.)

SECONDARY SOURCES
Halpenny, Bruce Barrymore *Action Stations — The Military Airfields of Yorkshire* (Patrick Stephens Ltd, 1984)
Kessler, L. and Taylor, Eric — *The York*

Blitz 1942 (William Sessions Ltd, York, 1986)

CANTERBURY

LETTERS
Evelyn Austin, Doris Black, Violet Brand, Maureen Clarke, Mrs L. Cullen, Mr C. A. Elphick, Hank Evans, Mrs D. Hillier, Mr P. Holmes, Mr B. A. Jordan, Janet Laing, Ian B. Moat, Mr F. Geo Perry, Mr L. Reynolds, Mr B. Sharpe, Peter Shirley.

CANTERBURY RECORD OFFICE
Emergency Committee: Rescue Reports; Damage Reports; Post-raid Conferences; Police Reports.

PUBLIC RECORD OFFICE
HO 186 2317   HO 192 1650
HO 188 456   HO 198 65
HO 192 969   HO 199 261
HO 192 971

PAPERS
Christchurch College Canterbury: Interviews by Jeremy McDermott with Winifred Hopper, Mercy Jordan, Kathleen Newton, Maria Theresa O'Callaghan.
Canterbury Cathedral: Lois Lang-Sims in Magazine of the Friends of Canterbury Cathedral, 1982.

NEWSPAPERS
Kentish Gazette, Kent Messenger, Kentish Observer and *Canterbury Chronicle.*

CONTEMPORARY SOURCES
Banner, H.S. *Kentish Fire* (1944)
Keable, G. and Lawrence, J. *St George the Martyr* (Broadwater Press, Welwyn, 1943)

SECONDARY SOURCES
Canterbury, June 1st, 1942 (*Kent Messenger*, 1962)
Killen, John *The Luftwaffe* (Frederick Muller Ltd, 1969)
Rootes, A. *Front Line County* (Robert Hale, 1980)
Williamson, Catherine *Though the Streets Burn* (Headley Bros, 1949)